David and Goliath

Ukrainian Research Institute
Harvard University

Harvard Series in Ukrainian Studies 83

HURI Editorial Board

Emily Channell-Justice
Michael S. Flier
Oleh Kotsyuba, *Director of Publications*
Serhii Plokhy, *Chairman*

Cambridge, Massachusetts

Serhii Plokhy

David and Goliath

Commentaries on the Russo-Ukrainian War

50 years ■ 1973–2023

HURI
UKRAINIAN RESEARCH INSTITUTE
HARVARD UNIVERSITY

Distributed by Harvard University Press
for the Ukrainian Research Institute
Harvard University

The Harvard Ukrainian Research Institute (HURI) was founded in 1973 thanks to the grassroots efforts of the American-Ukrainian community. The Institute does not receive any subventions from Harvard's Faculty of Arts and Sciences. To this day, HURI relies on small, restricted endowed funds established by its friends and benefactors to support its publications and other programs.

Published by the Harvard Ukrainian Research Institute in 2026
Copyright © 2026 by the President and Fellows of Harvard College

Book manuscript edited by Myroslav Yurkevich, Grace Mahoney, and Oleh Kotsyuba

Previously published texts reproduced here by permission
All rights reserved
Printed in India on acid-free paper

ISBN 9780674301092 (hardcover), 9780674301108 (paperback), 9780674301115 (epub), 9780674301122 (PDF)

Library of Congress Control Number has been applied for.
LC record available at https://lccn.loc.gov

Cover art and design by Lesyk Panasiuk, https://www.gladunpanasiuk.com
Book design by Andrii Kravchuk

Publication of this book has been made possible by the generous support of publications in Ukrainian studies at Harvard University by the following benefactors or funds endowed in their name:

>
> Ostap and Ursula Balaban
> Jaroslaw and Olha Duzey
> Vladimir Jurkowsky
> Myroslav and Irene Koltunik
> Damian Korduba Family
> Peter and Emily Kulyk
> Irena Lubchak
> Dr. Evhen Omelsky
> Eugene and Nila Steckiw
> Dr. Omeljan and Iryna Wolynec
> Wasyl and Natalia Yerega

You can support our work of publishing academic books and translations of Ukrainian literature and documents by making a tax-deductible donation in any amount, or by including HURI in your estate planning.

To find out more, please visit https://huri.harvard.edu/give.

Contents

Acknowledgments · ix
A Note on Transliteration · xi
Preface · xiii

I. **The Soviet Collapse**
   1. No End to History · 3
   2. The Collapse of the USSR Is Still Going On · 14
   3. Three Decades of Independence · 24
   4. Books on the War · 38

II. **The Empire Returns**
   5. The Long Shadow · 51
   6. What Is Happening in Ukraine Is Crucial · 58
   7. Putin's Revisionist History of Russia and Ukraine · 61
   8. Did Lenin Create Ukraine? · 67
   9. Ukraine's Dangerous Independence · 70

III. **The Big War**
   10. Appeasement · 85
   11. The Causes of the Russo-Ukrainian War · 95
   12. Putin's War Is Banishing an Outdated Myth · 99
   13. Annexation · 102
   14. The Russian Coup · 106

IV. Nuclear Roulette
15. The Ghosts of Chornobyl · 113
16. Who Is in Charge? · 117
17. Nuclear Terrorism · 120
18. Between a Rock and a Hard Place · 123
19. Atoms for Peace and Atoms for War · 130
20. Nuclear Plants Could Become Dirty Bombs · 137
21. Hiroshima Diary · 140

V. The Western Alliance
22. Magical Thinking · 145
23. Germany and Ukraine · 151
24. Why the Delays? · 161
25. Worrying Signs · 168
26. The War That Neither Ukraine nor the West Can Afford to Lose · 171
27. The Trump Card · 175

VI. Making Sense of War
28. Writing History as It Happens · 183
29. Not Since World War II · 191
30. Turning Back the Clock of History · 201
31. The Zelensky Effect · 208
32. The Sources of Russian Conduct · 211
33. Decolonizing the Past · 216
34. We Have to Make the Russians Think Differently · 223

References · 231
Index · 235

Acknowledgments

It is my distinct pleasure to give thanks to those who helped make this book a reality. These commentaries were born out of conversations and reflections published by institutions and media outlets across the world. My first thanks go to the teams behind those publications, especially my interlocutors for their thoughtfully formulated questions and dedicated assistance—even years later—in securing permissions to reprint these pieces for the present volume.

I am grateful to the staff, publications team, and editorial board of the Harvard Ukrainian Research Institute (HURI) for including this book in their continued efforts to increase the availability of Ukrainian studies materials in print. My special thanks go to Oleh Kotsyuba, HURI's director of publications and member of the editorial board, who spearheaded the entire project and shepherded it through every stage. I thank Anna Chukur of *Harvard Ukrainian Studies* who was diligent, persistent, and always gracious in tracking down rights holders and securing permissions for the texts included here. I'm indebted to Myroslav Yurkevich who, as always, did an excellent job editing the manuscript, and Grace Mahoney, who proofread the book in preparation for typesetting. Finally, I want to thank my other colleagues on the Institute's editorial board—Michael S. Flier and Emily Channell-Justice—as well as the Institute's executive director, Tymish Holowinsky, for adding this book to the impressive list of HURI's publications that have appeared in print in recent years.

A Note on Transliteration

In the text of this collection, a modified Library of Congress system is used to transliterate Ukrainian and other East Slavic personal names and toponyms. This system omits the soft sign (ь) and, in masculine surnames, the final "й" (thus, for example, Zelensky, not Zelenskyi). The exception to this is the transliteration of the name of the medieval princedom of Rusʹ. As a rule, personal names are given in forms characteristic of the cultural traditions to which the given person belonged. However, well-known personal names such as Yushchenko, Klitschko, and Yanukovych appear in spellings widely adopted in English-language texts, while the spelling of several other names of living authors follows their own preference. In bibliographic references, the full Library of Congress system (ligatures omitted) is used. Toponyms are usually transliterated from the language of the country in which the designated places are currently located. Rivers originating in one country and flowing through others are given in spellings widely adopted in English (thus Dnieper, not Dnipro).

Preface

David and Goliath is a collection of short essays, commentaries, and interviews written and spoken on the eve and during the first two years of Russia's full-scale invasion of Ukraine—the largest armed conflict in Europe since the end of World War II. They are reflections on the truly historic events of the war as they cross the boundary between past and present to become history and represent the work of a historian as a contributor to that process.

The commentaries presented here fall into several categories. The volume begins with reflections on the Soviet collapse: in the fall of 2021, the world marked the thirtieth anniversary of the disintegration of the Soviet Union and the emergence on its ruins of independent states, including Ukraine and Russia. The collection continues with a discussion of the uses and abuses of history by Vladimir Putin and Russian propaganda in the run-up to the Russian invasion of February 2022, followed by reflections on the origins of the war and assessments of its twists and turns considered in historical and comparative contexts. The volume ends with commentary on the process of writing history in the midst of the war: I had to answer numerous questions about the legitimacy, pluses, and minuses of such an undertaking after the publication of my book *The Russo-Ukrainian War* in May 2023.

Most of the interviews selected for this volume were written or given at the invitation of journalists who tend to ask questions not only about the past and present but also about the future. While resisting multiple attempts to turn me, as a historian, into a fortune teller, I recognized the benefit of placing everyday developments into a historical context. More than once I shared with my interlocutors my understanding of the long-term trajectories of events and processes that led to this horrible war and continue to drive it. As I worked on the volume, I selected and edited my commentary for length and style to avoid almost unavoidable repetitions, but I left all my predictions in place, whether they came true or not. They became, in this sense, witnesses to history, reflecting hopes, expectations, and prevailing moods among experts and the general public at various stages of the war.

Articles and interviews are inevitably collaborative efforts. After all, it is journalists and editors who decide what questions to ask, what to include or omit in the final version of the interview, and which op-ed to solicit and which to publish. My interviewers and editors come from various countries, ranging from the United States to the United Kingdom, Europe, China, and, of course, Ukraine. In that sense, a good part of this volume is a product not only of multiple but also international authorship. I would like to thank my partners in the "crime" of writing history on the fly for their contributions to this volume and to our understanding of one of the largest military conflicts in world history. I truly hope that this is the last collection of "as it happens" historical commentary on the subject of the Russo-Ukrainian war that I or anyone else will have to publish.

I. The Soviet Collapse

1. No End to History

In December 1991, as the Soviet Union was falling apart, I asked my students in a course entitled "The USSR in Crisis: The Nationality Question" to play a little game. Its basic premise was that, as of December 1991, all Soviet citizens had the right to move wherever they wished in their own republic or any other Union republic, an opportunity that would be lost once the republics became independent states. The students were asked to choose in which region or republic they would like to settle: in other words, which successor states of the Union of Soviet Socialist Republics (Soviet Union, USSR) would do best in the following decade or two.

The most popular choices were two regions of the Russian Federation: the Kaliningrad enclave, a part of East Prussia around the city of Königsberg seized by the Red Army in 1945, since it was considered a natural bridge for the political and economic integration of the new Russia into Europe, and the Far Eastern region around Vladivostok, which was expected to perform the same function with regard to the booming Pacific rim. Others chose Ukraine, for which experts at the Deutsche Bank had predicted the brightest economic future of any Soviet republic.

Thirty years later, the hopes and expectations of my students and of most experts and forecasters have failed to materialize. The regions that allegedly had the best chances of success are now among the worst in economic performance and standard of living. In assessing the economic potential of the post-Soviet space, it was not only my students but also the professors and pundits who proved mistaken about the prospects of economic and democratic development in the successor states. It was exactly at that time that Francis Fukuyama hailed the end of the Cold War and the Soviet collapse as "the end of history as such: that is, the endpoint of mankind's ideological evolution and the universalization of Western liberal democracy as the final form of human government."

Whatever one thought of Fukuyama's prognosis, the disintegration of the Soviet Union was generally perceived as a discrete event—one that seemed to have taken place miraculously, almost overnight; a turning point in some process or other but not a process in its own right. "I find it hard to think of any event more strange and startling, and at first glance more inexplicable, than the sudden and total disintegration and disappearance from the international scene… of the great power known successively as the Russian Empire and the Soviet Union," wrote the dean of American Sovietology, George F. Kennan, in 1995.

Looking back, we see that 1991 marked no end to history either as the ideological evolution of humankind or as the discipline that has, among other things, documented the lengthy and painful disintegration of the world's empires. What we see today in the post-Soviet space is the continuing process of the disintegration of the Union of Soviet Socialist Republics, complete with efforts to establish spheres of influence, border disputes, and open warfare. We also see Russia's return to the international scene as it attempts the role not only of a regional but also of a global power akin to that played by the Russian Empire and the Soviet Union.

*　*　*

With the euphoria of the early 1990s gone, we can now make a more sober assessment of the Soviet Union's disintegration and the reasons for it. We can also define the direction in which that process continues to develop and perhaps make better predictions about its future. One thing is immediately obvious: post-Soviet space has disintegrated into more than a dozen smaller polities that move to their own drumbeats, often in different directions.

History, pre-Soviet history in particular, played an important role in defining post-Soviet developments in the region. The downfall of the Soviet Union began in the most recent additions to its territory—the lands annexed in the course of World War II, first in the wake of the Molotov-Ribbentrop Pact and then recaptured from Nazi Germany in 1944–45 and integrated in the USSR as a result of the Yalta agreements. In the forefront of mobilization against the Soviet center were the Baltic states, especially Estonia and Lithuania. The former was the first Soviet republic to declare its sovereignty, meaning that its laws took precedence over those of the Union.

Lithuania, for its part, was the first republic to declare itself completely independent of the Soviet Union. It did so in March 1990 at the first session of the freely elected Lithuanian parliament. Even the Communist Party of Lithuania abandoned the USSR, declaring its secession from the Communist Party of the Soviet Union. Leadership passed to representatives of an alternative elite from the ranks of intellectuals and technocrats, not unlike the process in Eastern Europe a few years later.

The Baltic drive to regain the independence lost in the flames of World War II had a ripple effect throughout the Soviet Union. To deal with the Baltic "Popular Fronts"—pro-independence organizations that sent hundreds of thousands of people into the streets to achieve their goal—Moscow and the local party elites organized "International Fronts" that sought to mobilize Russian and Russian-speaking minorities in the republics.

Russian mobilization in the western borderlands of the USSR soon spilled over into Russia itself. The "Russia first" approach united Russian nationalists and democrats, propelling Gorbachev's former protégé and then his sworn enemy Boris Yeltsin to the position first of head of the Russian parliament and then to that of Russian president. Yeltsin's victory resulted from several mobilizations, first of nationalists and then of democratic activists in the major cities. Finally, there was the backing of newly organized workers who went on strike over economic conditions, expecting that Russian authorities could help them when Union officials had failed to do so.

By June 1991, Moscow had two presidents, one of Russia and the other of the USSR. But, in Russia, unlike in the Baltic republics, opposition to the center was led by a former party boss, not by an intellectual, as was the case in Lithuania, where the former music professor Vytautas Landsbergis led the charge toward independence. Even though Yeltsin publicly abandoned the Communist Party and then suspended its activities, the new Russian elite never made a clean break with the communist past, as did its counterparts in the Baltics. That was a consequential difference.

Mobilization in Ukraine, the second-largest Soviet republic after Russia in size of population and economy, combined elements of the Baltic and Russian mobilizations. In the parts of western Ukraine annexed by the Soviet Union on the basis of the Molotov-Ribbentrop Pact, it followed the Baltic model, focusing on issues of history, language, culture, and national sovereignty. Ukraine's declaration of independence from the Soviet Union in the wake of the failed August 1991 coup in Moscow came not only as a result of the alliance between nationalists, democrats, and striking workers in the Donbas (Donets Basin) region but also thanks to the support of the party apparatus, which had been threatened by Boris Yeltsin's suspension of Communist Party activity.

On 1 December 1991, Ukrainians delivered the final blow to the Soviet Union by voting overwhelmingly for independence. The Baltics were effectively gone by that time, as was Moldova and a good part of the Caucasus. But the Belarusians and Central Asians who counted on a continuing supply of subsidized gas and oil from Russia were in no hurry to leave. Even resource-rich Kazakhstan was hesitant about independence, partly because of its large Russian and Slavic population. But Russia's decision to recognize Ukrainian independence and not bear the economic burden of the Union without Ukraine's substantial human and economic resources spelled the end of the USSR. The Belarusians and Central Asians had to leave as well, willingly or not.

On 25 December 1991, Mikhail Gorbachev announced his resignation as president after the Soviet Union had already ceased to exist as a legal entity, having been formally dissolved by the leaders of the Union republics. That turned out to be the beginning of the process of disintegration, not its end.

* * *

The fall of the USSR, far from being a universal triumph of democracy as imagined back in 1991, was a victory to different degrees of nationalists, democrats, and party apparatchiks, with their roles and ideologies varying from one republic to another. In some cases, it was the most conservative elements of the Soviet elite that consolidated power.

The various paths to independence taken by different republics could not but influence the post-Soviet trajectory of the now formally independent states. With the notable exception of the majority of the Central Asian states, they began by democratizing their political life and institutions, but not every state was able to maintain or enhance that level of democracy throughout the tumultuous years of post-Soviet transition. In fact, most of them failed to do so.

Democracy was fully successful only in the Baltic states, where it turned out to be more durable and resistant to authoritarian pressures than even in the countries of the former East European communist bloc, most notably Hungary and Poland. Democracy in the form of competitive elections survived in Ukraine, Moldova, Georgia, Armenia and, to some extent, in Kyrgyzstan (an outlier among Central Asian states in that regard). It never took off in the rest of Central Asia, including Kazakhstan, Uzbekistan, Turkmenistan, and Tajikistan. In Belarus, the slide into authoritarianism began in the mid-1990s after the election of Alexander Lukashenko (Belarusian: Aliaksandar Lukashenka) as president. His regime became a virtual dictatorship by 2020, when he used unrestricted violence against peaceful demonstrators who protested the government's widespread electoral fraud committed to keep Lukashenko in office.

In Russia, the beacon of democracy for the more conservative republics in the late 1980s and early 1990s, authoritarianism began to gather strength after the failed coup of 1993 against Boris Yeltsin. The Russian president ordered his military to crush the coup with tanks and rewrote the Russian constitution to strengthen the powers of his office. On arriving in the Kremlin as president in 2000, Vladimir Putin made full use of those powers.

In 2021, having been prime minister twice and already serving his third term as president, Putin rewrote the constitution once again, allowing himself two more presidential terms, each extended from the original five years to seven.

Numerous indices of democratic development invariably put the three Baltic states far ahead of the other post-Soviet countries. The Bertelsmann Transformation Index divides them into three categories. Ukraine, with a score of 6.81, is followed by Armenia, Georgia, Kyrgyzstan, and Moldova in the so-called "limited democracy" camp. Russia, scoring 5.3, leads the "very limited democracy" group. It is followed by Kazakhstan, Belarus, Azerbaijan, and Uzbekistan. At the bottom are Tajikistan and Turkmenistan, with respective scores of 3.32 and 2.71. This is the "failed democracy" camp.

Contrary to expectations in 1991, liberal democracy failed to encompass most of the former Soviet Union, and the majority of post-Soviet states, including Russia, are now on the path of authoritarianism, not democracy.

* * *

History did appear to reach its end in 1991 in one respect—the abandonment of monopolistic state ownership and planning in every new polity and the adoption to different degrees of the principles of private property, free enterprise, and market economy.

Unfortunately, the rule of law did not generally become the defining principle of political, social, and economic life. Heavy state regulation and manipulation accompanied by corruption became ever-present features of economic life in the region. Once again, the Baltic states are the only exception to this general rule. There, democracy and the rule of law go hand in hand with the highest GDP per capita in the post-Soviet space (in 2020, Estonia led with 23,000 US dollars per annum).

Where democracy is not accompanied by the rule of law, the economic transformation of the last thirty years has produced less than modest results. Ukraine, with the highest level of democratic development, is close to the bottom of the list of post-Soviet countries, with a mere 3,500 US dollars GDP per capita. The same applies, in different degrees, to other countries of the "limited

1. No End to History

democracy" group: Georgia, Moldova, and Armenia, whose 2020 GDP per capita was less than 4,500 US dollars. All those countries are further disadvantaged by arrested or ongoing military conflicts: Russian forces remain in Transnistria, Armenia has a not so frozen conflict with Azerbaijan, Georgia was invaded by Russia in 2008, and Ukraine is in its eighth year [as of 2021—ed.] of fighting the Russian invasion of the Donbas and has lost the Crimea.

Russia, Kazakhstan, and Turkmenistan belong to the "very limited democracy" or even "failed democracy" group. In economic terms, they are behind the Baltics but ahead of Ukraine, Georgia, Moldova, and Armenia. GDP per capita is close to $10,000 in Russia, close to $9,000 in Kazakhstan, and slightly more than $8,000 in Turkmenistan. The relative wealth of those countries is due in no small measure to their natural resources and their ability to sell them in foreign markets. The profits of that trade help to support authoritarian rulers and limit the spread of democracy in all three countries. Russian and Azeri oil earnings also help to fund those countries' wars.

* * *

When the Soviet Union fell apart in 1991, one of the most encouraging features of its collapse was the absence of large-scale wars between the republics. The scenario that concerned many in the West, "Yugoslavia with nukes," never materialized.

The presence of nuclear weapons on Soviet territory should be credited not only with the peaceful end of the Cold War but also with the relatively peaceful dissolution of the Soviet Union, where four republics, Russia, Ukraine, Belarus, and Kazakhstan, found themselves in possession, although not always in control, of nuclear weapons. The United States worked hand in hand with Russia to bring about nuclear disarmament, forcing Ukraine and the other republics to give up their nuclear weapons in exchange for "security assurances." These turned out to be worthless once Russia invaded Ukraine in the spring of 2014.

The 1990s marked the high point of Russo-American cooperation. The two countries reached agreement on a number of key issues, from further cuts to nuclear arsenals to the resolution of regional conflicts in Africa, the Middle East, and Afghanistan, where Moscow stopped supporting its clients. But there was one major exception: Russia and the United States never reached an understanding about the future of the post-Soviet space.

Despite his decision in December 1991 to allow and even encourage the dissolution of the Soviet Union, Yeltsin never envisioned the post-Soviet space as an area in which the former republics of the USSR would acquire a free hand in deciding their affairs. The Commonwealth of Independent States, formed in December 1991, was there among other things to ensure Russia's leading role in the region. Other republics, Ukraine in particular, regarded the Commonwealth as an international institution that would make possible the orderly dissolution of the Union or, as they called it in Kyiv, a "civilized divorce."

The United States remained a strong supporter of Gorbachev and the Soviet Union until the last weeks of the Union's existence, but, once the USSR was gone, Washington endorsed the full independence of the post-Soviet states as opposed to the limited sovereignty advocated for them by Yeltsin and his advisers. The conflict between these two visions came to the forefront at the start of the twenty-first century.

Ukraine found itself at the very center of the battle for full sovereignty of the republics. It never fully joined the Commonwealth, which it had helped to create, and, with the departure of former party officials from the political scene, pro-democratic forces made a push to reorient Ukraine toward the West. The Orange Revolution—mass protests in Kyiv in the fall of 2004 triggered by the government's attempt to rig elections in favor of a presidential candidate supported by Russia—put membership in the European Union on Ukraine's political agenda. The United States supported Ukraine's democratic choice, but Russia considered the Orange Revolution a form of American aggression and encroachment on its sphere of influence.

While Putin's liberal allies, such as Anatoly Chubais, advocated the formation of a liberal Russian empire in which the other republics would be linked to Russia by economic dependence and soft power, Putin concluded that his only effective instrument to keep the post-Soviet space under Russian control was the use of military force. In the first months of 2014, as Ukrainians revolted against their president, Viktor Yanukovych, who had promised them to sign an association agreement with the European Union but reneged under pressure from Russia, Putin sent his troops into Ukraine's Crimea and seized the peninsula. A few months later, he opened another front in his war on Ukraine, this time in the eastern industrial region of the Donbas.

The war that began there in the spring and early summer of 2014 is still going on, claiming the lives of more than 14,000 people, with at least twice as many wounded, hundreds of thousands without shelter, and millions forced to become refugees. What are Russia's motives? First, to arrest Ukraine's drift toward the West: Putin claimed that, if he had not annexed the Crimea, it would have become a launching pad for North Atlantic Treaty Organization (NATO) forces. Second, to undermine and discredit Ukrainian democracy, whose success would send an undesirable signal to the Russians: if Ukraine can be democratic and successful, why cannot Russia do the same?

Moscow's efforts to establish or retain a Russian sphere of influence are not limited to Ukraine. The same rationale is apparent in neighboring Belarus where Russia supports the highly unpopular president Alexander Lukashenko whose legitimacy is not recognized by the country's European neighbors. The western front of Russia's confrontation with the collective West also includes the Baltic states, the post-Soviet success story. They joined both the European Union and NATO, but Russia considers them contested territory and is using new methods of cyber warfare against its former subjects.

Farther south, Russia maintains its military and economic support of Transnistria, a diplomatically unrecognized enclave created in Moldova to keep that country's Western aspirations in check. In the Caucasus, Russia invaded Georgia in 2008 and took over the region of South Ossetia, adding it to another Georgian enclave already under Russian control, the republic of Abkhazia. The war was a direct response to Georgia's desire to join NATO.

Many observers speak of a return of the Cold War to the now redefined Eastern Europe, consisting of the former Soviet republics of the USSR's western and, in part, southern periphery. But, in reality, the new Cold War started there as soon as the original one was over. What is truly unprecedented in the developments of the last decade is the emergence of new international actors in the post-Soviet space. The recent resumption of the military conflict between Azerbaijan and Armenia in the contested area of Nagorno-Karabakh ended with Azerbaijan's victory, thanks in large part to the backing of its ally, Turkey. Russia brought its "peacekeepers" into the area but was constrained to accept the defeat of its client, Armenia.

A considerable part of the post-Soviet space is emerging as a new battleground of a different Cold War, that between the United States and China, in which Moscow figures as a junior partner of Beijing—a return to the old Sino-Soviet alliance, with the partners' roles reversed. China, which is extending its economic and political influence in Central Asia and beyond (it is Ukraine's largest trading partner), refrains from challenging Russia directly in those areas, but its growing economic power, as opposed to Russia's stagnant economy, leaves little doubt about the eventual winner of that contest.

**

This is hardly a scenario that anyone envisioned thirty years ago. Nor did observers accurately foresee the fate of democracy, the economy, and the rule of law in the post-Soviet space. The triumph of democracy materialized in some republics but not in others. And Russia, after some hesitation, simply refused to give up its ambitions as the sole master of the post-Soviet space.

But not all the news is grim. The scale of the new Cold War is much smaller than that of the old one. The Iron Curtain has fallen, and people are free to travel. The dictates of communist ideology are gone, along with its social experiments and the Gulag. No one is forcing farmers to join collectives by starving them to death, nor is anyone killing writers to arrest the development of non-Russian cultures. Most of the post-Soviet countries are much freer today than they were even during Gorbachev's perestroika, to say nothing of Stalin's murderous dictatorship. The rule of law is slowly making progress in the region, and the vast majority

1. No End to History

of post-Soviet economies have grown since 1991, with concomitant improvements in the standard of living. All this allows us to look to the future without the euphoria of 1991, but with cautious optimism.

History did not end in 1991, the empire did not collapse overnight, and we no longer expect miracles. In that sense, the return of history comes with a bonus: we can now learn from experience and guess what comes next. Historical developments in similar post-imperial situations elsewhere in the world leave no doubt about the direction of the processes taking place today in the region once called the USSR. No empire has ever managed to revive itself and keep imposing its will or ideology on its former subjects indefinitely. One freedom that the former republics of the USSR have won and are not willing to give up is freedom of choice. That freedom should be supported by the international community not just with words but with deeds.

November 2021

2. The Collapse of the USSR Is Still Going On

Interview conducted by
Adam Reichardt, *New Eastern Europe*

Adam Reichardt (AR): This year [2021–ed.], we commemorate the thirtieth anniversary of the fall of the Soviet Union, an event that brought an end to the Cold War as well as what Francis Fukuyama called "the end of history." Yet this event also led to social, economic, and political instability; nation and identity building; the creation of new states and divides; and conflicts and wars among neighbors, just to name a few of the key processes. But maybe let's start with the positives. When you look back over the past thirty years, after the collapse of the USSR, what would you say were the most important achievements or milestones in the post-Soviet space throughout those decades?

Serhii Plokhy (SP): I will start with something that sounds controversial but is not. The collapse of the Soviet Union signaled the "end of history," but the history that I am talking about is not associated with the victory of liberal democracy. It was the victory of private property and market economics. With democracy we have a mixed record at best, but the late 1980s and early 1990s truly marked the end of economies that were not based to one degree or another on private property and the market. Even China, which survived as a party-run state and preserved a form of communist ideology, did so by adopting the principles of the market economy. So that is certainly one very clear turning point of global significance, for throughout most of the twentieth century that

2. The Collapse of the USSR Is Still Going On

economic model was often directly challenged. If we look at different countries, the degree of state limitations on the principle of private property and control over the market is different, and the way it is controlled is different, yet the foundations are basically the same. We must have some form of private non-state property and some form of market in order to survive and move ahead.

The fall of the USSR indicated another change of global significance, as it brought an end to the history of European empires in the modern era. The disintegration of those modern empires began with the First World War, and the Soviet Union was the last major European empire to fall. This process started even earlier if we include the gradual collapse of the Ottoman Empire, which began in the eighteenth century. It underlines even more the importance of the Soviet collapse as the last chapter of that historical era. It can, of course, be claimed that empires did not disappear per se, as they can persist in a metaphorical sense. Yes, the core countries of those empires, which are now often great powers, did not disappear. But it is clear that empire as a form of organization of a multiethnic space did not survive the twentieth century. The strongest signal that this era has receded into the past was the fall of the Soviet Union.

AR: *So can we regard the USSR as a continuation of the Russian Empire into the twentieth century in the sense that it had central control and many different nations within its territory?*

SP: The most obvious continuity between those states is the shape of their borders on the map. If you compare the map of the Russian Empire with that of the Soviet Union, there is huge overlap. But there are also differences on the map and otherwise. They are related to the fact that many borders were adjusted to fall along ethnic lines. The Curzon Line established on that principle is present on today's map and was certainly there before 1991, indicating that the Soviet Union integrated and accumulated some elements of nationalism and recognized some of its claims in order to manage it. The last Soviet leaders, including Mikhail Gorbachev, did not see the collapse coming until the very end because they were absolutely convinced that the USSR had solved the nationality question. They believed that the level of accommodation given to each nationality was sufficient and that the multiethnic state would continue. Well, history proved that this whole line of thinking was wrong.

AR: *At the outset, I mentioned various processes that took place immediately after the declared end of the Soviet Union, some of which were quite negative. I wanted to ask, from your perspective, what can we identify as the most tragic consequences of the collapse.*

SP: The most tragic outcome of the fall of the Soviet Union is the violence and wars, which continue today. For a long time, there was a belief or myth of a peaceful disintegration of the USSR. In my opinion, it was mostly a result of the surprise of Western leaders and publics that Eastern Europe was allowed to leave the Soviet bloc without conflict. That colored the perception of what was really happening within the borders of the Soviet Union before and after the collapse. The exodus of Russian and other Slavic populations from non-Slavic republics was provoked by fear of violence, and it started even before the fall. There were major interethnic clashes in Baku, as well as the larger Azeri and Armenian conflict. Meskhetian Turks had to flee Uzbekistan after the Fergana massacre of 1989. The fact that Gorbachev ordered troops into the streets of Vilnius and the Baltic states was conveniently overlooked.

Russia not having enough political will or resources to use force at the moment of disintegration was another reason why the whole process was considered peaceful. In fact, Boris Yeltsin had already ordered troops to Chechnya in the autumn of 1991. The problem was that those troops were immediately surrounded by Chechens. They were simply unable to fight, so the conflict was postponed for a few years. The subsequent two Chechen wars fit the paradigm of the violent fall of empires and certainly do not resemble peaceful disintegration. The frozen conflicts in Moldova and in the Caucasus that deteriorated into hot wars such as Russia's invasion of Georgia and the Azeri-Armenian war in Nagorno-Karabakh do not fit the model of peaceful disintegration. Russia's aggression against Ukraine and its annexation of the Crimea are basically part of the long-term consequences of

2. The Collapse of the USSR Is Still Going On

this collapse. Thus, the disintegration of the Soviet Union is still going on, and it is not peaceful.

AR: *You mentioned these long-drawn-out processes of conflicts and wars. Is this in line with historical precedent if we look at the fall of other empires? Does this match up with the Ottoman Empire or the British Empire, for example? Can we see some historical similarities?*

SP: The Soviet Union is collapsing along ethnonational lines and borders drawn and redrawn on their basis. From that point of view, there is no doubt that it is dying the death of a classic empire. What is not present, or less obvious, is the collapse of an imperial polity in the middle of a major war with other empires or great powers. This partially explains the myth of the peaceful disintegration of the USSR. The First World War spelled the end for the Austro-Hungarian and Ottoman empires. The Second World War set out the path for the disintegration of the British and French empires. Even earlier, it put an end to the Japanese empire in the Pacific and the projected German empire in Eastern Europe and parts of Russia. The USSR arguably lost the Cold War but never lost a military confrontation with the United States. That is because the fall of the Soviet empire took place in a different context—that of the nuclear age. This was an era of nuclear weapons, which made it difficult for any leader to believe that there could be another world war and that any country had good chances of surviving it.

AR: *We talked about this long process of collapse, with conflicts in the South Caucasus, Ukraine, and Moldova. I am curious: at what point can we say that this process is over? Will there be a point where we can say this collapse has finally ended?*

SP: Everything comes to an end at some point. If we continue this line of comparing the history of the Soviet collapse with the collapse of other empires, it is very clear that, at some point, the former metropolis will decide that the costs are too high to continue. The former imperial center will then adjust accordingly. Also, over time, the new colonies can become more powerful than the former metropolis. The best-known case of such change is, of course, the relationship between Britain and the United States. The tensions associated with the disintegration of the British Empire persisted on a psychological and cultural level all the way up to the Second World War, when the United States replaced the United Kingdom as the dominant power that controlled the world's waterways. At that point, resentment of Britain's imperial nature became much less central to American identity. So, things change. Former colonies or peripheries become new centers in their own right, and this is what will happen in the post-Soviet space as well. It is difficult to say when exactly that will take place, but it will happen. After all, Russia emerged as an empire after conquering the Tatar khanates that had ruled over it.

AR: *I would now like to shift focus a bit and look specifically at Ukraine, one of the countries in which you specialize. It celebrated thirty years of independence in August of this year [2021–ed.]. Various events that unfolded soon after the collapse of the Soviet Union were crucial in forming the system that Ukraine has today, which includes elements of a strong oligarchic presence as well as an inherent system of corruption. I want to ask you, from your perspective, what is the Soviet legacy there today?*

SP: One of the key international issues related to Ukraine in the last few months has been the controversy over Nord Stream 2. One of the major issues involved is that Russia will be making less use of the Soviet infrastructure that goes through Ukraine. Thus, we are still dealing with the issue of the Soviet legacy in very practical terms, with the physical pipeline there. This line extends to Europe and is at the center of international debate. Overall, the pipeline really can serve as a metaphor for Ukraine being tied to the Soviet legacy. In a sense, the pipeline is also largely responsible for the creation of the oligarchic class whose money has been associated with gas and oil in one way or another since the start of the 1990s. A lot of corruption is also associated with that oil and gas. So, again, this is just one but perhaps the most obvious example of the country being a hostage of the Soviet legacy.

Another big issue associated with the Soviet legacy is certainly the creation of Ukraine in cultural terms as a Russo-Ukrainian condominium. The Second World War, the Holocaust, and Stalin's policy of forced resettlement and state-sponsored

2. The Collapse of the USSR Is Still Going On

ethnic cleansing made Ukraine less multiethnic than it was before the war. As a result, it was turned into a Russo-Ukrainian entity to an unprecedented degree, largely through the processes of industrialization, labor-force migration, and so on. In the last decades of the Soviet Union, state policies promoted the ethnic, linguistic, and cultural unity of Russia and Ukraine, with cultural unification a major factor. All these issues are now at the center of the ongoing Russo-Ukrainian war in the Donbas. None of them can be understood only in the context of the last thirty years; those processes have deep roots.

Last but not least, I will return to the critical infrastructure associated with the Soviet Union in Ukraine. Overall, the war in the Donbas reminds us of another part of the legacy of Soviet industrialization. It is the pipeline, so to speak, that stopped working a long time ago: by that I mean the coal-mining industry, which has not been profitable for decades and decades. This is the fate of many "rust belts" all over the world, which are often associated with social dislocation, trauma, and tragedy. But Ukraine offers perhaps the world's only case in which the collapse of a rust belt not only produces social tensions but also facilitates a war, creating conditions for foreign invasion. The social issues produced by the collapse of nineteenth-century infrastructure, exploited by the USSR and then passed on to independent Ukraine, are an important component of the war in the Donbas.

AR: *Certainly, there is this physical element that is very interesting to consider. But you also mentioned Russification during the Soviet period—the promotion of Russian unity with Ukraine. I am reminded of Vladimir Putin's recent essay, published in July, titled "On the Historical Unity of Russians and Ukrainians," where he made the argument that "modern Ukraine is entirely a product of the Soviet era … that it was shaped—for a significant part—on the lands of historical Russia." Is this still the attempt of the metropolis to maintain an imperial narrative? As a Ukrainian historian, what was your reaction when you read this essay?*

SP: There are two levels to this issue. One involves actual policies conducted, and the other relates to the arguments used to justify such actions. Russia historically, for centuries and centuries, linked the concept of national security or imperial expansion to the creation of "friendly" states on its periphery. No state was friendly enough not to be integrated or incorporated into the empire, and, eventually, the next candidate for a friendly state would emerge. In that sense, there is no difference between Uzbekistan and Ukraine, for example. Yet, on another level, there is a huge difference between those two countries, and that is what Putin's article was mostly about. For a long time, especially in the nineteenth century, Ukrainians, Russians, and Belarusians were regarded as members of one big Russian nation. Owing to this, such people as Prince Volodymyr (Russian: Vladimir) or Bohdan Khmelnytsky were imagined as key figures in Russian history. Go to Kyiv today, and there are monuments to those personalities who are now perceived as Ukrainian national figures. But those monuments were erected in the nineteenth century by the Russian imperial authorities. They were built at the initiative of people who believed in one indivisible Russia.

What Putin says, in fact, is that he wants to go back to the pre-1917 model of the big Russian nation. He rejects the Soviet experience and blames Soviet nationality policies for actually creating today's divisions. Of course, this is just a result of Putin's rejection of the parts of history that do not fit his paradigm. The Soviet Union tried to preserve the empire by accommodating the national movements that were already there. It is not that the Soviet Union appeared first and the Ukrainian national movement or the idea of Ukrainian independence came second. It was the other way around, and anyone who has even a cursory knowledge of the history of the region understands that. Otherwise, we would have to assume that the USSR was also responsible for the creation of the Organization of Ukrainian Nationalists.

AR: *Looking at the trend in Ukraine's political development since the Soviet collapse, we can see this back-and-forth between a more pro-Western path versus a kind of stepping back, which can be characterized as more pro-Russian. That was probably the case until Petro Poroshenko's victory after the Revolution of Dignity. But I was wondering how we should understand Volodymyr Zelensky's rise in this process. Zelensky seems to lie a little bit outside this East-West tug of war.*

SP: There are really two Ukraines: one dating from before the war that began in 2014 and another one currently being forged by the war in the Donbas. If you look at the presidential elections before 2014, you see that Ukraine was divided almost down the middle. This division was very clearly defined in geographic terms between eastern and western Ukraine. The electoral border could move a little bit here and there, and different presidents would be elected with the support of one side or the other. But the war changed that pattern as well as the entire political map of Ukraine. First of all, the loss of the Crimea and part of the Donbas removed millions of voters with a post-Soviet identity, oriented toward Russia, from the electorate. Another difference came with the fact that the rest of Ukraine, which remained under Kyiv's control, became increasingly mobilized in an attempt to protect itself against Russian aggression. Both processes contributed to Ukrainian society, with the electorate becoming much more homogeneous.

The first sign that this was really happening came in 2014, when Petro Poroshenko won the presidency with an unprecedented majority. It was not clear whether this was the start of a new trend, because there was, of course, the shock of war, and many unusual things were happening at the time. The election of President Zelensky demonstrated that we were probably dealing with a new tendency in the country, because he also gained an absolute majority. While Poroshenko lost a little bit in the east, Zelensky lost a little bit in the west. But basically, since 2014, both presidents have been elected by an overwhelming majority of the electorate. That is the new reality. This increase in homogeneity also resulted in the fact that, for the first time in Ukraine's post-Soviet history, a majority in parliament belongs to one party. Consequently, accusations of authoritarianism are becoming part of Ukrainian political vocabulary to an unprecedented degree. This is the new reality produced by changes in Ukrainian geography and society that came with the war.

AR: *Certainly, the war played a huge role in consolidating Ukrainian society and identity, pushing Ukraine even further away from the Soviet legacy and the imperial past.*

SP: Ukraine is being pushed away from Russia to a degree that was really unimaginable before 2014. And there is a real disconnect between what Vladimir Putin is saying in terms of Russo-Ukrainian unity and the impact that his actions are having on Russo-Ukrainian relations.

AR: *In the context of our conversation about the consequences of the collapse of the Soviet Union, it seems that Belarus is a bit of an outlier in terms of developments. Yet something has changed with the most recent falsified election and the outbreak of mass protests and demonstrations there. Is this also part of the processes that we have been talking about?*

SP: In many ways, Belarus is basically catching up with the rest of the region. There, the original push for a more nationalizing state that started in 1991 and 1992 was partly stopped by the arrival of Alexander Lukashenko (Alyaksandr Lukashenka). The refusal to nationalize led Belarus to become a kind of relic of the Soviet period. Others in the neighborhood, Russia and Ukraine in particular, were progressing on the path of nationalization. Ironically, Belarus was becoming ever more different from those republics by refusing to nationalize. What we see now, especially in the last year or two, is actually a major step in this nationalization process, which has been triggered by two factors. The first is society's rejection of Lukashenko's authoritarian regime, which is associated with this anti-national position. Almost by default, the pre-Soviet national flag of Belarus became the flag of the protesters, bringing along all the values, myths, and other features associated with the Belarusian national project.

This is somewhat similar to the Ukrainian story, which involves the political importance of symbols and elements of national culture. The Ukrainian language was quite marginal on the streets of Kyiv through the 1990s up to the early 2000s. But Ukrainian would consistently become the language of revolution, opposition, and the Maidan. Now we are dealing with a form of Belarusian Maidan. Various Belarusian national values and symbols are closely associated with this movement. The second influence is that of Russia, which remains a very important factor in the whole post-Soviet space, affecting the processes taking place there. Russia's backing of the discredited Lukashenko regime has now created disillusionment in Belarusian opposition circles that were oriented in one way or another toward Russia. Now they have little choice but to embrace Belarusian identity. We will see in time whether current events turn out to be just a moment in history or the beginning of a trend setting Belarus on the same track as the rest of the region.

AR: *For the last question, I want to ask about terminology and approach to the region. It is now thirty years since the collapse of the Soviet Union, and I wonder what you think about the expression "post-Soviet." This is something I have been asking myself and others. Do you consider this term outdated? Is it time that we abandon this expression?*

SP: Like "Soviet," "post-Soviet" is becoming—and this should be encouraged more and more—part of the vocabulary of historians. Post-Soviet and Soviet legacies are still with us, but they are becoming less important with every passing day. Just look at the different former republics of the Soviet Union, with various groups embarking on very different tracks and directions. On the one hand, you have the Baltic states, which belong to the European Union and NATO. They are successful democracies and, at this point, even more successful than some democracies of the former Eastern bloc, including Poland and Hungary. Then you have mostly authoritarian Central Asia and a mixed bag in terms of democracy in the South Caucasus. Ukraine and Moldova are democratic but face huge economic challenges. In many ways, all these countries have a common Soviet legacy but have chosen different paths of development. Less and less can now be explained by reference to the Soviet legacy alone. What we also see now is that pre-Soviet history is becoming ever more important in explaining what is happening in the region and the choices being made today. So I would not call the term illegitimate, but it loses much of its legitimacy when it comes to explaining contemporary developments in the region.

December 2021

3. Three Decades of Independence

Interview conducted by
Nadia McConnell, US-Ukraine Foundation

Nadia McConnell (NM): *Ukraine will soon [as of August 2021—ed.] celebrate the thirtieth anniversary of its independence. Looking back, what do you see as the greatest achievements and greatest failures of these thirty years of independence?*

Serhii Plokhy (SP): I think that both successes and failures become quite clear when you look at the current map of Ukraine. That is, Ukraine has existed on this map for thirty years since its Declaration of Independence and referendum on independence. This is a major achievement. Ukraine exists as a state; as a nation, it is taking shape and continuing to develop, even if that process is still far from completion. The shortcomings that we see include the fact that the Crimea is part of Ukraine de jure but not de facto. Similarly, part of the Donbas has been lost. These parts of the map show great failures of the period of independence, which are related to the fact that, for twenty-five or thirty years before 2014, Ukraine did not manage to create a strong national identity binding its citizens to the state and inspiring them to protect their country. Nor has Ukraine created an economic system that people would consider fair. Recall the old issue of oligarchic power. The situation in the Donbas is at least in part a result both of the weakness of Ukrainian national identity in certain regions and of popular protest against the economic vulnerability in which people find themselves. These

3. Three Decades of Independence

are two major problems that exist in Ukraine today and are reflected on its map.

NM: *This is indeed a very important achievement—that Ukraine is finally on the map, with its territory and borders that Putin is trying to attack. After all, for a very long time, people nurtured the idea of Ukraine when it had no state dimension. We must be aware of it and appreciate such an achievement. Regarding the problem of oligarchs and corruption, what ways do you see to solve this problem in order to avoid social division and destruction of the Ukrainian economy, since oligarchs control most of it?*

SP: A better organization of the economy to make it free and fair and to begin the process of deoligarchization are important tasks facing Ukraine. I don't think that anything can be solved in a revolutionary manner. Ukraine's loss of the Donbas is due, on the one hand, of course, to Putin's actions, but, on the other hand, it manifests the rejection of the oligarchic model by a large part of the population. As a result, the Donbas has turned into an economic desert. This clearly demonstrates that revolutionary, "proletarian" methods of reform in the spirit of the Bolshevik revolution of 1917 are absolutely useless and bring nothing but ruin to Ukraine.

Changes should take place gradually and be supported by appropriate legislation. Since oligarchs own the largest assets in Ukraine, transformation of the Ukrainian economy will be destructive unless oligarchs themselves take part in this transformative process. For this reason, legislation should create conditions making it advantageous for oligarchs to give up some influence in order to preserve their principal assets in full or in part. I like to joke that I support the oligarchization of the whole country. I mean, let there be ten or fifteen thousand so-called oligarchs, and that will allow us to solve the problem of oligarchic influence in Ukraine. We need legislation that would allow the average business to rise to that level, which would ensure real competition. In my opinion, an effective means of deoligarchization is to establish real economic competition and a market economy.

NM: *This is not just an interesting idea but a wise one, too: that we should not fight oligarchs but give everyone an opportunity* to increase their wealth. *Promote development of a strong middle class in Ukraine so that more people can contribute to the country's economic development and success. Obviously, Ukraine's development strategy should place more emphasis on this opportunity. And how would you describe the development of Ukrainian civil society over these thirty years, especially in the period since the Revolution of Dignity?*

SP: I'd say that, over the past thirty years, Ukrainian society has tried to understand how it should live in its own state. What is it like to live in your own home? This is a departure from the past, when society lacked the skill and knowledge required for independent living. It used to have a dream, but that dream was shared by only one part of society. Now the whole society—those who dreamed and those who did not—has ended up sharing this new home. Society needs to understand what it consists of, understand what was there on this territory, in order to begin creating a new common identity. It is a very difficult process that must be carried out at a time when the old economy has collapsed but the new one has not yet emerged.

There is an online resource at the Harvard Ukrainian Research Institute called Digital Atlas of Ukraine that presents the results of our research projects in the form of electronic maps. One of the projects concerned the views of people from different regions about Ukraine's attitude toward Russia and what Ukraine's relations with Russia should be. The picture was worst in the 1990s. At the end of that decade, the percentage of those who actually supported Ukraine's independence or believed that relations between Ukraine and Russia should be like those between sovereign states was lowest. At the same time, Ukraine was in the depths of its economic crisis. But, since the 2000s, a new society has begun to emerge, and the economy has begun to emerge as well.

In 2013–14, we found ourselves in a situation that few could have imagined in 1991: many Ukrainians proved willing to risk their lives to preserve a concept called Ukraine, and not only the concept but also the country's political institutions, territory, borders, and so on. Many people have sacrificed their lives for it. It was a difficult path. For many, it was a surprise that such a volunteer movement appeared, and that there were people ready to defend Ukraine. It was no longer a question of defending only the language or culture: these were just components of the people's overall motivation. Their self-mobilization was cross-linguistic and cross-cultural.

In the events of 2013–15, a community took shape in Ukraine—a political nation—that no longer considered the state something accidental or insignificant. The nation matured and Ukrainian consciousness developed. Although this wave of mobilization receded a few years later, it did not fall back to pre-2013 levels.

I think that 2014 is as important a year in Ukrainian history as 1991. In 1991, Ukraine gained its statehood; in 2014, in my opinion, Ukraine gained a new majority of people who associated themselves with the Ukrainian nation and considered this country their home. Not everyone shared this belief; hence the map as we see it now. Even today, there is a significant percentage of people in Ukraine who do not believe that the events in the Donbas are a war with Russia. So this process of identity formation is far from complete and can be reversed. But the country has passed a very important turning point.

NM: *Comparing 1991 and 2014, I remember how Rukh impressed me with its ability to unite not only different political forces but also different ethnic groups. All Ukraine's ethnic groups, including Russians, were represented in its leadership and coordination councils. Now, although you say that there are still people in Ukraine who do not support its statehood or do not believe in it, let us remember that the volunteers and soldiers who rose to defend Ukraine also came from different ethnic groups. Many of them speak Russian. Nevertheless, they feel Ukrainian. It seems to me that you underestimate these important changes in Ukrainian society. In my opinion, these changes are already irreversible.*

SP: I believe that the formation of Ukraine as an independent nation-state is irreversible in historical perspective. This issue has been resolved. The question of Ukraine's borders remains a problem. We didn't think about it before 2014 but need to do so today. And questions remain about the effectiveness of the Ukrainian state: how well it will be able to represent and protect the interests of the people? But the existence of the Ukrainian state and nation is no longer a question: it was answered first in 1991 and then in 2014.

NM: *Speaking of Ukraine's independence, I would like to ask you how many times Ukraine was an independent state in the past, for how long, and is its present-day independence historically the longest?*

SP: Indeed, the Act of Independence adopted in 1991 was the fifth attempt to proclaim Ukraine's independence in the course of the twentieth century. The previous attempts were unsuccessful; some of them were particularly futile. For instance, independent Carpatho-Ukraine existed only a few days. The Ukrainian state proclaimed by the Organization of Ukrainian Nationalists in 1941 did not last a single day. Even the Ukrainian People's Republic proclaimed in January 1918 had a complex history. It is therefore hard to say how many days Ukraine's independence lasted, all in all, prior to 1991. For one thing, it was intermittent. Besides, in order to gain partial independence from Russia, Ukraine had to become more dependent on other states, as was the case under Hetman Pavlo Skoropadsky in 1918. There is no doubt that, in August 1991, we obtained the longest period of Ukrainian independence since the times of Kyivan Rus'. In other words, independence under Hetman Bohdan Khmelnytsky and Hetman Ivan Vyhovsky was much shorter than what we have today. The present generation of Ukrainians has been politically independent longer than any other generation for centuries.

NM: *I do not believe that everyone appreciates the fact that we will soon be able to celebrate thirty years of Ukraine's independence, while previous attempts were very short-lived. We therefore need to consider why this declaration of independence has been more successful. I would like to talk about the events of 1989–91, which preceded the Act of Independence. Let us talk about those events and their impact on Ukraine's civil society as it later endorsed the call for independence. The events of that period range from the impact of the Chornobyl disaster to the movement of "soldiers' mothers" to protect the rights of their sons who had been sent to fight in Afghanistan. I think that the commemoration of the*

3. Three Decades of Independence

Millennium of Christianity saw a sort of awakening in Ukrainian society. How do you think those events or others contributed to the strength of Ukraine's independence proclaimed in 1991?

SP: All those factors contributed to the advancement of independence. Chornobyl (Russian: Chernobyl) became the starting point of Ukraine's modern politics, with the establishment of Green World, the first political party other than the ruling communist one. It produced mass mobilization embodied in Rukh. Another factor that facilitated mass mobilization was the return of legal status to the Ukrainian Greek Catholic Church (UGCC). That event brought people into the streets and helped to delegitimize established authority. It was linked to the Millennium of Christianity—a first step that was followed by UGCC legalization.

There were two things that the government could not ban. One was social mobilization on environmental issues related to Chornobyl. The other was freedom of religion. The government acknowledged both those demands as legitimate. A third factor promoting mass mobilization was industrial workers' strikes, especially in the Donbas. Those three factors were the most salient. There were other, less significant ones as well. You mentioned Afghanistan and the movement of soldiers' mothers. For the most part, Afghanistan remained an unknown war. The government managed to hide the truth about that war better than about Chornobyl. Mobilization around that issue was limited to small groups, such as soldiers' mothers protecting their sons. That movement also mattered, but it was less significant than the three other factors that brought people into the streets to defy communist rule.

NM: *You have had lifelong experience of living in Ukraine and then observing it intensely even after you moved away. My first trip to Ukraine took place in 1990, when I traveled to take part in the Human Chain for Unity. Over the next two years, I must have made eight or nine additional trips, and I observed events as an outsider. I was struck by the strategic approach of Rukh under the leadership of Ivan Drach and Mykhailo Horyn, considering how they activated and mobilized supporters. It was extraordinary how they organized the Human Chain itself in every detail. They had buses to bring people from cities such as Ivano-Frankivsk to* remote locations, so that the Human Chain would stretch continuously from Lviv to Kyiv.

But I could also see that there was no overall strategic plan of selecting candidates for the elections of March 1990; some of that process became spontaneous as different people decided that it might be an opportunity to win, and some of them did win, of course. In parliament, they ended up with 125 members of the Narodna Rada (the Democratic Bloc) against 239 communists. These numbers show that the Democratic Bloc was a relatively small minority in the legislature. Yet, a few months later, in July, they were able to pass the Declaration of Sovereignty, which, for me, was a phenomenal success! And then, just a year later, the Declaration of Independence came in August 1991, with the condition that it be approved by referendum on 1 December. How do you analyze that period, and how do you explain this success of the democratic forces, despite having such a small number in parliament?

SP: It goes without saying: there would have been no independence without Rukh. And indeed, Rukh was a minority. World events are usually determined by a minority, as long as it is mobilized and has a viable alternative to propose. Although Rukh was a minority, it had an idea, a viable alternative vision—first sovereignty and then independence—that no one else could propose. In 1990–91, it appealed to many different groups as a solution to their problems, from the national communists who decided that they would benefit from independence to the Donbas coal miners who assumed that the government in Kyiv would be closer and more responsive to them than the one in Moscow, to ordinary residents in the East who had never thought about independence but, faced with a collapsing economy, began to consider that Ukraine would do better on its own than within the Soviet Union. Thus, an idea proposed by a minority became very timely and showed strong mobilizing power. One might say that this situation repeated the Ukrainian success of March 1917 when Hrushevsky could not believe his eyes on seeing how many people had turned out for a pro-Ukraine political rally. At that time, the Central Rada came up with an alternative—autonomy for Ukraine—that no one else could propose. So I totally agree with you.

You mentioned the amazing Human Chain that stretched from Lviv to Kyiv. And we know that it did not extend across all Ukraine—as far as Kharkiv, Simferopol, or Donetsk. This indicates that, nationwide, Rukh remained a minority, even though it was an important political actor. Its influence was regionally limited. Independence became possible in 1991 because that idea was accepted by other actors who had not previously supported it—most importantly, the national communists of Leonid Kravchuk. That was an example of the power of ideas, mobilization, and political leadership.

NM: *Yes, that was something I really grasped then: the leadership of Rukh included both Communist Party members such as Ivan Drach, a prominent member of the Writers' Union, and recent political prisoners such as Mykhailo Horyn, who had spent fifteen or eighteen years in the Gulag. Remarkably, this was a very strong partnership, and they were able to bring all those groups together.*

SP: They all started in the ranks of the same Komsomol, together with Viacheslav Chornovil, but then some of them decided to conceal their views and remain in the party, while others spoke out. But one might say that there was no fundamental chasm between Drach and Horyn. That is why, when the Communist Party of the Soviet Union (CPSU) was banned, no one came out in protest. We have spoken about mass movements related to Chornobyl, the Ukrainian Greek Catholic Church, coal miners' strikes… But there was never a movement or mass mobilization to defend the CPSU. For most people, membership in the CPSU was a required formality that did not reflect their own choice of ideas or orientations.

NM: *Going on to the referendum vote, its sheer numbers were phenomenal: nearly 93 percent of the people of Ukraine voted for independence, more than 50 percent in the Crimea, and in the Donbas as well—and that is what secured Ukraine's independence. So why has Ukraine chosen to celebrate its Independence holiday as an anniversary of the parliamentary vote in August rather than the day when the people democratically voted for their independence?*

SP: I don't think I can explain this factually, because I was not involved in those decisions. But this is how I explain it to myself: throughout the referendum campaign, it was emphasized that independence had been proclaimed, and now the popular vote only had to confirm it. Once that vote took place, it was hard to turn around and say that we were not independent then but are only getting there now. Those who led the campaign for independence believed that 24 August was the day on which they broke the shackles that bound them to Moscow, or to the Soviet Union, or to Russia, or to the Empire. That was the turning point. And then, once the "marriage" had been dissolved, it only remained to do the paperwork, so to speak.

NM: *Thirty years after the country's independence was proclaimed and internationally recognized, Ukraine continues to struggle bitterly against Russia's efforts to maintain its imperial dominance. Do you foresee a time when Putin and the Kremlin may come to the realization that Ukraine is an independent state? It just seems that they have a psychological inability to do so.*

SP: I do not believe that Putin and his circle are ready to accept Ukraine as an independent state. This also applies to their generation as a whole. But a new generation will no longer understand the thinking of Putin and his contemporaries. After all, Putin's thinking was shaped in the 1970s, so his idea of normality was the Soviet Union as a superpower. And, for that generation, everything that has happened since the 1970s is not normal. This is how we all are made: we develop a frame of reference about this world when we are twenty or thirty years old, and then it guides us for the rest of our lives. The generation on the streets of Moscow and other Russian cities these days is completely different. They cannot understand Putin's mindset of the 1970s, nor even his mindset of the 1990s.

This change of generations does not mean that some of Russia's imperial ambitions or claims to a dominant role in the region will suddenly disappear. But there will be a change in the perceived legitimacy of independent statehood for other Soviet republics. Of course, they will still try to manipulate, influence psychologically, or apply military force. In that sense, a new generation will not change anything. But there will be a change in their perception of Ukraine's independence, and they will come to terms with it. Even Putin's thinking has changed since Soviet times: he might try to manipulate Poland or Hungary, but no one would question whether Poland and Hungary are entitled to independent statehood. By the way, even in 2014, Putin never made claims to western Ukraine, because it is obviously non-Russian in language and culture. Russian perceptions are changing, but very slowly, so I do not foresee visible change for another decade, or as long as Putin and his group remain in power. But eventually this policy will change, or at least there will come a fundamental political understanding that Ukraine is entitled to independent statehood.

NM: *Putin seems unable to believe that Ukraine's development as an independent state comes from within, not from outside. He seems to think that it was a conspiracy of Western countries. I wish he knew that Taras Shevchenko's words, "When will we have a Washington of our own, with new and righteous laws?" were written in 1857. In those times, there was no CIA or international assistance programs. So the idea expressed by Shevchenko has been maintained for at least a century and a half. But Putin cannot rid himself of the notion that Ukraine and Russia are one people, one nation. I would like to hope that your prediction will finally come true.*

SP: Putin's words about "one nation" reflect the thinking of a large part of Russian society. Putin is a big problem, of course, but a much bigger problem is that he is not the only Russian who thinks so. This is a consequence of two factors: Ukraine's long existence within the Russian Empire and then in the Soviet Union, as well as its russification. Before the current war, Russians who went to the Baltics did not ask whether the people there belonged to Russia. But on going to the Crimea, the Donbas, or Kyiv and hearing Russian speech, they would ask themselves: "How are these people different from us?" And very often they would decide that there is no difference.

In today's world, the legitimacy of a state is linked to a distinct nation, and a nation is distinguished by its own culture, language, and so on. And so Ukraine finds itself in a challenging situation. On the other hand, Ukraine is answering that challenge in a way that Putin never expected. For him, the Russian language and Russian-speaking culture equals Russian identity and loyalty to Moscow. In [Russian-speaking—ed.] Dnipro, however, the people's answer to him was "no," and in [Russian-speaking—ed.] Kharkiv the answer was also "no." That is, the Ukrainian response was that of a political nation. There are different ethnic groups and languages in Ukraine, but its citizens are loyal to their country and to the political and economic system that it has chosen.

This system is very different from that of Russia with regard to democracy, to a relatively free economic space not completely controlled by the government (despite all the problems with oligarchs), and so on. The political and economic institutions of Ukraine and Russia differ dramatically, and this has become the basis for their different identities. Of course, language and culture remain important, but Ukraine is also a textbook example of the influence of political institutions on identity: since 2013–14, we see the growing loyalty of Ukraine's population to those institutions and the people's willingness to protect them.

NM: *What can you say about expectations of "Russia without Putin"? What impact would that have on Ukraine and Russia's relations with Ukraine?*

SP: Like all post-Soviet countries, Russia is shaping a new national identity. Russian nationalism will continue to grow. But, as a result of the war in the Donbas and the problems that Russia has encountered in dealing with Ukraine, it will discover, to its surprise, that this Russian nationalism can no longer be built around an "all-Slavic people" that includes Ukrainians and others. Instead, it will be purely Russian. I expect that these changes will go further and lead to a psychological recognition of Ukraine's entitlement to its own statehood. I also expect that the so-called Russian World project, which placed Russia and Ukraine under one umbrella, will be revised. It is far too costly for Russia, in terms of economic and political losses, as well as losses in its relations with the West. This policy cannot continue indefinitely, since it is detrimental to Russia and the Russian economy.

But I do not anticipate that Russia will leave Ukraine alone. It will behave like a great power dealing with a smaller neighbor. However, this won't be a policy of absorption, or attempts to seize territory, and so on. There will be a more or less normal great-power policy rooted in historical ties with neighbors. It seems to me that there will be some normalization on new terms, which still may not be fully normal and equal. But at least there will be no more confusion as to whether Kyiv is a Russian city or not. I think that Ukraine has already given the answer to that question, and that the next generation of Russian leaders will accept it.

NM: *The war in Ukraine's east is on the minds of most people these days. Do you think there is a solution to that conflict other than military? Is it possible to have a diplomatic solution?*

SP: There is no military solution to that war. There is only a diplomatic solution, and the main issue is how to recover Ukrainian territory occupied by Russia. The question is how that will come about, and on what terms. As long as Putin and his circle remain in the Kremlin, I doubt that the terms will be acceptable to Ukraine. Thus, while I see no solution other than a diplomatic one, it cannot come soon. This complicates the situation, because, with every passing year, the Donbas and Ukraine are moving further and further apart.

NM: *I would like to discuss another important question with you. What do you think we can do for Ukraine—the people of the West, particularly those in the diaspora? In other words, what should we do and what should we not do?*

SP: It seems to me that the trend, which began in the late 1980s, of every visitor from the diaspora setting out to impart "basic wisdom" to people in Ukraine has run its course. Today, we have people in Ukraine who are competent in economics, business, and governance. So the initial mission of integrating Ukrainian elites into the Western world, which was extremely important, has been accomplished. Also, there were times when material support from the Ukrainian diaspora could play an important role in politics. For example, the diaspora could raise money for Rukh—say, $10,000—to buy some critically important equipment or supplies and thus make a big impact. But, today, there is much more money in Ukraine's politics and economy, so that page has been turned as well.

What remains to be done? There is still the matter of representing Ukraine and helping with so-called soft power. However, the whole model needs to be changed and is already changing: namely, not only does Ukraine need the help of the diaspora, but the diaspora needs the help of Ukraine. This is an important point that needs to transform in the diaspora's perception.

NM: *You know, it has taken a united community here to stand up for the idea of Ukraine throughout the decades and on a variety of issues—the Holodomor, the Captive Nations resolution, the Shevchenko monument in DC, and much more. We were representing the concept of Ukraine, I guess. So now that there's an independent Ukraine with its own government, we no longer speak on behalf of what we think Ukraine is. We can now speak just as citizens of the United States or any other country of residence. And yes, I recall that there was a tendency to patronize, sometimes great resentment on the Ukrainian side, and a love-hate relationship with those of us from the diaspora. They loved us, but at times they were not very happy with the way in which we dealt with them.*

SP: What we need now are joint projects, truly mutual ones. It is very positive that Ukraine understands this. I can see it, for example, in the establishment of the Ukrainian Institute, which is now headed by Volodymyr Sheiko. There is not much money there, but it shows that Ukraine is an active participant. I think that the task for the diaspora today is to develop an effective partnership with Ukraine, first of all in regard to humanitarian matters, and then to Ukraine's international image. This is where the diaspora can really help and contribute something useful. But, fundamentally, these relations must change from patronage and paternalism to partnership. And they are changing already. I'm not saying anything revolutionary; I'm talking about already existing trends, and I think that they indicate the future.

NM: *We've talked about whether there will come a time when Russia or the Kremlin will accept the idea of Ukraine as a sovereign*

3. Three Decades of Independence

country that has the right to choose its own path. How do we see that perception changing in other countries? It seems to me that some countries are still looking at Ukraine through the lens of Moscow, and Ukraine may sometimes look like a pawn sacrificed on the altar of geopolitics. How do you see things, let's say, in Germany and France, developing more toward understanding and supporting Ukraine as an independent state?

SP: Every state acts first and foremost in its own interests. Presidents and governments are elected for that purpose, and, if they don't take care of the country's interests, in democratic systems, they are voted out in elections. Therefore we cannot expect that the United States, or France, or Germany would act against their own interests for the sake of Ukraine. We don't see that today, we didn't see that thirty years ago, and we surely won't see it thirty years from now. Ukraine must therefore develop a capacity to survive, at least to some extent, relying on its own resources. Others can help if it is in their interest, but no one will do the job that Ukraine must do for itself.

In this sense, Ukraine's international situation has generally been very favorable for thirty years, and that facilitated its independence. It has been much more favorable than during the liberation struggle of 1917–20 or after World War II. That favorable situation continues at present. The United States is involved in one way or another, and Europe is involved. I don't think that it's worth hoping for more. The question is how to take advantage of these favorable conditions to build up the Ukrainian state, democracy, and economy. That's what we should hope for. And this applies just as well to any other country. Expectations that someone would do certain things for us, support us, or fight for us are not only naive but also very harmful.

August 2021

4. Books on the War

*Interview conducted by
Sophie Roell, Five Books*

Sophie Roell (SR): *Before we get to the books, could you explain what, in your view, the conflict between Russia and Ukraine is about?*

Serhii Plokhy (SP): It has been framed again and again in terms of Russia and NATO. That pertains to some elements of the conflict, but there are also deeper roots. It is a situation that could be recognized throughout the world, because we are watching the disintegration of one of the last empires. The Russian Empire began to fall apart when the Austro-Hungarian, Ottoman, and other empires were crumbling. The Bolsheviks held it together, but, in 1991, it collapsed almost overnight. Everyone was surprised. Miraculously, there was no major war or bloodshed. Now we realize that the war was just postponed. This has been a terrible but very familiar situation for many countries that have found it necessary to fight wars of independence.

It is complicated by the fact that both Russians and Ukrainians have unresolved issues of identity and nation formation, as well as contested history. For example, Russians believe that they come from Kyiv ("Kiev" in Russian), which happens, today, to be the capital of an independent state, Ukraine. Vladimir Putin wrote an article "On the Historical Unity of Russians and Ukrainians." How many presidents plunging into war write such articles and make arguments of that kind? It's an attempt to delegitimize the

Ukrainian claim to statehood. If we are historically the same people, what right do you have to a state of your own? You have none! That doesn't normally happen with the disintegration of empires. The British never claimed that they somehow came from Delhi, nor vice versa. But you do see that with Russia and Ukraine.

So those are the deep roots and overall structure of the conflict. With the end of the Cold War, the Soviet Union fell apart. It was not a hot war, but it was one that Moscow lost economically, geostrategically, and so on. Now there is an attempt to reassemble the Russian empire as a belt of dependencies. Russia tried to accomplish it by economic and political means, and now we've reached the war stage. It's the last instrument in Russia's hands.

Ukraine is important because it's the second-largest post-Soviet republic. If Ukraine resists successfully, that puts in question the Russian claim to the rest of the post-Soviet space. It gives the lie not to Moscow's supposed attempt to recreate the Soviet Union—no one wants a reprise of such an expensive imperial project—but to establish an effective sphere of influence. Without the second-largest republic, there would be a huge gap in the entire structure. The media are concentrating on Russia-NATO relations, which are important, but they are just at the apex of a great many other political, historical, and cultural problems that define the current crisis.

SR: *Before speaking with you, I was looking at a* New York Times *map of where the Russian troops are, and I could see them in Belarus and Transnistria. Earlier in 2021, Russian troops were invited to intervene in Kazakhstan. It seems that quite a few ex-Soviet countries are quite happy to stay in the Russian sphere of influence. I guess the problem for Ukraine is that, since 2013 or perhaps earlier, since 2004, it's been trying to go down a different route.*

SP: You're absolutely right. The Soviet Union fell apart on the issue of Ukraine. The first to raise the banner of independence were the Baltic states, but they're small and not Slavic. The Ukrainian referendum of December 1991 did not ask, like the all-Union March referendum, what was to be done with the Soviet Union. It concerned Ukraine alone: "Do you want Ukraine to be independent?" After more than 90 percent of Ukrainian voters responded in the affirmative, the USSR was gone within a week. The Central Asian republics were pushed out of the Soviet Union because Russia was not interested in a union with them that did not include Ukraine. That's the beginning of the most recent part of the story: the Soviet Union disintegrated over the issue of Ukraine. If Russia is to have effective political, economic, and military spheres of influence, it must include Ukraine, as it did before the collapse of 1991.

SR: *Let's talk about the books you've chosen, and maybe you can say a bit about each of them and what they bring to the picture. The first one on your list is* Ukraine and Russia: From Civilized Divorce to Uncivil War *by Paul D'Anieri, a political scientist. I think he's a specialist on this relationship, is that right?*

SP: This is D'Anieri's first book dealing with Ukraine-Russia relations. Before that, he studied internal processes in Ukraine and, to a degree, in Russia. That's what he brings to the table. This book concerns more than just international relations theory or diplomatic history: D'Anieri knows a lot about both countries. He starts in the late 1980s and goes up to 2019, when the book was published. By that time, the war in Ukraine's east had begun, and its first stage was over. His argument is basically twofold. First, his history is rooted in the disintegration of the Soviet Union and in the way it fell apart. He stresses the importance of Ukraine in that process, something I was just talking about.

His other big argument is that the war became almost inevitable because of the different political tracks chosen by Ukraine and Russia, in particular the issue of nation-building and the creation and consolidation of the Ukrainian state. Ukraine became a democracy, while Russia moved in an authoritarian direction. This automatically made Russia's relations with Europe difficult, and security issues became very important. D'Anieri is very good at documenting and chronicling how security problems have affected Russo-Ukrainian relations since the 1990s, into the 2000s with the arrival of Putin, and subsequently. He gives a good explanation of the war and its background, not looking for sensationalist explanations or dwelling on personalities but concentrating on structural reasons.

4. Books on the War

D'Anieri is a political scientist, and the book is very well organized and well written. It explains a lot about the two countries and their political development, the choices made in both cases, and how they led to the current confrontation.

SR: *Yes, because we may talk about foreign policy, but, if you look at how leaders act, it's almost always to do with domestic politics.*

SP: Yes, indeed—and he really brings this point home.

SR: *Let's move on to* Ukraine: What Everyone Needs to Know *by Serhy Yekelchyk, a Ukrainian historian based in Canada. Are you recommending this as the best introductory book?*

SP: Exactly. It's part of an Oxford University Press series, *What Everyone Needs to Know* (supposedly, that is). The first edition appeared in 2015 under the title *The Conflict in Ukraine*. It was done almost like a catechism: the author collected the most commonly asked questions and answered them. The book was exceptionally important, given that the war in Ukraine is a hybrid one: it discusses disinformation, false narratives, false-flag operations, and so on. The book does a very good job of explaining whatever questions were raised in the media. Was the Ukrainian Maidan protest "fascist"? What was happening with the Crimea? What is the attitude of the population in the Donbas?

This is a revised edition, which also, according to the title, is a broader book. If people are interested in the subject, that's where I suggest they start. Yekelchyk's argument explaining the war contradicts the Kremlin's narrative. In the media, one can read that Ukraine is engaged in a civil war, that the country is divided between east and west, and these people speak Russian, while those speak Ukrainian. He argues that this is not an issue. Yes, the languages are different, but Ukrainians have mobilized across linguistic lines. A good many of the soldiers now fighting at the front speak Russian. The Russian language doesn't automatically mean Russian identity and loyalty to Russia. In the 2020 edition, Yekelchyk brings in more recent developments, including the Trump impeachment trial, the role of Paul Manafort, and claims about Ukrainian interference in the American elections.

It's a book that deals with all the issues and controversies that have appeared in the media since the start of the war.

This book is meant for a broad audience. The author recently advertised a new edition, saying, "The book is out there. It is not for my Facebook friends, because you probably know all of it, but please recommend it to your friends." It's an ABC of the current conflict and the war, written by a very good historian.

SR: *Let's go on to* Ukraine's Nuclear Disarmament *by Yuri Kostenko. He's a Ukrainian politician who was involved in the negotiations that led to the Budapest Memorandum after Ukraine gave up the third-largest nuclear arsenal in the world. Tell me about the book and how it fits in.*

SP: At the start of the war, Russia violated a lot of treaties. Among the key ones was the Budapest Memorandum, signed by Ukraine in December 1994 with the United States, the United Kingdom, and Russia. There were also separate agreements signed with Kazakhstan and Belarus. According to the agreements, those republics gave up the nuclear arsenals that they had inherited from the Soviet Union in exchange for "assurances," not guarantees, from the other three powers of their sovereignty, the inviolability of their borders, and so on. In 2014, Russia, one of the countries that gave those assurances—and to which Ukraine transferred its nuclear arsenal—violated Ukraine's territorial integrity and occupied the Crimea.

It was in this context that Kostenko wrote his book, which is half memoir and half an account based on all the documents that he accumulated. It's a really interesting story, almost unknown in the West. Ukraine was very reluctant to give up its nuclear arsenal, over which it had physical but not operational control. Kazakhstan and Belarus were much more agreeable. Once again, Ukraine was a troublemaker, if you look at it from a Russian perspective. But everyone took the view that it was a good thing, a great success of denuclearization.

Kostenko provides a different perspective. It's the first work in English with so much detail that goes against the mainstream, Western interpretation of the story. His argument is not that Ukraine should have kept nuclear weapons but that Ukrainians were forced to give them up without getting proper guarantees

4. Books on the War

of their country's independence or adequate financial compensation. Nuclear weapons were Ukraine's security, and Ukraine gave them up because the US and Russia were working together.

This is a perspective that has received very little attention in the West, and it is especially interesting because it comes from someone who was right there, in the middle of the denuclearization process. You might also say, "Thank God that the current war is not nuclear—because it could have been if there were no Budapest Memorandum." But one way or another, our understanding of the Budapest Memorandum and what is happening today is absolutely incomplete without this very important book.

SR: *Is he suggesting Ukraine should perhaps have kept its nuclear weapons?*

SP: No, and that wasn't his position in the 1990s. He was involved as Minister of Environmental Protection and Nuclear Safety; he also dealt with Chornobyl. He is saying that Ukraine was cheated out of its nukes. The price was wrong. The price should have been either membership in NATO or something else actually meaningful that would have saved Ukraine from Russian aggression. What has happened to Ukraine since it was disarmed has and will have a negative impact on the global story of denuclearization. Countries are going to think twice next time someone comes along proposing to give them a piece of paper in exchange for their nuclear weapons. It's a huge disincentive to denuclearize. That's the global importance of this story, beyond just the current crisis.

SR: *Let's go on to* Ukraine in Histories and Stories: Essays by Ukrainian Intellectuals. *Tell me about this book.*

SP: This book, in a way, is on par with Yekelchyk's in the sense that it is an introduction to Ukraine, but it's an introduction using Ukrainian voices. The foreword is by Peter Pomerantsev, and there are essays by other expats (I'm also one of the contributors). But mostly the essays are the work of Ukrainian intellectuals living in Ukraine. They talk about their country and about stereotypes, mythology, history, and literature. It's an introduction to Ukraine for those who read not only nonfiction but also fiction, who are interested in the local cultural and academic scene.

What do Ukrainian philosophers think about their country? Or the writers? Many of the contributors are writers, such as Andrei Kurkov. If a person is even slightly known in the West, he'll be in there. There's Volodymyr Rafeyenko, one of the best new Ukrainian writers. There's an essay by Yuri Andrukhovych, one of the most recognizable names in Ukrainian literature. There is a piece by Alim Aliev on Ukraine and Crimean Tatars, another important issue. This book is for people interested not just in politics but also in the cultural scene, who perhaps have read some Ukrainian authors in translation and want to know a little more about the country.

SR: *And does the book deal with how people feel about Russia and the relationship with Russia?*

SP: It's all about that in one way or another. It's about Ukrainian identity, what it means, and how different or not it is from Russian. The authors are all, in a sense, bilingual. Andrei Kurkov has published a couple of books in Ukrainian, but he is basically a Russian-language writer. As for the Crimean Tatars, the younger generation speaks and writes in Ukrainian, but, for the older generation, it's Russian. The Polish-Ukrainian connection is represented in a piece by Ola Hnatiuk.

SR: *So is it a combination of fiction and nonfiction?*

SP: No, these are all essays. Andriy Kulakov writes the introduction, "Tabula rasa, or How to Find a Ukrainian Terra Incognita." A historian, Yaroslav Hrytsak, writes "Ukraine: A Brief but Global History of Ukrainian Bread." They interviewed me about Cossack identity in Ukraine and Yuri Andrukhovych on Ukrainian culture and literature. There is also an essay entitled "Steppe, Empire, and Cruelty" by Volodymyr Yermolenko who is a very good philosopher. Larysa Denysenko, a lawyer and activist, writes "Majority as a Minority." "Gaining a Motherland" by Vakhtang Kebuladze, a philosopher, is all about attitudes toward the Soviet past, the current war, and where you belong. There is an essay titled "Donbas–Ukraine, a Life Journey" by Volodymyr Rafeyenko, a writer who is one of the refugees from the Donbas. The last one is entitled "Insecure Security of Ukraine" by Hanna Shelest, an essayistic take on the current security situation—or lack thereof.

SR: *Lastly, you've chosen a work of fiction,* The Orphanage, *a novel by Serhiy Zhadan. Is he one of the most famous Ukrainian novelists?*

SP: Yes, in Ukraine, he is probably the leading contemporary author; outside Ukraine, I think Andrei Kurkov is better known. Both Kurkov and Zhadan have written about the current war. Kurkov's book is *Grey Bees*. I didn't include it because I haven't read it yet, but I do want to.

The Orphanage is an extremely interesting book. Serhiy Zhadan comes from eastern Ukraine, and, during the Maidan of 2013–14, he took part in clashes in the second-largest Ukrainian city, Kharkiv, which is now under threat of attack. He is a multitalented person: he has his own band and sings, writes novels and poems, and draws. To me, it's a brave book because it talks about things that one is not supposed to discuss in wartime. The war says, "This is us, and we are in the right. We're the heroes, and the other guys are the opposite of that. And certainly we are Ukrainians, Ukrainian patriots."

But, in the novel, he writes about a guy, Pasha, who has a post-Soviet identity. He is ethnically Ukrainian but not really Ukrainian or Russian. Exclusive identity is not his. That's very much the story of the Donbas, which is now beyond Ukrainian control, and many parts of eastern Ukraine as well. National identities there are not really formed. Pasha, a teacher, does not take sides in the conflict, but he has a nephew who happens to be on the other side of the dividing line, in the area controlled by separatists. Pasha feels that he has to return, get his nephew, and bring him back to the family. In the process of traveling there and back, he realizes where his home is. This is also another big, important thing: the war shapes Ukraine and Ukrainian identity. It leads to attachment to a nation that perhaps was not there previously in those eastern parts of Ukraine. It's a story of discovering where you belong, on which side of that divide.

Again, I was saying that it is a brave book, because, if you read about this guy, you sympathize with him. The novel is a kind of explanation of this blurred identity that is neither here nor there: of course, it opens up all kinds of possibilities for manipulation.

The novel is also very well done. It reads well. It's almost a photographic portrayal and presentation of the society in which the war is taking place, with no attempt to paint it ideologically one way or another or pretend that it is not what it is. It is a very honest book in that sense as well.

SR: *I read the first part, where he gets into trouble because he's avoiding listening to the news. He doesn't want to hear about what's going on; he just wants to go about his day.*

SP: This is another part of the coping mechanism in Ukraine, that people just stopped listening or watching. It's a form of denial, but it's also a way of coping with the situation. Will Putin attack today or not? Or maybe tomorrow? A person can't live like that for four or five or six months. Right now, in Ukraine, I understand there is no panic. Everything that is normally in the stores is there. People are not stocking up on toilet paper, as we did when Covid came. Everything is there in abundance. The only things unavailable are hunting weapons and guns to buy. That's the only thing there's been a run on. It's interesting, the way society reacts. For whatever reason, they're not stocking up on anything except weapons, which means that they want to stay and resist. They want to be able to protect themselves.

SR: *Do you understand what Putin hopes to achieve in Ukraine with the current buildup? It's slightly confusing to me because I'd always been led to believe that surprise was a key element in military strategy. If he was going to invade, shouldn't he already have done so?*

SP: The point is to finish unfinished business from 2014. His goal is either to make Ukraine pro-Russian or dismember it. He didn't succeed in 2014. He grabbed part of Ukrainian territory, but that mobilized the rest against Russia. In Ukraine, the number of people who want to join NATO increased threefold. Ukraine drew closer to the West, conducting joint military exercises with NATO, and so on. It's the absolute opposite of what Putin wanted to achieve. So the plan now is to come back and threaten the Ukrainian government, to create internal crisis, to grab more territory—basically, the goals are the same.

SR: *It's a war in which 13,000 people have already died since 2014, is that right?*

SP: Yes, between thirteen and fourteen thousand. Also, in such wars, it's not the military but the civil population that is most vulnerable. It's average citizens who suffer most from bombings and airstrikes.

February 2022

II. The Empire Returns

5. The Long Shadow

As Russian troops mass on the approaches to Ukraine, Ukrainian citizens are bracing themselves for war. "Emergency kit" is a phrase I hear used more and more among my friends and acquaintances all over the country; the question on everyone's mind is whether there will be an attack. I have been asked this numerous times over the past few weeks, and I cannot provide a satisfactory answer. The only thing I am sure about is that every bit of moral, political, and military support that Ukraine gets from its friends and allies makes an invasion less likely.

The crisis erupted on 17 December 2021, when Russia presented the West with an unexpected ultimatum. Its list of demands included a commitment in writing to halt any further eastward expansion of NATO, the removal of multinational NATO troops from Poland and the Baltic states, and the possible withdrawal of US nuclear weapons from Europe. Most crucial was that Ukraine never be allowed to join the alliance. The demands were considered non-starters in Washington and found unacceptable by all members of NATO. The result is that we now find ourselves locked in the most intense diplomatic confrontation between East and West since the end of the Cold War.

There are significant differences between this crisis and previous ones. Most important is the emergence of China as the leading partner in what began as the Sino-Soviet alliance, accompanied by the reduction of the former Soviet Union to the territory of Russia — a state whose economy is not in the world's top ten. These changes are crucial for understanding Russia's foreign policy today. Its aggression toward Ukraine can be seen as part of an attempt to turn the clock back to Soviet times and reinstate Russian control over the former Soviet space—or at least limit Western influence over what used to be Moscow's East European empire.

So, does Vladimir Putin want to reestablish the Soviet Union, as is occasionally suggested today? Not really. His goal is rather to reinstate or maintain the Kremlin's control over the former Soviet space more efficiently by creating dependencies, preferably ruled by autocrats, in place of the former Soviet republics—an imperial power structure with him as ruler of rulers at the top. The current crisis is a reminder that the dissolution of the Soviet Union, closely associated in the public mind with Mikhail Gorbachev's resignation as president of an already nonexistent country on Christmas Day 1991, was not a one-act play. It is, rather, a continuing saga with numerous sequels; a process rather than an event.

History cannot tell us what might or might not happen tomorrow. But it can provide a better understanding of how we reached the situation we are in today and what is at stake—especially as in this case the discipline of history, or at least a version of it, is at the very heart of the dispute. Last July, Putin published a long essay specifically dealing with the history of Russo-Ukrainian relations. The key argument of the article, entitled "On the Historical Unity of Russians and Ukrainians," was formulated in its very first paragraph. Referring to a recent press conference, Putin stated: "when I was asked about Russian-Ukrainian relations, I said that Russians and Ukrainians were one people—a single whole. These words were not driven by some short-term considerations or prompted by the current political context."

What the essay suggested was that there had been no such thing as a separate Ukrainian nation. The argument, which swept aside differences in language, history, and culture—especially political culture—between Russians and Ukrainians, was perceived by many as a denial of Ukraine's right to statehood. But the claim that Russians and Ukrainians constitute one people is not new, either in Putin's pronouncements or in the history of Russian political thought. The origins of that claim go back at least to the mid-nineteenth century when, in order to accommodate the rising Ukrainian national movement, Russian imperial thinkers formulated the concept of a tripartite Russian nation consisting of Great

5. The Long Shadow 53

Russians (or Russians in today's understanding of the term), Little Russians, or Ukrainians, and White Russians, or Belarusians.

It was also around this time that the imperial authorities prohibited Ukrainian-language publications in the empire, all but arresting the development of the Ukrainian political and cultural movement. That policy had its limits. It slowed down the development of a modern Ukrainian national project but did not stop it altogether. As the empire fell in the flames of the Russian Revolution, Ukrainian activists created a state of their own and declared independence in January 1918. In neighboring Austria-Hungary, Ukrainians declared independence as the Western Ukrainian People's Republic. This independence turned out to be short-lived, but it set the agenda for generations of Ukrainian leaders.

By 1920, when the Bolsheviks took over most of what had been Russian-ruled Ukraine, the idea of independence had gained popularity among the Ukrainian masses and could not simply be dismissed by the new authorities. The Bolsheviks found themselves obliged to recognize Ukraine as a separate nation and even grant pro forma independence to the Ukrainian Soviet republic. Indeed, the Soviet Union was created in 1922–23 as a pseudo-federal rather than a unitary state precisely in order to accommodate Ukraine and Georgia, the two most independent-minded republics, whose communist leaders simply refused to join the Russian Federation.

Ukraine, as the most populous republic after the Russian Federation, played a key role not only in the creation of the Soviet Union (Union of Soviet Socialist Republics) but also in its dissolution. It was the Ukrainian referendum of 1 December 1991, in which more than 90 percent of participants voted to leave the USSR, that spelled the end of the Cold War superpower. Importantly, the Ukrainians had answered the question of whether they wanted their country to be independent, not whether they wanted to dissolve the USSR. But the USSR fell apart within a week when Russia's parliament approved an agreement negotiated by Boris Yeltsin and his Ukrainian and Belarusian counterparts, Leonid Kravchuk and Stanislav Shushkevich, in the hunting lodge of Viskuli in western Belarus. That agreement dissolved the Soviet Union, recognized the independence of the former Soviet republics, and established the Commonwealth of Independent States (CIS) in place of the now defunct USSR.

Boris Yeltsin explained this development more than once in conversations with President George H. W. Bush: without Ukraine, Russia would have been outnumbered in Mikhail Gorbachev's Union by the Muslim Central Asian republics. Demographic and cultural factors certainly figured in that calculation, but so did economics. Russia was not prepared to bear the burden of the Union without its second-largest economy, that of Ukraine. So the old Union had to go.

Addressing the Russian parliament on 12 December 1991, Yeltsin stated that the formation of the CIS was the only way to "ensure the preservation of the political, legal, and economic space built up over centuries but now almost lost." Yeltsin did not want Gorbachev's reformed Union: his preferred political model was confederation, not full independence for the republics. The Commonwealth, whose creation was a compromise forced on Yeltsin by Ukraine, became central to Russia's bid to reestablish control over the post-Soviet space and its status as a global power.

It seemed that the leaders of the Soviet republics, the Russians in particular, had managed to avoid the usual violent disintegration of empires, preventing not only a widely feared nuclear war between the newly minted nuclear powers of Russia, Ukraine, Belarus, and Kazakhstan but also a conventional war between the main post-Soviet successor states. But the subsequent years found Russia involved in conflicts with post-Soviet states, offering support to separatist movements and eventually using its military forces outside its own borders. That was hardly a scenario imagined in the euphoria of the early post-Cold War years, given the victory of democratic forces in Russia and some other former Soviet republics.

The Soviet Union ceased its existence in a manner reminiscent of other continental empires, including its neighbors, the Ottoman Empire and Austria-Hungary, disintegrating along ethnic lines. But the end of the competition between Moscow and Washington never included a political settlement concerning the post-Soviet space. The United States, having sought to prevent the disintegration of the USSR as long as possible, ultimately decided to recognize and support the independence of the former Soviet republics. Russia, for its part, never accepted anything but the conditional independence of the former republics, predicated on an alliance with Moscow and belonging to Russia's sphere of influence.

Although the CIS was devised for the specific purpose of accommodating Ukraine, the Ukrainian leadership was not interested in any form of joint statehood with Russia. It even formally refused to join the Commonwealth that it had helped to create. But Kyiv's stubborn reluctance to give up the nuclear weapons it had inherited from the USSR—the third-largest arsenal in the world after those of the US and Russia—was based on its concern about possible Russian aggression. When the Ukrainians finally agreed to give up nuclear weapons in 1994, they insisted on guarantees of their territorial integrity and sovereignty. The Budapest Memorandum, which provided Ukraine with assurances instead of guarantees, was the result. One of the "assurers," apart from the US and the United Kingdom, was Russia.

Yeltsin's Russia attempted to keep Ukraine within its sphere of influence by means of economic ties, especially Ukraine's dependence on Russian gas. Putin's Russia tried to follow suit, and, as Ukraine continued its drift away from Russia toward the European Union, attempted to bribe President Viktor Yanukovych with a 15 billion loan to prevent him from signing an association agreement with the European Union. A popular uprising drove Yanukovych out of the country when he ultimately refused to sign such an agreement with the EU, although he had promised Ukrainian voters that he would do so. Russia accepted the fugitive, blamed the US and Europe for provoking and supporting the popular revolt, and annexed the Crimea. Moscow then began its destabilization of the Donets Basin (Donbas), the easternmost part of Ukraine, bordering on Russia. The resulting war is still going on, and many expect the Donbas to be the flashpoint of a new conflagration if a Russian invasion takes place. Some are concerned that the conflict could engulf other European countries and go global.

How does NATO fit into this story? As the Second World War drew to a close, Soviet armies conquered Eastern Europe and occupied it for two generations. NATO was established in 1949 as a defensive alliance to prevent further Soviet westward penetration. Russia's annexation of the Crimea drove a majority of Ukrainians into the pro-NATO camp. If less than 20 per cent of those polled supported joining NATO in 2013, almost 60 per cent favor it today. Not surprisingly, after the disintegration of the USSR, East European nations joined the alliance in order to prevent a recurrence of their long political and economic subjection—a process that Russia now deliberately misrepresents as an aggressive "eastward expansion" of NATO led by Washington and Brussels. Poland offers a particularly striking illustration of East European insistence on joining NATO: the Poles threatened Washington with the development of their own nuclear capabilities if they were not offered membership.

Russia's invasion of 2014 became the driving force behind Ukraine's insistence on joining the alliance. Immediately after the fall of Viktor Yanukovych's government in February of that year, the new Ukrainian leadership declared that it had no plans to join NATO. But the annexation of the Crimea and the war in the Donbas brought the majority of Ukrainians into the pro-NATO camp. Despite this change of attitude, NATO continues to deny Ukraine a Membership Action Plan. But Russia's current demand to bar Ukraine from NATO forever may very well backfire, leading ultimately to the opposite result.

Russia now gives the impression of moving faster than ever before to reestablish its control over the post-Soviet space. The Kremlin's support for Alexander Lukashenko of Belarus has helped him to quash peaceful protests against his corrupt rule. Russian military intervention in Kazakhstan this month helped President Kassym-Jomart Tokayev put an end to the violent protests in his country. But Russia is paying a price for its support of authoritarian regimes in the post-Soviet space. The Belarusian opposition, which had regarded Russia as an ally, has ceased to do so and is now looking more than ever toward the West. It remains to be seen how soon Tokayev will manage to repair the damage done to his reputation in the eyes of Kazakh elites and citizens for inviting foreign troops into his country.

5. The Long Shadow

Russia today is following in the footsteps of former imperial powers, from the Ottomans to the French, who lost political, financial, and cultural capital the more they clung to their imperial possessions. Attempts to resuscitate a failing empire alienate neighbors and even potential allies, leading to isolation. And, if history shows us anything, it is that eventually every empire must fall.

January 2022

6. What Is Happening in Ukraine Is Crucial

Interview conducted by
Adrien Jaulmes, *Le Figaro*

Adrien Jaulmes (AJ): *What is Russia looking for in Ukraine?*

Serhii Plokhy (SP): We are facing a major crisis. It is an attempt by Russia to overthrow and renegotiate the international order established in 1991. Ukraine is at the center of this crisis, not only because of its location next to Russia but also for broader reasons that go beyond that. What is happening now is crucial and will have consequences for decades to come. It is also a crisis on several levels.

The first level concerns the relationship between Russia and Ukraine. This is a centuries-old issue that touches on Russian identity and the idea that Ukraine and Belarus can have a history separate from that of Russia. In his historical essay published last summer, Putin made it clear that, in his opinion, there has never been a Ukrainian history in the past, nor will there be one in the future.

Yet the events that have unfolded in Ukraine since 2014, with the annexation of the Crimea and the occupation of the Donbas, have led a generation of Russian speakers to embrace a Ukrainian identity—for reasons that have nothing to do with NATO. It is a matter of domestic politics, with deep, ancient roots. This crisis of Russian identity is right in front of us: ironically, it is so obvious that it is easy to overlook. But we have to take it very seriously.

AJ: *What are the other levels of this crisis?*

SP: The second level is the broader issue of Russia's relations with the entire post-Soviet space, including Kazakhstan, Belarus, and Georgia. This issue goes back to the dissolution of the USSR more than 30 years ago. On 1 December 1991, 92 percent of Ukrainians voted for Ukrainian independence, a result that led to the dissolution of the Soviet Union one week later. The USSR collapsed over the issue of Ukrainian independence. Since then, the future of the post-Soviet space and the question of Russian influence in that space continues to depend on the position of Ukraine. This issue, which goes far beyond relations between Moscow and Kyiv, concerns all the other ex-Soviet republics.

The third level of the crisis—the one that everyone is talking about today—concerns NATO and Russia's sphere of influence. However, it is often forgotten that it was not NATO that chose to expand eastward but rather Moscow's former East-European allies who asked to be accepted into the organization. Membership was the only way of ensuring their defense, and one of their arguments was that they would otherwise have to develop nuclear programs themselves. The driving force behind NATO's expansion was never the will of the alliance but the demand of Eastern Europeans to be defended against Russia. Much the same scenario is playing out today in Ukraine. Before 2014, only a minority of Ukrainians wanted to join NATO. Now it is the majority. As happened thirty years ago, it is Russia that is driving this process—the memory of Russia's past dominance and the threat it poses.

AJ: *Does this complexity make a negotiated solution more difficult?*

SP: These three levels of the crisis are linked and act on one another. That is why neutralizing Ukraine, as was done with Austria in 1955, is not an option. While Moscow may have been satisfied with the creation of a neutral state in Austria at the time, or even a neutral Finland, simply keeping Ukraine out of NATO would not solve the other two problems—recognition of Ukraine's right to independent statehood and Moscow's control over post-Soviet states previously subject to it.

The analogy that is often made with the Cuban missile crisis of 1961 is not helpful either. In order to draw a parallel between the two crises, there would have had to be American atomic missiles deployed in Ukraine. Perhaps the best parallel is the Berlin crisis of 1948–49, when Moscow tested American willingness to protect the part of Europe under Allied jurisdiction. The two adversaries never resorted to military force, but the crisis also marked the beginning of the Cold War.

AJ: *Is Putin counting on a lack of American motivation to defend Europe?*

SP: Undoubtedly, and this is where the Cuban crisis offers an interesting parallel, because it was triggered by Nikita Khrushchev's misjudgment of John F. Kennedy, whom he considered inexperienced and indecisive, without understanding that the American political class was united behind its president on the issue of security. Certainly, Putin is counting on Biden's weakness after the withdrawal from Afghanistan. But has he really assessed the consensus that exists in the American establishment on the Ukrainian issue, one of the few subjects on which Republicans and Democrats agree?

AJ: *Is Europe once again left out of it?*

SP: On the contrary, Europe plays a crucial role. It is at the center of the action, and its position will be decisive. The main problem for the Europeans is to reach a decision, which is almost more difficult than finding agreement between Democrats and Republicans in Washington. But Russia's lack of ambiguity in its aggressive policy toward Ukraine gives the Europeans an incentive to do so.

January 2022

7. Putin's Revisionist History of Russia and Ukraine

Interview conducted by
Isaac Chotiner, *The New Yorker*

Isaac Chotiner (IC): *How far back do you trace a type of Ukrainian identity that we would recognize today?*

Serhii Plokhy (SP): It depends on what element of that identity you are speaking of. If you are talking about language, that would be pretty much primordial. In terms of an identity with religious components, that would be more than a thousand years old. But the first modern Ukrainian political project started in the mid-nineteenth century, as with many other ethnic groups. Ukraine's problem was its division between two powers, the Russian Empire and Austria-Hungary. And, very early, the Russian Empire recognized the threat posed by a separate and particular literary Ukrainian language to the unity of the empire. So, starting in the 1860s, there was a prohibition on Ukrainian-language publications that lasted more than forty years, basically arresting the development of the literary language. That prohibition, along with Ukraine's position between the two powers, retarded the country's political development. In the middle of World War I and the revolutions of 1917–18, as other nationalities strove for independence and sometimes gained it, Ukrainians tried to do the same but were ultimately defeated.

IC: *Why was Russia so threatened by Ukrainian identity and, specifically, language? Was it just typical imperial distrust and dislike of minority groups or languages?*

SP: The Russians looked at what was happening in Europe at that time—in France, in particular, where there was a notion of creating one language out of different dialects or languages, which was seen as directly related to the unity of the state. So that is something global. What is specific and certainly resonates today is the idea that there is one big Russian or Slavic nation, perhaps with different tribes, but basically constituting a single nation. That is the model, conceived in the nineteenth and early twentieth centuries, to which Vladimir Putin subscribes when he says that Ukraine has no legitimacy as a nation. That model has a direct connection with what is happening today.

IC: *You recently wrote, "The Soviet Union was created in 1922–23 as a pseudo-federal rather than a unitary state precisely in order to accommodate Ukraine and Georgia, the two most independent-minded republics." Can you talk more about this?*

SP: The Bolsheviks took control of most of the Russian Empire by recognizing, at least pro forma, the independence of the different republics that they were including in the Soviet Union. Until 1922, Ukraine was briefly an independent country or state. When the Bolsheviks signed the Treaty of Rapallo with Germany in 1922, Ukrainians questioned why representatives of the Russian Federation had any right to sign agreements for them. The Russians decided that something had to be done, so they discussed the creation of one, united state. Joseph Stalin's idea was to establish such a state, with various republics joining it. But Vladimir Lenin sided with the Ukrainians and Georgians, who protested against such a concept, saying that they should create a "union state," because he had a vision of world revolution.

IC: *Can you define a "union state" a little more fully?*

SP: Formally, the Soviet Union was conceived as a polity of equal republics ranging in size from huge Russia to small Estonia. The reason even to play such political games about equality was that

7. Putin's Revisionist History of Russia and Ukraine

some prospective republics had declared or fought for their independence. The Bolsheviks took them over by accommodating some national and cultural aspirations, including language rights.

IC: *How did the Russo-Ukrainian relationship change once Lenin died and Stalin took power?*

SP: It didn't change right after Lenin's death, because Stalin continued Lenin's policies. He launched a campaign to accommodate Ukrainians and others and their national languages and cultures. Georgians spoke Georgian and Armenians spoke Armenian, but the idea was to accommodate them as long as they bought into the communist idea and the communist project. And then, in the early 1930s, Stalin began to change that idea. There was a gradual revival of the symbolic importance of the Russian language and culture, which had previously been considered imperial and retrograde. But even then, the authorities did not yet discriminate against non-Russian languages. The Ukrainian famine of 1932–33 was in many ways a turning point, because the Stalin regime did more than confiscate supplies of grain. It went after the Ukrainian language.

In a decree of 1932, Stalin ended support for Ukrainian-language instruction and publishing outside the Ukrainian republic, whether in Russia or elsewhere. And there was even stricter control of Ukrainian cultural activities in Ukraine. This was done to check the potential rise of Ukrainian nationalism. The regime also went after key figures in the Communist Party of Ukraine and the cultural establishment, at least two of whom ended up committing suicide in 1933. The Holodomor was not just a famine but a broader phenomenon. The father of the concept of genocide, Raphael Lemkin, said that, in the Ukrainian case, genocide included not only starvation by man-made famine but a broader attack on institutions, language, and culture.

IC: *I want to move ahead to the end of the Soviet Union sixty years later, when we see an independent Ukraine. How do you look back on what happened in 1991 and those first few years of Ukrainian independence?*

SP: There was a huge difference between that period and 1917–18, when the idea of a Ukrainian nation and a Ukrainian revolution was basically about ethnicity, even though many ethnic minorities lived on Ukraine's territory, including Russians and Poles, and many of them viewed the idea of Ukrainian independence with suspicion. But, by 1991, the idea of a nation and its connection to language and culture had changed. Ukrainians were now imagined more as a civic nation in the making. By that time, the big industrial cities were Russian-speaking, but support for independence in the referendum of December 1991 was more than ninety per cent. Ethnicity and language mattered, but they were secondary. The majority in every region supported independence.

IC: *In what ways do language divisions manifest themselves among the population, beyond west vs. east of Ukraine?*

SP: Historically, Ukrainian was the language of the countryside. The twentieth century brought modernization and urbanization, along with the integration of former peasants into urban culture through the Russian language. So there was a large group of people who considered Ukrainian their mother tongue and had a Ukrainian identity, even though they spoke Russian.

IC: *I would imagine that this has reversed a bit today in terms of what language people speak in the big cities.*

SP: This is a development of the past eight years. There may have been some movement earlier, but this is really a reaction to the war. And the war started in 2014. The argument on the Russian side was made thus: we came to save you from cultural and various other types of oppression, and you are Russian speakers, so our assumption is that you should be loyal to us—that is, Russia. But, in many big cities, among young people and especially university students, there was a conscious choice to switch to Ukrainian. For people who grew up with both languages, the barrier to switching is quite low. So there has been a tendency to switch languages, or to associate oneself with the Ukrainian language and send children to Ukrainian-language schools.

IC: *How did Putin's speech this week fit into this conversation that we're having?*

7. Putin's Revisionist History of Russia and Ukraine

SP: It fits very well in the sense that what you see in his speech is a rejection of Soviet-era policies. He blamed the Soviet Union for everything, even the creation of Ukraine. So what you see now is a return to a pre-revolutionary understanding of what Russians are. It is a very imperial idea of the Russian nation as consisting of Russians, Ukrainians, and Belarusians. The last two groups don't have a right to exist as separate nations. We are almost back to the mid-nineteenth century, with imperial officers trying to hinder the development of Ukrainian culture and ideas.

IC: *Does the idea of a Russian imperial posture, with Ukrainian identity existing only within it, appeal to large groups of Ukrainians, even if they are far from a majority?*

SP: Certainly that idea found traction in the Crimea in 2014. Most of the population there consisted of ethnic Russians. And it got traction among some of those living in the Donbas, where Soviet identity was popular. There, people rejected the idea of an exclusionary identity, and there were grounds for the idea that, yes, maybe we are Ukrainians, but there is a place for a larger Russian role.

IC: *Is it your sense that, within Russia, even among people who may not like Putin, there is a certain amount of jingoism about the Ukrainian question? Or do you sense more division within Russia?*

SP: There was a very strong feeling about Crimea being Russian. Putin had high approval ratings after the annexation. With the rest of Ukraine, I think there is more ambiguity. The distance between Russia and Ukraine, from the perspective of how the populations view each other, has grown since the war began. I am not a sociologist, but my sense is that the Russian narrative of history around Ukraine is in decline. According to that narrative, Russian history begins in Kyiv. You go to school and learn about that. So that stuff is there, but realities make this historical mythology problematic.

IC: *You seem to be suggesting that, by waging this war with Ukraine, Putin has made his own population less interested in thinking of the two sides as one country.*

SP: Yes, that is my impression, and there is also a Russian resistance that has contributed to that. If Putin keeps talking about fascists and such, it doesn't help to create a sense of unity. The Maidan protesters were described by Russian propaganda as radical nationalists. When you present the citizens of another country that way, it doesn't support a discourse of brotherhood and unity.

IC: *If Russia does invade much or all of Ukraine, how much resistance do you think there will be? Is your sense that it will be hard to tamp down even if the Ukrainian military is formally defeated?*

SP: Yes, that is my feeling. In part, it depends on the region. Putin may never come to western Ukraine. I imagine that there will be extremely strong resistance in central Ukraine. What happened as a result of this war was not just that a Ukrainian identity grew stronger, and Ukrainians connected more with their culture, but that many strata of the population no longer see the idea of bearing arms for their country as radical. Thousands of people underwent military training, and they will fight. I don't know when and how, but I have no doubt that there will be resistance.

IC: *What have you made of how President Zelensky has handled this? It's been eye-opening how he went from trying to tamp down panic to traveling to Germany and talking about appeasement.*

SP: There was a sort of denial for a long, long period of time. I don't know exactly what the foundations of it were, but Zelensky was in tune with Ukrainian society in that people did not want war, were unprepared for it, and didn't want to think about it. And there was hopeful speculation that, with all this attention focused on Putin, he would not dare to do anything. But, in the past couple of weeks, a sense developed that the threat was real. And that's the reason for the change at the top.

February 2022

8. Did Lenin Create Ukraine?

Vladimir Putin has justified his war against Ukraine on the basis of a bizarre reading of history and accusations that Ukraine is at the same time Vladimir Lenin's creation and the homeland of Nazis.

Much has been said in the last few years to show the fraudulent nature of the "Nazi" claim. But the Lenin theme fully emerged only recently, in Putin's speech of 21 February 2022, in which he recognized the "independence" of the two puppet states created by Russia in eastern Ukraine at the start of the Russo-Ukrainian war in 2014. The bizarre nature of that claim is underlined by the fact that at least one of those "republics," that of Donetsk, claimed at its creation the legacy of an earlier puppet state, the Donetsk-Kryvyi Rih Republic, which was formed by the Bolsheviks in 1918 to prevent that territory from being included in the Ukrainian state.

In his de facto declaration of war, Putin stated that "modern Ukraine was entirely created by Russia or, to be more precise, by Bolshevik, Communist Russia. This process started practically right after the 1917 revolution, and Lenin and his associates did it in a way that was extremely harsh on Russia—by separating, severing what is historically Russian land." He developed that idea by stating: "Soviet Ukraine is the result of the Bolsheviks' policy and can rightfully be called 'Vladimir Lenin's Ukraine.' He was its creator and architect."

In Ukrainian social media, reaction to Putin's statement was almost immediate. Within a few hours, Facebook was flooded with images of Vladimir Lenin surprised to learn that he had created Ukraine. Another montage inserted Lenin into the monument to the legendary founders of Kyiv, the brothers Kyi, Shchek, and Khoryv and their sister, Lybid. Lenin replaced Lybid at the prow of the boat carrying the founders of the Ukrainian capital. The monument expresses Ukrainians' belief that their country's roots go back to the Middle Ages.

But what about modern Ukraine, a state that, according to Mr. Putin, came into existence at the expense of historical Russian lands? Even a cursory acquaintance with the history of the Russian Revolution and the fall of the Russian Empire that accompanied it indicates that the modern Ukrainian state came into existence not thanks to Lenin but against his wishes and in direct reaction to the Bolshevik putsch in Petrograd in October (according to the Gregorian calendar, November) of 1917. The Bolsheviks tried to take control of Kyiv as well but were defeated, jumpstarting the process of modern Ukrainian state-building.

In January 1918, the Central Rada (Council), the revolutionary Ukrainian parliament, dominated by socialist and leftist parties and led by Ukraine's most prominent historian, Mykhailo Hrushevsky, declared the creation of the Ukrainian People's Republic. It encompassed most of today's Ukrainian territories within the borders of the Russian Empire, including the mining region of the Donbas (Donets Basin). The new state wanted to maintain federal ties with Russia, but, after the Bolshevik invasion of January 1918, the Central Rada declared Ukraine's independence.

The Bolsheviks waged war on the Ukrainian government under the banner of their own Ukrainian People's Republic—a fiction created to provide a degree of legitimacy for the Bolshevik takeover of Ukraine. Bolshevik troops massacred the population of Kyiv, killing hundreds if not thousands of its citizens, including Metropolitan Vladimir (Bogoiavlensky) of the Orthodox Church. The Bolshevik commander in Kyiv, Mikhail Muraviev, sent Lenin the following telegram: "Order has been restored in Kyiv."

The Central Rada had to flee Kyiv but soon returned, having signed an agreement with Germany and Austria-Hungary whose troops moved into Ukraine in the spring of 1918 and drove the Bolsheviks out of its territory, including the Donbas. The Germans soon replaced the democratic Central Rada with the authoritarian regime of Hetman Pavlo Skoropadsky, but the democratic

8. Did Lenin Create Ukraine?

Ukrainian People's Republic was restored when the Germans withdrew from Ukraine late in 1918. The Bolsheviks moved in once again, this time under the banner of their adversary Ukrainian People's Republic, formally independent of Russia.

After the original defeats in Ukraine, Lenin concluded that the formal independence of the Ukrainian state, coupled with concessions in the realm of language and culture, was absolutely necessary if the Bolsheviks were to maintain control over Ukraine. He felt that Ukrainian aspirations to independence were so strong, not only among Ukrainians in general but even among the Bolsheviks themselves, as to require the granting of a degree of autonomy and a status equal to Russia within the Soviet Union, the new state whose creation was declared in 1922.

Lenin was indeed central to the formation of the USSR, as Mr. Putin has claimed. But Lenin's main contribution to the history of Russo-Ukrainian relations was not the formation of a modern Ukrainian state but the endowment of the Russian Federation—the name under which it entered the Soviet Union—with a territory and institutions of its own, distinct for the first time in centuries from the territory and institutions of the empire that it was seeking to preserve. If anything, Lenin laid the foundations for the formation of modern Russia, not Ukraine. Boris Yeltsin, Mr. Putin's patron, took that state, the Russian Federation, out of the Soviet Union in 1991. It is over that state, not pre-revolutionary Russia, that Mr. Putin presides.

February 2022

9. Ukraine's Dangerous Independence

Conversation with
Rund Abdelfatah and Ramtin Arablouei,
hosts of "Throughline," National Public Radio

Rund Abdelfatah: *It seems that Ukraine is one of those places where past and present are almost not happening in sequence; they're virtually simultaneous in people's minds because both are so prominent in conversation and identity today.*

Serhii Plokhy (SP): It is because history is a very important part of our identity, either our personal history or that of the group with which we are associated. What you see in Ukraine today is something that many other nations have experienced. It is a war for independence, which greatly influences the formation of this new identity. And that makes history very important. From that point of view, you're absolutely right. Ukrainians place themselves in that historical continuum—how they think about themselves, about their country, and their imagined future. These things are interconnected in the minds of many Ukrainians today.

Ramtin Arablouei: *Who controls the past controls the future; who controls the present controls the past. This is a famous mantra from George Orwell's dystopian novel 1984. It points to the constant evolution and tension affecting our self-image in the continuum of the past, present, and future. We are prisoners of the moment. And, for that reason, it's very difficult to recognize how alive the past is in everything, to see it in the machinery of our* daily lives, especially when our perception is obscured by the complexity of current events. But sometimes developments clarify our perception.

Abdelfatah: Last July, months before Vladimir Putin launched a full-scale military invasion of Ukraine, he published an essay on the Kremlin website titled "On the Historical Unity of Russians and Ukrainians."

SP: And what Vladimir Putin suggested was that Ukrainians don't have a history of their own.

Abdelfatah: Putin's essay alleges a lot of things, but it's this idea of Ukraine's lack of identity as a distinct country and people that's at the core of his sprawling historical argument that Ukraine should lean more toward Russia than toward Europe or the United States.

SP: His suggestion is that the Ukrainians are really Russians; therefore no history, no identity, no legitimacy for the Ukrainian state, no right for Ukrainians to exist.

Abdelfatah: Putin laid out a vast, epic vision of Ukraine and Russia's shared history, pointing out their cultural and linguistic similarities. But the way he pointed it out fitted perfectly into his narrative that the two countries belong together—under his rule, of course. It was exactly what George Orwell warned of—who controls the past controls the present. And, when Russia's invasion began and columns of tanks rolled into Ukraine, we saw the past crashing into the present.

Arablouei: But how do Ukrainians understand their history? How does it interact with their identity? What can that view of history teach us about why Ukrainians have opted to fight instead of surrender, to stay or, in some cases, return to face a more powerful enemy?

SP: I would say that Ukrainian identity is developing at a deeper level. That's the deep part of the story, which is very often overlooked. So it is extremely important from the viewpoint of Ukrainians in Ukraine, their response and thinking about themselves.

Arablouei: *Ukraine lies on the western edge of a vast flat grassland called the Eurasian Steppe. Nomadic groups migrated around this area and would periodically move farther into Eastern Europe to conduct raids. In the thirteenth century, a federation of these nomads, known as the Mongols, attacked the peoples of today's Ukraine and Russia and destroyed most of the Kyivan Rus´ state. It was a violent, brutal affair, but Mongol power would also wane. By the fifteenth century, the Mongols had been mostly expelled from Ukraine. And, according to Serhii Plokhy, that's when modern Ukrainian identity began to take shape.*

SP: Ukrainian history, early modern history is focused not so much on the Scandinavian Vikings or Kyivan Rus´ but on a social category known as the Cossacks.

Arablouei: *The Cossacks...*

SP: And the Cossacks were an advanced group of the settled population that moved into the steppe and tried, for lack of a better word, to colonize it as agriculturalists. Of course, they became involved in conflict with the nomads who controlled the steppe. The Cossacks, then, were Slavs who moved into the steppelands common to Ukrainians and Russians. But the Cossacks of Ukraine, unlike their Russian counterparts, managed to create a state of their own, independent at first, then a dependency of the Russian tsars, which existed until the final decades of the eighteenth century.

Arablouei: *The Cossack elite created a high culture, including literature and the first modern university in the East Slavic lands. Its descendant, the Kyiv Mohyla Academy, exists today. And, for Ukrainians, that legacy is expressed in a single word, and that word is freedom. But we should be clear—the Cossacks weren't just some homogenous, heroic group of freedom fighters; they could also be quite brutal. They also carried out massacres of Jews in the region in the seventeenth century. Yet today, for many Ukrainians, the Cossacks represent resistance to external control.*

SP: Cossacks became the symbol of this freedom and liberty because they inhabited the frontiers of established states, societies, and empires, from the Russian Empire to the Polish-Lithuanian

Commonwealth to the Ottoman Empire, all of which they challenged. So Cossackdom is a very important symbol of Ukrainian historical and cultural identity, historical identity; it's a national myth about freedom-loving Ukrainians. So, on the one hand, Ukraine has deep roots in Kyivan Rus´. On the other hand, there is the Cossack legacy, which sets Ukrainians apart, in their own view, from the Russians. For Ukrainians, this is the central part of their early modern history.

Arablouei: *And that history is part of the present, woven into the Ukrainian national anthem.*

SP: The present-day Ukrainian anthem was written in the mid-nineteenth century. And it starts with the words "Ukraine has not yet perished." The reference is to the fact that there was once a Cossack state. It was integrated by the Russian Empire. The Cossack army was disbanded. The institutions were abolished. The office of hetman, or ruler of the Cossack state, was gone. But Ukraine has not yet perished: it is now something new. Ukraine is about who we are, how we feel. So we can exist as a nation, even though the state has perished. It sounds like a very pessimistic beginning of an anthem, but, in reality, it is very, very optimistic in the sense that, again, despite the fact that we have lost the state, we are still alive.

Arablouei: *The last line translates as "We are brothers of Cossack descent." It's important to note here that Ukraine achieved independence and sovereignty during relatively brief periods of its history. Ukrainians spent much of the rest of that time under the rule of major powers, trying to achieve independence. And identifying with the Cossacks remains a powerful symbol of that fight to this day.*

Abdelfatah: *For an American hearing this and thinking about what was going on as the Cossacks of Ukraine were defying the Russian Empire, it's impossible to know what that meant without fully understanding what the empire looked like at the time and the tensions between the Cossacks and the empire.*

SP: A Cossack state came into existence in the mid-seventeenth century, in the process of a Cossack revolt against the state to which most of Ukraine then belonged. That state was the Kingdom of Poland, which was part of a larger federation, the Polish-Lithuanian Commonwealth. The Cossacks rebelled in 1648 and fought a number of battles with the Poles. And that's how the state began to take shape. But the war continued. And the Cossacks didn't think that they were strong enough to maintain the state on their own. They established relations with Muscovy, the state northeast of Ukraine—the predecessor of today's Russia. And they entered into an agreement with the Muscovite tsar who took them under his protection in 1654. That was the beginning of relations between the Ukrainian Cossack state and what would later become the Russian Empire.

Those relations were based on certain agreements and understandings—that the tsar would allow the Cossacks to have their own army and enjoy their liberties and freedoms. Basically, a Muscovite protectorate was established, and that was the Cossack state, already known as Ukraine. But, in the second half of the seventeenth century and particularly in the eighteenth, the empire violated more and more of the conditions of those agreements, limiting the freedoms of the Cossack state. And as the Muscovites/Russians grew more powerful, they became less and less interested in maintaining the freedoms that they had once guaranteed to the Cossacks. Then, in the 1780s, the successful empire, led by Empress Catherine II, abolished the Cossack liberties and Cossack statehood entirely. What had begun as a military alliance and protectorate thus ended with the full integration of the Cossack state.

Arablouei: *Soon after the Cossack state was integrated into the Russian Empire, the Russian language and culture became more dominant in Ukraine. Many historians call this process Russification, and it happened in many parts of the empire. Many Ukrainians resented that process. And, along with language, came the expansion of Russian serfdom into Ukraine.*

Abdelfatah: *Serfdom was the prevailing economic system in medieval Europe. By the 1300s, it had mostly gone away in Western Europe. But the leaders of Russia were strengthening serfdom in their empire around the same time as American slavery developed. The peasants were more or less turned into economic slaves legally* bound to the land that they worked, allowing the Russian elites to extract more wealth from their lands. And, as you can imagine, many peasants would do anything to escape it. One of the places to which they escaped were the lands of the defiant Cossacks.

SP: I mentioned that the Cossacks were a symbol of freedom, and now we need to define what that meant at the time, in the seventeenth and eighteenth centuries. It was perhaps about democracy. It was about independence. But freedom had a very specific meaning then—freedom from serfdom. Not all Cossacks were former serfs, but a significant number were runaways. For them, becoming a Cossack meant personal freedom. The steppes, which were very dangerous for the conduct of any economic activity, whether agriculture or trade, were the lands to which the serfs were moving, even after the abolition of the Cossack state in the late eighteenth and early nineteenth centuries.

Serfdom reached southern Ukraine, in this area north of the Sea of Azov and the Black Sea, only in the first half of the nineteenth century, some ten or twenty years before serfdom as an institution was abandoned in the Russian Empire. What did this mean? While in the rest of the Russian Empire a good part of the population, at least one-third, were serfs, in Ukraine, most of the inhabitants had no experience of serfdom. They managed to live, from one generation to another, either as Cossacks or runaway serfs. It's hard to overestimate the importance of this tradition, this mentality, this attitude toward personal freedom that comes with not having experienced much serfdom in your history, including your family history.

Abdelfatah: *The Ukrainian Cossacks had a complex relationship with the Russian Empire that wavered between alliance and outright rebellion. And, when the Ukrainians rebelled, they rebelled against outside control, both political and economic. And that spirit would come back in full force when the Russian Empire fell during one of the most important revolutions of the twentieth century, in which Ukraine played a key part.*

Arablouei: *When the Russian Empire ends, Ukraine faces a whole new century of turmoil.*

Abdelfatah: *By the early twentieth century, the Russian Empire, which included much of Ukraine, was one of the poorest countries in Europe. The institution of serfdom was abolished in the nineteenth century, but the vast majority of the people were still poor, economically oppressed peasants and urban laborers. Yet they were able to organize, and, by 1917, after several decades of hardship and war, the people of the Russian Empire had had enough. An empire-wide revolution erupted. And, when it was all done, the Bolsheviks, a Marxist group led by Vladimir Lenin, had seized control of the country. While some people in Ukraine supported getting rid of the Russian Empire, after the Bolsheviks took control, things changed. According to Plokhy, once again, many Ukrainians resisted centralizing power from Russia and its Red Army.*

SP: They rebelled against the Bolsheviks. They fought against the Red Army. And, when you look at Ukraine, southern Ukraine in particular, you see peasant uprisings against the rule of the Communist Party on a much greater scale than those that occurred in Russia. Once again, the lived experience of freedom made for partisan warfare and rejection of authority, especially outside authority.

Arablouei: *So a lot of what you've described is a tug of war between Ukrainian independence and defiance of external control. How did that play out once the Soviet Union was formed?*

SP: The Russian Empire began to disintegrate in the middle of World War I and the Russian Revolution. But the Bolsheviks were able to glue it back together. They did so not only by means of a new ideology that was no longer nationalist—it was some form of Marxism—but also by making concessions to ethnic groups in the empire, recognizing their status as nations at least rhetorically, as well as their right to use their language and develop their culture. This was a concession of cultural but not political rights.

Abdelfatah: *By 1922, the Soviet Union was formed. You can think of it as a collection of states under one central government in Moscow. Vladimir Lenin was the leader, and republics such as Ukraine, Georgia, Azerbaijan, and Lithuania would belong to the union.*

9. Ukraine's Dangerous Independence

SP: Ukraine was a separate state and Russia was a separate state, and then they formed one Soviet Union. Again, as I said, that was a façade. Cultural rights were given, but political rights were not. Vladimir Putin alleges that the artificiality of the Ukrainian state and Ukrainian statehood stems from its creation by the Bolsheviks, which is as divorced from reality, historical reality, as could be. For the first time, Lenin and the Bolsheviks created a separate state, separate institutions, and a separate territory for Russia, which became known as the Russian Federation, thereby separating Russia proper, at least symbolically, from what used to be the Russian Empire. Before that, there had been no such separation.

Arablouei: *That is a really important point. What Serhii is saying is that the Bolshevik Revolution and the formation of the Soviet Union didn't create Ukraine, as Vladimir Putin claims. If anything, the Bolsheviks laid the foundation for a Russian state by endowing it with territory and declaring Russians a people separate from the Ukrainians. And that Russian state had more or less the same geographic boundaries as today's Russia, the one that Putin leads. So during the post-revolution years, Ukraine became a very important part of the Soviet Union. Ukrainians made up the Soviet Union's second-largest ethnic group after the Russians. Ukraine was a major agricultural and manufacturing center. And a lot of Ukrainians became key players in the Soviet power structure. And after the death of the Soviet Union's leader, Joseph Stalin, in 1953…*

SP: …the regime had to accommodate the Ukrainian party elite, making it a junior partner of the Russians in the running of this Soviet empire. Thus, from the 1950s to the early 1980s, the leaders of the Soviet Union were actually products of the Ukrainian Communist Party machine. For example, Nikita Khrushchev came from eastern Ukraine.

Arablouei: *An ethnic Russian born just a few miles from Ukraine, Nikita Khrushchev rose through the ranks of Ukraine's Communist Party to become Stalin's successor, leading the Soviet Union from 1953 to 1964.*

SP: Leonid Brezhnev, too, came from eastern Ukraine…

Arablouei: Leonid Brezhnev succeeded Khrushchev as leader from 1964 to 1982.

SP: So Khrushchev and Brezhnev, whose names, I assume, are known to the listeners, are the best to remember when one thinks of the role of Ukraine in the Soviet Union.

Abdelfatah: What about the role of the Soviet Union in Ukraine? Let's go back to the 1930s, when one of the darkest events of Soviet history happened in Ukraine.

SP: The man-made famine of 1932–33, in which as many as four million Ukrainians perished.

Abdelfatah: The event to which Serhii refers is known as the Holodomor, which comes from the Ukrainian words for hunger and extermination. This is basically what happened. There was not enough food produced to feed the people of Ukraine in 1932 and 1933. Millions of people starved. The causes of this catastrophe are still debated by historians. Some believe it was the result of incompetent policies undertaken by the Soviet Union to collectivize agriculture. Others claim that it was an intentional policy under Joseph Stalin's leadership to kill Ukrainians in order to put down any potential independence movement, or a combination of the two.

SP: And the famine was an extremely important part of a broader shift in government policy at the time because it came with an attack on Ukrainian culture, on Ukrainian institutions. So the famine is just one big symbol of the horrendous crimes of the regime against Ukraine in particular.

Arablouei: This was a key turning point in Ukraine's relationship with the Soviet Union. Another happened many decades later.

Abdelfatah: There was a moment in 1986, the nuclear disaster at Chornobyl. Obviously, it shook the world, but, I think, a lot of people don't realize that Chornobyl is in Ukraine. And, I guess, I'm wondering how that moment impacted the Ukrainian people's assessment of their place in the Soviet Union.

9. Ukraine's Dangerous Independence

SP: Chornobyl is one of two events associated with the Soviet Union that are mourned and commemorated in today's Ukraine. It is another example of the same story. Because industry in the Soviet Union in general and the nuclear industry in particular were highly centralized and run from Moscow, the Chornobyl disaster has been perceived in Ukraine as a crime committed by Moscow against the Ukrainian nation and people.

Arablouei: *In the Chornobyl disaster, a reactor at a huge nuclear power facility blew up and spewed tons of toxic material into the nearby ecosystem. Up to 50 people died immediately. And, in 2004, the United Nations predicted that as many as 4,000 more might eventually die from radiation exposure. Countless others became very ill, and the Soviet government tried to cover it up. It didn't work. It became international news and was seen as a clear signal of just how badly the Soviet Union was failing.*

SP: Chornobyl was the most important issue for Ukrainians at the time, and they demanded that the state tell them the truth about what had happened. They wanted to see the map. And the first mass mobilization against the Soviet state was a response to the disaster. Out of that mobilization came Rukh, the Popular Movement of Ukraine, a large umbrella organization for a number of groups and parties that eventually demanded Ukrainian independence. So it would be impossible to imagine Ukraine's path toward independence without that wake-up call.

Abdelfatah: *The Ukrainian independence movement gained momentum after Chornobyl. And, at the same time, other Soviet republics were beginning to leave the union. Soon there was a call for a referendum on whether Ukraine should leave the Soviet Union and become an independent state.*

SP: So Ukrainians went to vote in their referendum for independence on 1 December 1991. Slightly more than 92 percent of them voted for it. Within a week, the Soviet Union fell apart. By choosing independence, the Ukrainians also decided the future of the Soviet Union, because Russia did not want to continue the Soviet project without its largest partner in population and economy, which was also culturally quite close. But Ukraine's centrality for the future of Russia did not disappear. What is happening today, this horrendous war, is a continuation of that story, with Russia trying to restore some form of control over the post-Soviet space. And that project cannot be successful, even semi-successful, if the second-largest player in the region is not on board.

Abdelfatah: *Ukraine emerged as an independent country with the fall of the Soviet Union in 1991, but it was not as if the whole world was immediately supportive of the idea. In fact, in the years leading up to independence, the opposing powers in the Cold War—the United States and the Soviet Union—had different and sometimes surprising reasons to view Ukrainian independence with skepticism.*

SP: The United States didn't want the disintegration of the Soviet Union and did everything in its power diplomatically and financially to keep it going as long as possible. It may sound counterintuitive, given that the Soviet Union and the United States were the major adversaries in the Cold War, but it makes perfect sense when you recall that there was no hot war, although both sides had nuclear weapons. And the main concern of the United States was to prevent the devolution of control over nuclear weapons, which might lead to war between republics, like the one now going on between Russia and Ukraine, possibly involving nuclear exchanges.

Arablouei: *During the Cold War, the Soviet Union placed a significant number of nuclear weapons in Ukraine. So, if Ukraine became independent, those weapons would become part of its defensive capability, and there would be a few nuclear states with a contentious history neighboring one another. Everyone was worried about that, including the United States. But just before Ukrainians went to the polls...*

SP: ...the United States changed track and sent signals that it would recognize independent Ukraine. America has a very particular understanding of what the world is or should be—a world of independent states. And Ukrainians are, in that sense, on the same page as Americans. The Russians, wanting to maintain their control of their region, think quite differently. From the very beginning, the Russian model is that of limited sovereignty for the former Soviet republics. When Putin took power at the beginning of this century and this millennium, in the year 2000, his liberal economic advisers suggested that the former republics become part of a Russian liberal empire, with Moscow controlling them economically and keeping them friendly and dependent. That didn't work. So Putin changed track, shifted gears, and actually used the military option. Hence the invasion of Georgia in 2008, the invasion of Ukraine in 2014, and all-out war in 2022. That is the only instrument remaining in the imperial toolbox, which Putin has used so indiscriminately.

Abdelfatah: *You know, going back to the idea of lived history, you were born in Russia, and your family is originally from Ukraine, where you grew up. So this is very close to home for you. Reflecting on these last few decades, what does this moment, this all-out war, mean to Ukrainians and to you personally?*

SP: It is really difficult to comprehend what is going on. There was an assumption that the world had changed dramatically around the year 1991. Liberal democracy arrived, wars came to an end, and the Cold War was over. Power was now in the hands of the people who could vote one way or another. Ukraine acquired independence through a referendum and without a military confrontation, continuing to exist as a very peaceful state with no enclaves, no mobilized minority movements or clashes. And then, in 2014, because Ukrainians demanded that their government fulfill its promise to sign an association agreement with the European Union, not even joining it, they were attacked and invaded by Russia.

Abdelfatah: *In 2014, Russia invaded the southern Ukrainian region of the Crimea, eventually annexing it and assuming control.*

SP: Ukrainians could not comprehend that something like that might happen. Nor were they prepared to shoot at others, particularly at Russians, who were considered to be not only near neighbors but also close relatives in cultural and ethnic terms. But Ukraine really mobilized after 2014, having lost part of its territory. Still, until the very end, no one in Ukraine believed that there could be another major war. Both wars, those of 2014 and now of

2022, caught Ukrainian society by surprise. And that, on many levels, was also my reaction.

Arablouei: *Surprise, shock, sadness, and anger—these are emotions we have heard from Serhii and many other Ukrainians and Russians watching this conflict unfold. The complicated dimensions of identity and geopolitics are all interacting and playing out in tragic fashion. Yes, Ukrainians have developed a distinct identity since the time of the Cossacks, but Russia and Ukraine are clearly two countries that share culture and history, which cannot always be defined by borders and politics, or wars. And, for that reason, the destruction and chaos created by the invasion of Ukraine become more painful to watch.*

March 2022

III. The Big War

10. Appeasement

Vladimir Putin began his all-out war on Ukraine on 24 February 2022. I took part in my first anti-war rally on 27 February 2022, three days after the start of the invasion.

There were approximately three hundred people in downtown Vienna protesting the war and holding anti-war signs. A friend of mine pointed out one of the signs carried by a young woman clad in a Ukrainian blue-and-yellow flag. The poster, held high above her head, bore the legend: "Hey Putin, Let's Fast-Forward to the Part Where You Kill Yourself in a Bunker!" The allusion was unmistakably to Hitler. After returning home and searching the web, I saw that an almost identical sign had been carried at a protest rally in Berlin on 25 February, the day after the invasion. But the idea of comparing Putin's actions to those of Hitler was by no means new.[1]

In March 2014, on the eve of the pseudo-referendum conducted by the Russian authorities in the recently occupied Crimea, the historian Andrei Zubov, a professor at the elite Moscow Institute of International Relations, compared Putin's planned annexation of the peninsula to Hitler's *Anschluss* of Austria in 1938. Zubov drew parallels between Hitler's vision of Greater Germany and Russia's reunification rhetoric, pointing out that both annexations had been justified to the public as measures to protect allegedly persecuted minorities, German (in Czechoslovakia) in the first case and Russian in the second. Zubov went on to call the

---

[1] *Influx News*, Twitter, 25 February 2022, https://twitter.com/InfluxNewsLive/status/1497347387958108160.

staged referendum a sham intended to provide legal cover for the forcible annexation.[2]

The official results of the Russian referendum, which no independent observer was allowed to attend, claimed 97 percent support for the annexation of the peninsula, slightly less than the 99.73 percent support reported in Hitler's referendum. The Crimea was promptly integrated into the Russian Federation as the "Republic of the Crimea," losing the autonomous status it had enjoyed as part of Ukraine. Zubov was soon dismissed, losing his prestigious position at the country's top diplomatic school. But he did not lose the argument. In March 2015, on the first anniversary of the Crimean "referendum," the economist Klaus Friedrich, writing in The Globalist, added to Zubov's parallels a couple of his own, including the theme of personal and national humiliation exploited by Hitler and Putin, and their shared disdain for Western culture.[3]

Meanwhile, Putin and his propaganda machine insisted that the Russian "liberators" of the Crimea were fighting Nazism and accused the victim, Ukraine, of having been captured by Hitler's heirs. The same argument was used in 2022, during the run-up to the all-out invasion of Ukraine. In his television address broadcast at the start of the invasion early in the morning of 24 February, Putin accused the Ukrainian leaders of being "neo-Nazis" and the West of supporting a "neo-Nazi" regime.

"Focused on their own goals, the leading NATO countries are supporting the far-right nationalists and neo-Nazis in Ukraine, those who will never forgive the people of the Crimea and Sevastopol for freely making a choice to reunite with Russia," claimed Putin. "They will undoubtedly try to bring war to the Crimea just as they have done in the Donbas, to kill innocent people just as members of the punitive units of Ukrainian nationalists

---

[2] Andrei Zubov, "Ėto uzhe bylo," Vedomosti, 1 March 2014.
[3] "Anschluss and World War II," Britannica, https://www.britannica.com/place/Austria/Anschluss-and-World-War-II; "Iz MGIMO uvolen professor Andrei Zubov," BBC News, 24 March 2014, https://www.bbc.com/russian/rolling_news/2014/03/140324_rn_professor_mgimo_fired; Klaus Friedrich, "Uncomfortable Parallels: Hitler and Putin," The Globalist, 21 March 2015, https://www.theglobalist.com/uncomfortable-parallels-hitler-and-putin/.

10. Appeasement

and Hitler's accomplices did during the Great Patriotic War. They have also openly laid claim to several other Russian regions." Putin formulated the goal of his "special military operation" as follows: "demilitarize and denazify Ukraine, as well as bring to trial those who perpetrated numerous bloody crimes against civilians, including against citizens of the Russian Federation."[4]

Putin's propaganda had spent years portraying some of the Ukrainian volunteer military formations of 2014 as Nazi. But more was at stake than those battalions. A few days earlier, the United States had warned the United Nations that Russian intelligence services were compiling lists of people "to be killed or sent to camps." They included "Russian and Belarusian dissidents in exile in Ukraine, journalists and anti-corruption activists, and vulnerable populations such as religious and ethnic minorities, and LGBTQI+ persons." There was also little doubt that anyone resisting the invasion would be killed or put on trial.[5]

The Russian invasion of Ukraine in February 2022 produced immediate pushback from opponents of the war on the issue of Nazism. Posters like those I had seen in Vienna flooded the streets of European capitals; politicians and academics became less reticent about Putin-Hitler comparisons. In late February 2022, a few days after the start of the war, Janne Haaland Matlary, a professor of international politics at the Institute of Oslo and a former politician, compared Hitler and Putin in an interview given to a Norwegian newspaper. If Hitler denounced the Treaty of Versailles, Putin opposed the rise of sovereign democratic states after the fall of the USSR, and both termed the invasion an act self-defense, argued Matlary.[6]

---

[4] The "Great Patriotic War" refers to World War II (editor's note). "Address by the President of the Russian Federation," President of Russia, 24 February 2022, http://en.kremlin.ru/events/president/news/67843.

[5] Dan Sabbagh, "Russia is creating lists of Ukrainians 'to be killed or sent to camps,' US claims," *Guardian*, 21 February 2022.

[6] Anne Lise Stranden, "Invasion of Ukraine: 'A lot of historical parallels to Hitler-Germany in the 1930s,' says Norwegian professor," *sciencenorway.no*, 28 February 2022, https://sciencenorway.no/russia-war/invasion-of-ukraine-a-lot-of-historical-parallels-to-hitler-germany-in-the-1930s-says-norwegian-professor/1989909.

While Zubov, Friedrich, and Matlary pointed out the similar motives behind Putin's and Hitler's actions, a comparison of Western policies toward the ever more aggressive ambitions of Hitler's Germany and Putin's Russia may be even more productive. As I shall demonstrate in this essay, policies of appeasement were adopted in both cases for comparable reasons and with comparable outcomes, suggesting that lessons learned by the West after the failure of those policies to prevent World War II were poorly absorbed or subsequently unlearned by democratic leaders and societies.

* * *

In January 2022, on the eve of the Russian invasion of Ukraine, viewers of the German/British drama *Munich—The Edge of War*, released by Netflix, were glued to television and computer screens throughout the world. The *New York Times* characterized the film as "a feature-length attempt to glorify Neville Chamberlain," the British prime minister who engaged in the much-debated diplomatic strategy of appeasement in the run-up to World War II.

The wisdom of Chamberlain's policy was soon questioned in most public fashion by President Volodymyr Zelensky of Ukraine, speaking to world leaders at the annual security conference in Munich. "The current policy of appeasement has to be turned into one of guarantees of security and peace," declared Zelensky on 19 February, five days before the start of the all-out war. "No one was foolish enough to compare Russia to national socialism," wrote the Guardian's correspondent, commenting on the mood in the conference hall, "but underlying every discussion was the question of Vladimir Putin's true intentions and whether the Western response is moral and a sufficient deterrent, or instead a betrayal and a repeat of the appeasement of the 30s."[7]

---

[7] Manohla Dragis, "'Munich: The Edge of War' Review: 'Well Navigated, Sir' (Not!)," *New York Times*, 20 January 2022; "Zelensky's full speech at Munich Security Conference," *Kyiv Independent*, 19 February 2022; Patrick Wintour, "Memory of 1938 hangs heavy in Munich as Ukrainian president calls for action," *Guardian*, 20 February 2022.

10. Appeasement

The answer to those questions came in less than a week. Putin was getting ready to attack, and the Western response was a repeat of its policy in the 1930s. The appeasement of Hitler by the governments of Britain and France, which dominated Europe at the time, began in 1936. Without firing a shot, they allowed Hitler to reoccupy the Rhineland, which had been demilitarized after World War I, with his inferior forces. Appeasement continued with the acceptance of Germany's *Anschluss* of Austria in 1938 and subsequent takeover of Czechoslovakia's Sudetenland, negotiated by Prime Minister Neville Chamberlain. He believed that the Munich Agreement of 30 September 1938, which permitted Germany's annexation of the Sudetenland and led to the dismemberment of the independent Czechoslovak state in the center of Europe, would secure "peace in our time." He was mistaken.[8]

After the dismemberment, Britain and France formally abandoned their policy of appeasement, signing agreements with Poland and other East European countries to guarantee their territorial integrity in case of German attack. In fact, however, the policy was maintained after the start of World War II. The "Phony War" of 1939–40, in which neither the French nor the British moved against Germany, bore all the hallmarks of the appeasement of the previous era and was predetermined by it. Once again, it was a mistaken policy. By June 1940, Hitler's forces were in Paris, the British were leaving Europe in panic at Dunkirk, and soon London and other British cities found themselves under attack by the Luftwaffe. World War II ceased to be phony and became real for the West.[9]

Western appeasement of Russia early in this century began in the same way as the appeasement of Germany—by turning a blind eye to the Russian government's use of military force at home. That policy predated Putin's accession to power, beginning with Western refusal to criticize his predecessor, Boris Yeltsin, for starting the brutal Chechen War: according to official estimates, it

---

[8] David Reynolds, "Munich 1938: Chamberlain and Hitler," in idem, *Summits: Six Meetings that Shaped the Twentieth Century* (New York, 2007), 37–102.

[9] Ernest R. May, *Strange Victory: Hitler's Conquest of France* (New York, 2015).

saw up to 40,000 civilians killed and as many as half a million displaced. In 1999, Putin, then Yeltsin's prime minister, launched the Second Chechen War. The Russian siege of Grozny in late 1999 and early 2000 caused the death of as many as 8,000 civilians and left the city in ruins. Amnesty International estimated a total death toll of 30,000 civilians. But this time Russia succeeded in subjugating Chechnya.[10]

In March 2000, Putin won the Russian presidential elections with 53 percent of the vote, as opposed to 30 percent for his communist opponent. Putin's path to the Kremlin led through the massacre of civilians in Grozny, but the world welcomed a new face in the Kremlin, hoping that Russia would finally break with communism and stay on the democratic track. To keep Putin happy, the new masters of Europe, Germany and France, drew a line at the three Baltic states when it came to the membership of former Soviet republics in the European Union and NATO.

The applications of Ukraine and Georgia for NATO membership were rejected at the alliance's Bucharest summit in 2008, despite strong advocacy of their membership by the United States. Before going to Bucharest, President George W. Bush made a stopover in Kyiv, where he told the Ukrainians: "Your nation has made a bold decision, and the United States strongly supports your request." But, as the leaders of Germany and France arrived for the Bucharest summit on 2 April 2008, Russia's vocal protests against membership for Ukraine and Georgia were on their minds. Putin came to the Romanian capital in person to take part in the Russia-NATO summit and warn the members of the alliance against extending invitations to the two post-Soviet republics. "The emergence of a powerful military bloc at our borders will be seen as a direct threat to Russian security," he said.[11]

---

[10] John B. Dunlop, *Russia Confronts Chechnya: Roots of a Separatist Conflict* (Cambridge, UK, 1998); James Hughes, *Chechnya: From Nationalism to Jihad* (Philadelphia, Pa., 2011), 1–93; Fiona Hill and Clifford G. Gaddy, *Mr. Putin: Operative in the Kremlin* (Washington, DC, 2015), 29–31.

[11] Samuel Charap and Timothy J. Colton, *Everyone Loses: The Ukraine Crisis and the Ruinous Contest for Post-Soviet Eurasia* (New York, 2016), 87.

10. Appeasement

London and Paris blocked the decision advocated by the United States and supported by the new East European members of the alliance to grant Ukraine and Georgia a Membership Action Plan (MAP). "We agreed today that these countries will become members of NATO," read the declaration before making it clear that no accession would take place anytime soon. The MAP was promised but not issued on the basis that the two potential applicants still had to meet some specific criteria in order to qualify. "We will now begin a period of intensive engagement with both at a high political level to address the questions still outstanding, pertaining to their MAP applications." [12]

The matter was postponed and would not return to the NATO agenda at the next summit or the one after that. Everyone knew that the decision to deny a MAP to the two post-Soviet republics was a concession to their former master, Russia. Otherwise it would have been impossible to explain why the participants in the Bucharest summit invited Croatia and Albania to join NATO. For the two countries now perceived as threats by Russia, NATO's nondecision on their membership was the worst possible outcome of the summit: their applications had been postponed indefinitely, leaving them with no protection from the alliance that they had publicly stated they wanted to join. While Russia would not dare to attack NATO itself, it could easily attack nations aspiring to join it and did so.

On 8 August 2008, a few months after the Bucharest summit, Russia launched a war on Georgia, ostensibly in defense of the enclave of South Ossetia, which had seceded from Georgia in the early 1990s. The Russian attack allegedly came as a response to actions of the Georgian army, which had been ordered into South Ossetia, but there was no doubt that the war was directly linked to the outcome of the Bucharest summit. Russia had established official relations with South Ossetia and Abkhazia, the two Georgian provinces that it was now "defending," almost immediately after Putin's return from the Bucharest summit. The Georgians

---

[12] "Bucharest Summit Declaration." Issued by the Heads of State and Government Participating in the Meeting of the North Atlantic Council in Bucharest on 3 April 2008, NATO, https://www.nato.int/cps/en/natolive/official_texts_8443.htm.

fought back under the leadership of President Mikheil Saakashvili who had been educated in Ukraine and the United States, but the Russian army, larger and superior to Georgia's, moved deep into the country and threatened to occupy its capital, Tbilisi.

The Russian advance was stopped four days into the invasion thanks to a cease-fire negotiated by President Nicolas Sarkozy of France. Russian troops eventually left a good part of the occupied territory but stayed in Abkhazia and South Ossetia, ostensibly protecting the independence of the two provinces from Georgia and perpetuating its territorial division. That undermined Georgia's chances of ever joining NATO, as the alliance was reluctant to accept any state with unresolved territorial issues. Russia's invasion of Georgia became the first instance of its initiating a major war beyond its borders in the post-Soviet period. It sent a clear signal to the West that Russia was prepared to use military force to stop any expansion of the alliance. It also demonstrated to other post-Soviet republics that NATO would not come to their rescue in case of Russian attack.[13]

The decision of the Bucharest NATO summit, coupled with the outcome of the Russo-Georgian War, dealt a devastating blow to Ukrainian aspirations to join the alliance. The changing of the guard in Washington and the inauguration of Barack Obama as president in January 2009 led to a thorough revision of all elements of US foreign policy and an attempted "reset" of US-Russia relations. The Bucharest summit put Ukraine in the most vulnerable position that it had experienced since declaring independence. Without nuclear weapons and NATO membership, Ukraine found itself at the mercy of Russia, which saw the ambiguous offer of membership extended to Ukraine by the Bucharest summit as a threat to its own security. Ukraine was a lone warrior on

---

[13] Jan Maksymiuk, "Is Ukraine Prepared to Maintain Its Tough Stand Against Russia?" Radio Free Europe/Radio Liberty, 15 August 2008, https://www.rferl.org/a/Is_Ukraine_Prepared_To_Maintain_Its_Tough_Stand_Against_Russia/1191251.html; Charap and Colton, *Everyone Loses*, 91–94; Svante E. Cornell and Frederick S. Starr, *The Guns of August 2008: Russia's War in Georgia* (Armonk, NY, 2009); Ronald D. Asmus, *A Little War That Shook the World: Georgia, Russia, and the Future of the West* (New York, 2010).

10. Appeasement

open ground pursued by hostile forces, running to take shelter in a secure fortress, only to find its gates closing because of disagreements among its defenders.[14]

***

The West had learned little from the experience of the 1930s, partly because comparing Putin to Hitler and present-day Russia to Nazi Germany remains an affront to political correctness.[15]

Yet there were clear parallels not only between the ways in which Hitler and Putin claimed foreign territory—similarities first pointed out by Andrei Zubov—but also between the reactions of Western countries to the aggressive behavior of Hitler and Putin. There was a widespread Western belief that the impulses, if not the actions, of the two authoritarian leaders were justified and their revisionist ambitions limited in scope. The West regarded Hitler's move into the demilitarized Rhineland as an understandable if illegal act of reclaiming full sovereignty over German territory after the allegedly unjust Treaty of Versailles had curtailed that sovereignty. Russia, for its part, had allegedly been right to wage its two wars in Chechnya in order to reassert its territorial integrity after losing its outer empire in Eastern Europe and its inner empire within the borders of the former USSR.

In 1938–39, the West considered Hitler's takeover of Austria and mostly German-speaking territories of Czechoslovakia justifiable, as the Versailles settlement had fully legitimized the principle that people speaking the same language belonged to the same nation and ought to live within the boundaries of a single state. The same sort of tacit understanding, if not approval, was extended to Putin's Russia after its illegal annexation of the Crimea, with

---

[14] Ivan Watson and Maxim Tkachenko, "Russia, Ukraine agree on naval-base-for-gas deal," CNN, 21 April 2010, http://www.cnn.com/2010/WORLD/europe/04/21/russia.ukraine/index.html; Rajan Menon and Eugene Rumer, *Conflict in Ukraine: The Unwinding of the Post-Cold War Order* (Cambridge, MA and London, 2015), 44-52.

[15] Birgit Jennen and Michael Nienaber, "Scholz Touts Latest Ukraine Arms Delivery after Criticism," *Bloomberg*, 1 June 2022, https://www.bloomberg.com/news/articles/2022-06-01/scholz-touts-latest-ukraine-arms-delivery-as-criticism-persists#xj4y7vzkg.

its ethnic Russian majority, and seizure of the predominantly Russian-speaking Donbas in eastern Ukraine.

In both cases, there was hope that Hitler and Putin would stop after claiming ethnically German territories of Central Europe and ethnically Russian territories of Ukraine. Such hopes proved unjustified: the takeover of ethnically German and Russian territories and the absence of decisive opposition from the international community only whetted the appetites of the aggressors. By the time Western policy changed, both aggressors had grown much stronger and more difficult to contain than had been the case during the years of appeasement. But even then, the West tried to outsource the war, leaving the actual fighting to the Poles and Ukrainians. Their sacrifices bought time for the West to prepare for an actual fight. If the West does not provide enough support for Ukraine to win this war, it will need to fight once again.

March 2022

11. The Causes of the Russo-Ukrainian War

Russia's attack on Ukraine came in the dawn of 24 February 2022, with missile strikes on targets all over the country. It marked the beginning of the greatest war in European history since the end of World War II. The conflict has claimed the lives of tens of thousands of innocent civilians and created the greatest refugee crisis in Europe, once again, since the end of World War II. The number of women, children, and elderly people who fled the fighting in Ukraine and found refuge in the countries of Eastern and Central Europe exceeded eight million. The Russian army occupied the Chornobyl nuclear power plant for several weeks and keeps the world hostage by maintaining its control over the Zaporizhzhia nuclear power plant, the largest in Europe. There are growing concerns about the possibility that Russia may use nuclear weapons as well.

What has caused a war of such proportions? Vladimir Putin, the Russian leader who made up his mind to go to war in secrecy even from his key advisers in Russia's National Security Council, went out of his way to present his aggression against a sovereign country as a defensive war, aimed allegedly against a threat posed to Russia by NATO. There was, however, no immediate threat to which Putin could point, as NATO, which had promised Ukraine a path to membership fourteen years earlier, has done precious little to act on that promise, and its leaders are not even hiding the fact that Ukraine has no chance of becoming a member of the alliance in the near future.

Putin's claim to have been concerned mainly about NATO was further undermined by his refusal to conduct meaningful negotiations with that organization on reducing the threat that NATO and

Russia pose to each other. His demands to roll back the borders of NATO to the 1997 line and effectively expel the East European countries that joined it after the fall of the USSR left little doubt that he was not serious about negotiations and that his primary concern in the coming war was not the threat posed by NATO. There was also little doubt that, if war broke out, it would only unite the NATO countries and harden the alliance's military posture on Russia's borders. Putin clearly did not consider even the increased presence of NATO in Eastern Europe a real threat to Russia.

If relations with NATO were not the key reason for Putin's decision to go to war, what was that reason? The answer to this question was provided by Putin himself in the long speech that he gave on the eve of his attack. The speech was dubbed a history lecture, as it focused so much on Russia's historical relations with Ukraine. That theme was anything but new for Putin, as in July 2021 he had published a long essay on the subject. The argument, both in the essay and in the speech, was the same and had been advanced by Putin for years: he alleged that Russians and Ukrainians were one people, suggesting that Ukrainians do not exist as a nation, and that the Ukrainian state, an artificial creation of Vladimir Lenin and the Bolsheviks, had no right of existence.

Putin's claim that Russians and Ukrainians are the same people was rooted in Russian imperial thinking of the prerevolutionary era, when tsarist officials not only denied the right of Ukrainians to exist as a distinct nation but also prohibited Ukrainian-language publications, including the Bible and school primers, for more than forty years. Their goal was to arrest the development of Ukrainian national identity and create one big Russian nation consisting of Russians, Ukrainians, and Belarusians. That project failed in the flames of the Russian Revolution, forcing Lenin to recognize the existence of Russians and Ukrainians as separate peoples, something that Putin has now set out to reverse.

The war in Ukraine is the latest chapter in the more than century-long disintegration of the Russian Empire and Russian efforts to arrest and reverse that process. During the Russian Revolution, Vladimir Lenin and the Bolsheviks managed to unite under their control most of the imperial Russian territories that had fallen away toward the end of World War I. Not only had Poland,

Finland, and the Baltic states declared their independence in the course of the revolution, but so had Ukraine, Belarus, Georgia, Armenia, and other parts of the former empire. The Bolsheviks managed to bring Ukraine, Belarus, and the Caucasus back under central control both by force and by a number of concessions, including the creation of a union state that would become known as the Soviet Union.

That state, which became a superpower after World War II and was the main adversary of the United States in the Cold War that followed it, fell apart in December 1991. The key factor in its collapse became the proclamation of Ukrainian independence. The Soviet Union was dissolved one week after the Ukrainian referendum of December 1991, in which the Ukrainian public—92 percent of those who took part in the referendum—voted for the independence of their country. Neither the Soviet president, Mikhail Gorbachev, nor the Russian president, Boris Yeltsin, could imagine the Soviet Union without Ukraine, the second-largest Soviet republic after Russia. And so the USSR was peacefully dissolved almost immediately after the Ukrainian referendum.

After 1991, Ukraine embarked on a path of development very different from Russia's. It remained democratic as Russia and most of the post-Soviet states succumbed to authoritarianism. Ukraine also sought to align itself with Europe and its institutions. Its democracy and westward orientation not only undermined Russia's geopolitical ambitions but also threatened the authoritarian regime in Moscow. If the Ukrainians could be democratic, why could the Russians not do likewise? The Kremlin responded by launching a war aimed at destroying Ukrainian democracy.

Given the importance of Ukraine in the collapse of the USSR, any project of reintegrating the post-Soviet space has depended on the position of Ukraine. Boris Yeltsin attempted to tie Ukraine to Russia by means of economic measures, exploiting its dependence on Russian oil and gas. Putin used force in an attempt to solve the same problem. In late 2013 and early 2014, when the Ukrainians rebelled against the government of President Viktor Yanukovych who bowed to Russian pressure and refused to sign an association agreement with the European Union long promised to Ukrainian citizens, Putin sent troops to annex the Crimean peninsula and then launched hybrid warfare in the Donbas. His intelligence services helped to form Russia-backed puppet states and launched a war that claimed the lives of more than 14,000 Ukrainian citizens.

The all-out invasion of Ukraine in February 2022 is just the latest incarnation of the war launched by Russia back in 2014. It has dwarfed the hybrid war of the previous decade. The Russian shelling of Ukrainian cities, which all but leveled Mariupol, a port city the size of Cleveland, horrified the world with its brutality and mobilized it in support of Ukraine. The Ukrainian people resisted and continue to resist this Russian aggression. They have been doing so despite the widespread prewar consensus, shared by the Kremlin and the White House alike, that Ukrainian resistance would be crushed within the first two or three days of the war. The key reason for the success of the resistance is the rise in Ukraine of a strong national identity and loyalty to the democratic state.

Ukrainians mobilized in defense of the values of sovereignty and democracy by working in solidarity across ethnic, linguistic, and cultural lines. Putin claimed that his invasion was meant to liberate Russians and Russian speakers from Ukrainian oppression. He met resistance not only from Ukrainian-speaking Ukrainians but also from Russian-speaking non-Ukrainians, including Russians and Jews. They risked their lives to stop the aggression and trolled Putin on social media, saying "One does not send slaves to liberate the free." The slaves in this case were Russian soldiers, while the free were Ukrainians of various social and cultural backgrounds.

May 2023

12. Putin's War Is Banishing an Outdated Myth

As I write these words, Russian missiles are striking Kyiv, and Russian troops are trying to breach the lines of the city's defenders. This is not only tragic but also a surreal situation that few citizens of Ukraine or Russia could have imagined only a few weeks ago. Vladimir Putin launched the war on Ukraine under the banner of protecting the imagined unity of Russians and Ukrainians, whom he has repeatedly called one and the same people. But the invasion in general and the assault on Kyiv in particular are destroying the last vestiges of his claim that Ukrainians and Russians are fraternal peoples, to say nothing of their being the very same people.

Cracks have appeared even in the supreme leadership of the Orthodox Church, which serves as one of the last institutional and spiritual links uniting many Ukrainian citizens with Russia. When the war broke out, Patriarch Kirill of Moscow, the head of the Russian Orthodox Church, issued a statement calling on "all parties to the conflict to do everything possible to avoid civilian casualties" and invoked the tenth-century baptism of Kyivan Rus´, a state from which both Ukrainians and Russians trace their origins, as part of a tradition that should help to overcome "the divisions and contradictions that have arisen and have led to the current conflict."

But Kirill's formal subordinate and ally in Ukraine, Metropolitan Onuphry, the head of the Ukrainian Orthodox Church under the jurisdiction of the Moscow Patriarchate, had little tolerance for his superior's refusal to name and condemn the aggressor. "Russia has launched military actions against Ukraine, and, at this fateful time, I urge you not to panic, to be courageous, and to show love for your homeland and for each other," stated the metropolitan who has been considered a staunch supporter of Ukraine's ties with Moscow, in an address to his flock. He then appealed to the Russian president and all but accused him of the "sin of Cain" by offering a very different interpretation of the common baptism of Rus′ in 988 by Prince Volodymyr of Kyiv, to which Patriarch Kirill had alluded. "Defending the sovereignty and integrity of Ukraine," continued Onuphry, "we appeal to the President of Russia and ask him to stop the fratricidal war immediately. The Ukrainian and Russian peoples came out of the Dnieper baptismal font, and the war between these peoples is a repetition of the sin of Cain who killed his own brother out of envy. Such a war has no justification either from God or from people."

Metropolitan Onuphry's statement is just one of many similar pronouncements, public and private, issued in Kyiv and other cities of Ukraine since the Russian attack. Onuphry's own clergy are demanding that he declare autocephaly—the independence of his metropolitanate from Moscow. "No one will ever forget or forgive Russia for what is happening now" is a common leitmotif of Facebook posts and private exchanges. In such statements, one can see not only defiance but also a sense of betrayal.

The stubborn resistance of the Ukrainian government and public to Western warnings about the coming invasion was at least partly based on the belief that Russia, historically and culturally close to Ukraine, might launch a new round of hybrid warfare but would not dare to wage a large-scale war against Ukraine. And surely Russia would never attack Kyiv, which Putin had called "the mother of Russian cities." That quotation comes from the medieval Kyivan Chronicle, which refers to Kyiv as the mother, or capital, of Rus′ rather than Russian cities.

There is a profound difference between the Rus′ tribes of the medieval era, which included all Eastern Slavs, and the Russians of today. But Putin has been following in the footsteps of the Russian imperial tradition that treated Kyivan Rus′ as a Russian state. In the nineteenth century, some Russian historians even argued that medieval Kyiv was in fact settled by ethnic Russians who migrated from the area during the Mongol invasion of the thirteenth century. No such outmigration had actually taken place, as has been proved by historical and linguistic data.

There is also no proof to suggest the existence of a unified nationality in the medieval Kyivan state, which extended from the Carpathian Mountains in the west to the Don River in the east, and from the Baltic Sea in the north to the shores of the Black Sea in the south. It was originally ruled by Viking princes and included Slavs and non-Slavs alike. But the imperial mythology claimed that there was one such nationality, and it was Russian. That nineteenth-century understanding of history is at the core of Putin's claim about the existence of one Russian people that includes Russians and Ukrainians. It now faces its demise in the skies of Kyiv.

The Russian assault on Kyiv has destroyed another symbolic bond between Russians and a good many Ukrainians—that of the history and mythology of their common resistance to Nazi Germany during the Second World War. One of the most famous Soviet songs about the start of the German attack referred to Kyiv in its first line: "On June the 22nd, precisely at four in the morning, they bombed Kyiv, and we were told that the war had begun." The "they" of the song were the Nazis; now, those attacking Kyiv are the Russians, claiming that their purpose is to "liberate" the Ukrainians from Nazis in their own midst. The Ukrainians are now defending Kyiv, invoking its status as a Hero City, which it received from the Soviet government for its resistance to the Nazi invasion in 1941.

Far from inspiring gratitude for ostensible "fraternal assistance," the current war is helping to destroy a number of Russian imperial and Soviet myths. Instead of slowing down the development of the Ukrainian nation and destroying its commitment to sovereignty, the Russian invasion in general and the assault on Kyiv in particular are strengthening the Ukrainian people's sense of identity and unity, while endowing it with a new raison d'être, new narratives, and new heroes and martyrs, among whom a place of honor is already reserved for the defenders of Kyiv.

March 2022

13. Annexation

Interview conducted by
Jerzy Sobotta, *Die Welt*

Jerzy Sobotta (JB): *Last Friday, President Vladimir Putin of Russia completed the annexation of Russian-occupied territories in front of running cameras. Why?*

Serhii Plokhy (SP): The annexation is part of Putin's "Greater Russia" project. This is similar to Hitler's "Greater German Reich" (*Großdeutsches Reich*): the idea is to conquer as much territory as possible. But we must not forget that this is only Putin's Plan B. At first, he wanted to annex Ukraine as a whole. That didn't work out, so now he has to repeat the scenario of 2014: the annexation of the Crimea and the de facto occupation of the Donbas.

JB: *Then, as now, Putin legitimized the annexation, which violated international law, by claiming to bring Russians back into their country. How Russian are the people in the occupied territories?*

SP: The Kremlin's version is that, if you speak the Russian language, then you are Russian. You should therefore be loyal to Russia: we even have a right to your loyalty and can send you to the trenches. But propaganda and reality have little to do with each other. You can see this in the fabricated results of the "referenda" that Putin now presents with a straight face as the will of millions of people.

13. Annexation

JB: *What is your version?*

SP: When Putin attacked in February, he thought that Ukraine was still the same as it had been in 2014. At that time, many people were confused about their national self-image. Many saw themselves as neither Russian nor Ukrainian but as former Soviet citizens. Russia exploited that confusion for its brutal politics.

JB: *The Kremlin has called this the Russian World (*russkii mir*). All who speak Russian should feel Russian. There is less of that now. Why?*

SP: Putin has destroyed the idea of the "Russian World" with his own missiles. He is shelling Kharkiv and Zaporizhzhia—Russian-speaking cities in southern and eastern Ukraine. He is killing the people he calls "Russians" (russkie), which makes the "Russian World" absurd. Many Ukrainian citizens who have felt Russian all their lives now see themselves as Ukrainians. No one wants anything to do with this destructive, aggressive Russia anymore. Neither in Ukraine nor elsewhere in the world.

JB: *What does it mean that these people have become Ukrainians?*

SP: In Ukraine, a completely different understanding of nationality has been developing for eight years. It is based neither on language nor on religion. Russian-speaking Ukrainians are fighting against this aggression just as heroically as those who speak Ukrainian. It is the birth of Ukraine as a political nation. This process was enormously accelerated by the Russian aggression. It is patriotic loyalty to our democratic institutions: we can vote and express our opinions freely. None of this exists in Russia, least of all in the occupied territories.

JB: *Putin calls Ukrainians "Little Russians." What does he mean by that?*

SP: This is the idea of the "triune Russian people," a nineteenth-century imperialist concept. According to it, the Russian people consisted of Great Russians, Little Russians, and White Russians. As Little Russians, Ukrainians are considered only a tribe, a subgroup, not a political nation. This idea was a reaction to the first Ukrainian national movement, by which the tsars felt threatened. Putin has returned to the ideology of this tsarist imperialism because he is an imperialist.

JB: *In Germany, too, many have long considered Ukraine part of Russia.*

SP: Absolutely. Here, the imperialist thinking of the nineteenth century has continued, as it did in communist Russia, although the Bolsheviks pretended that the Soviet Union was not an empire. The name "Russia" has stuck to this part of Eurasia, not only in Germany. That is why many in the West were so surprised by the fall of the Soviet Union. They suddenly realized: wait a minute, there are not only Russians living there. But this view belongs to the past.

JB: *Putin accuses the West of wanting the Russian Federation to disintegrate. Would such a thing even be conceivable?*

SP: Even now, we are still witnessing the disintegration of the Russian Empire! It started with the revolutions at the end of the First World War. The Bolsheviks then cobbled the empire back together by making major concessions to non-Russian nationalities, especially to the Ukrainians, who were able to maintain their language and culture at first, but not later. But this empire crumbled again in 1991. And now we see the worst attempt to regain control over the lost territory.

JB: *The war is not going well for Putin. What consequences can that have?*

SP: The very survival of his regime is at stake. It is threatened by chaos, which opens the door to the disintegration of the Russian Federation. Now he has even declared parts of Ukraine that he does not control at all to be Russian territory. While he was signing the document annexing Donetsk, Ukrainian troops surrounded the town of Lyman, located on annexed territory in the Donetsk region. So the Russian Federation has already lost parts of its territory.

13. Annexation

JB: *The disputed and annexed territories are one thing. The other is the Russian Federation.*

SP: Parts of it might secede if the crisis in Russia intensifies. That happened in 1991 and could happen again, for example, in the Caucasus. We are already seeing protests against mobilization in Chechnya, in Dagestan, and in parts of Siberia. People there are starting to revolt against the Russian center. They now feel like nothing more than cannon fodder.

October 2022

14. The Russian Coup

As Yevgeny Prigozhin's columns headed toward Moscow in late June 2023, threatening the very center of Russian state power, Vladimir Putin invoked a historical analogy: calling the actions of Prighozin's Wagner mercenaries a betrayal, he likened the situation to 1917, when "intrigues, squabbles and politicking behind the backs of the army and the nation turned into the greatest turmoil." Without naming names, Putin was comparing himself to Tsar Nicholas II during World War I, on the verge of the fall of the Russian Empire and not long before the Bolsheviks seized power and established the Soviet Union.

There were indeed many parallels between the two situations. World War I was not going well for Nicholas Romanov in 1917, and Putin's invasion of Ukraine has been going badly since its beginning in February 2022. Then as now, both nationalists and liberals—to say nothing of communists and the Russian people at large—were unhappy, and many in the army believed that they needed a new leader and strategy.

But, although Putin may have been right to invoke Russia's imperial history—he clearly drew a number of lessons from the demise of dynasty and empire in 1917—he seemed to be missing the lessons of Russia's post-Romanov past. What brought down the successor regimes in Russia's twentieth century were not attacks by their opponents: it was the "saviors" who rescued the weakened central power and thus found themselves dramatically strengthened. That pattern could be playing out yet again today, and the regime's saviors might quickly become its gravediggers.

14. The Russian Coup

In 1917, Nicholas II was urged to step down by two representatives of the Duma (parliament), the nationalist Vasily Shulgin and the conservative liberal Aleksandr Guchkov. But those who convinced him to do so were military men—the commander of the northern front, General Nikolai Ruzsky who acted on the instructions of General Mikhail Alekseev, commander of the General Staff. Alekseev had the backing of the commanders of the military districts. The brass wanted Nicholas to be succeeded by a government responsible to parliament. Their position sealed the fate not only of the tsar but also of the Romanov dynasty, the institution of the monarchy, and the Russian Empire itself. The abdication of Nicholas II was in essence the result of the military and political opposition finding a common language. That may have been what Putin had in mind—and sought to prevent—when he referred to 1917.

But Prighozin himself had failed to learn this lesson of 1917: he targeted the military brass without obtaining support from the political elite entrenched in the Russian Duma (which, unlike the Duma of 1917, is fully controlled by Russia's political executive). Prigozhin, a St. Petersburg businessman with a criminal background, was a creation of Putin; Wagner often functioned as Putin's private army, operating outside Russian law and often in conflict with the Russian Ministry of Defense. Putin encouraged or tolerated that conflict in order to apply pressure on his underperforming official army. But, when Putin decided to restore the state's monopoly on the use of armed force by subordinating Wagner to the Ministry of Defense, Prigozhin rebelled. His "march for justice" was supposed to convince Putin that the military commanders were worthless—that Prigozhin was the real military power and should take their place. But Putin refused to separate himself from his military commanders and declared his former protégé a traitor.

While Prigozhin's story differs from that of Generals Alekseev and Ruzsky, it has much in common with the fate of their successor at the helm of the Russian army, General Lavr Kornilov. In August 1917, Kornilov, upset that the Russian Provisional Government, led by Aleksandr Kerensky, had proved incapable of eliminating dual power in the capital and crushing the competing Soviet of Workers' and Soldiers' Deputies, marched on Petrograd to do the job for the government and dissolve the Soviet. Kornilov's vanguard, the "Wild Division," was composed largely of volunteers from the Caucasus, including a regiment from Chechnya.

The march on Petrograd was later labeled a coup, although Kornilov never planned to remove Kerensky's government. But he failed to achieve his more limited goal—the dissolution of the Soviet. The "Wild Division" refused to follow his orders. The Soviet and the Bolshevik leaders recruited Muslim politicians to convince the Caucasian mountaineers to remain neutral. The alleged coup failed, but Kerensky's power was significantly weakened by his "rescuers," the Bolsheviks. They emerged in the wake of the coup as the real victors, gaining a majority in the Soviets of Petrograd and Moscow, and then using the Soviets controlled by them and their allies to further destabilize Kerensky's government and provide a veneer of legitimacy to their coup against it in October 1917.

There are many echoes of Kornilov's coup in the one launched by Prigozhin, the most important being that they were allegedly undertaken in defense of legitimate authority—a tactic also used by leaders of Cossack uprisings during the Time of Troubles in Russia in the first decades of the seventeenth century. An even closer parallel may be found in the August coup of 1991, in which the military backed the KGB in a revolt against Mikhail Gorbachev. The 1991 coup began like Kornilov's, with the alleged goal of saving the legitimate authorities from their enemies.

Having learned that their positions in government were threatened by a deal reached by Gorbachev and his archrival, Boris Yeltsin, in late July 1991, the plotters asked Gorbachev to sign a decree allowing them to crush Yeltsin and his backers and restore order in the interests of Gorbachev himself. When Gorbachev refused, the plotters reluctantly launched a coup despite their own lack of unity, which left such military commanders as Generals Pavel Grachev and Aleksandr Lebed sitting on two stools.

Once blood was spilled on the streets of Moscow, the minister of defense, Marshal Dmitry Yazov, pulled his troops out of the capital, effectively ending the coup. Its leaders, with Vladimir Kriuchkov of the KGB at their head, rushed to negotiate with their former patron, Mikhail Gorbachev, then vacationing in the Crimea. They hoped to convince him that the coup was directed

14. The Russian Coup

not against him but against Yeltsin. It was too late. Yeltsin had already won, not only against them but, much more importantly, against Gorbachev. He was so weakened by the attempted coup that Yeltsin forced him to cancel his appointments of new ministers in the government's "security bloc" and appointed his own loyalists to those positions instead.

That was just the beginning. After taking control over Russian natural resources and the Soviet financial institutions, Yeltsin deprived Gorbachev of government funds, took away his power to print money, and eventually got the army on his side by promising salary increases and a new decisive, steady leadership that Gorbachev did not offer. The dissolution of the Soviet Union, triggered by Ukraine's referendum of 1 December 1991 for independence, became the final act of the coup launched by Gorbachev's closest aides in August 1991.

There is a common thread in the history of failed coups in revolutionary and late Soviet Russia that may be helpful for understanding the possible consequences of this latest attempt. While not aimed explicitly at the ruler holding supreme office, such coups significantly weaken the officeholders who become hostages of their "rescuers" and eventually leave the political scene. Observers should watch whose power rises and whose falls in Russia as a result of Prigozhin's attempt. The group that gains more power will obtain it less at the expense of its fallen rivals than at the expense of Putin himself.

Prigozhin's coup has demonstrated the weakness of Putin's political regime. It proved extremely easy for a unit ten thousand strong to capture key facilities in two of Russia's major cities and regions and to threaten the capital itself. Not only did the military under Moscow's control not resist the Wagner fighters, but many ordinary people welcomed the rebels. Prigozhin's halfhearted coup showed that the Russian army and society are ready for real change, and his march may have been only a rehearsal.

The news coming from Russia suggests that, while the attempted coup challenged the power of Putin, it helped to increase the power of his security apparatus, particularly the FSB (Federal Security Service, the Russian-state successor agency of the KGB), which is investigating Ministry of Defense involvement. The

Rosgvardiia, Russia's National Guard, under the command of the former Yeltsin and Putin bodyguard Viktor Zolotov, is in the process of acquiring tanks and airplanes. The Rosgvardiia is an internal military force directly controlled by the president. But so was the Wagner Group. The loyalty of such troops and their leaders is anything but a given.

Putin's best strategy under the circumstances would be to end the war with Ukraine as soon as possible—the most effective way of preventing future cases of disgruntled military units turning their weapons on the government. But that is an unlikely scenario. Both Nicholas II and Kerensky bet on the next big offensive to save their regimes. Putin will most probably do the same. Historically speaking, that is the wrong choice. After Kornilov came the Bolsheviks; after the leaders of the August 1991 coup came Yeltsin. Who will come after Yevgeny Prigozhin is not yet apparent, but the door to change has already been opened.

June 2023

IV. Nuclear Roulette

15. The Ghosts of Chornobyl

I visited the Chornobyl exclusion zone many times while researching my book on the Chornobyl nuclear disaster and immediately recognized the familiar landscape on my television screen. An armored personnel carrier was moving along a snow-covered road a few miles away from the damaged reactor no. 4. Men in military camouflage armed with assault rifles jumped out of the vehicle and took positions along the road. The Ukrainian minister of defense, Oleksii Reznikov, who had invited journalists to the zone, explained that Ukrainian troops were getting ready to protect it against a possible Russian invasion.

The expected invasion happened. On the afternoon of 24 February, soldiers in unmarked uniforms entered the Ukrainian part of the exclusion zone from its northern, Belarusian side—the two countries, now de facto at war, have been sharing it since April 1986. The unidentified soldiers overpowered the Ukrainian national guardsmen who were protecting the radioactive waste stored in the zone. They took over the rest of the zone as well, including the decommissioned nuclear reactors and the new containment structure over the damaged reactor no. 4. The structure, which cost 1.5 billion Euros, was opened in the summer of 2019, soon after the release of the HBO/Sky blockbuster *Chernobyl*.

Anton Herashchenko, an adviser to the Ukrainian minister of internal affairs, posted an announcement on his Facebook page stating that the Ukrainian guardsmen in the zone had been attacked. He wrote that a battle for control of the zone was going on and that Russian shelling could damage the storage facilities, producing a radioactive plume that might cover much of

Ukraine, Belarus, and the countries of the European Union. That did not happen. The unidentified military force, equipped with tanks and armored military vehicles, took control of the zone and its installations by early evening of 26 February without an exchange of fire.

By 8:30 p.m. Ukraine's State Nuclear Regulatory Inspectorate had lost control of all facilities in the zone and sent an alarm in that regard to the Vienna-based International Atomic Energy Agency (IAEA). The IAEA issued its own statement but offered little more public information. The agency's director general, Rafael Mariano Grossi, expressed "grave concern" and appealed "for maximum restraint to avoid any action that may put the country's nuclear facilities at risk," but his appeal was not addressed to anyone in particular. Russia, one of the major donors to the IAEA, was not mentioned at all, leaving the impression that the site had been seized by some non-governmental entity.

That day, monitoring equipment in the exclusion zone showed rising levels of radiation. Gamma irradiation in some parts of the zone increased dramatically. In the village of Mashevo on the border with Belarus, it rose tenfold above the yearly average. Fortunately, it turned out that the rising levels had nothing to do with any damage to nuclear storage facilities or leakage from reactor no. 4. Military vehicles entering the zone, including tanks, had stirred up radioactive dust from the 1986 accident and raised it into the air. The IAEA breathed a sigh of relief, declaring that radiation levels were "within the operational range measured in the Exclusion Zone since it was established."

The Ukrainian authorities issued a statement pointing out that, according to international agreements, military operations were banned in nuclear power plants and at nuclear radiation sites. They could still monitor radiation levels in the zone but had lost contact with their personnel there, who were being held by the Russian military. President Volodymyr Zelensky called the Russian takeover of the station "a declaration of war against the whole of Europe." "The capture of the station and the conduct there of any military activities threatens another Chornobyl disaster," went the Ukrainian statement issued on 25 February, the second day of the invasion.

On that day, Russian officials admitted that the site of the world's worst nuclear disaster was under their control. What is going on there remains very little known today. The Russian side claims that its military is patrolling the premises together with the Ukrainian armed forces. The Ukrainians deny that and claim that the personnel has been kidnapped, and no change of shifts has taken place since Kyiv lost control of the area. Meanwhile, experts are worried not only about the safety of the nuclear waste stored in the zone but also about the state of the new confinement structure, which may start leaking radiation if it has been damaged.

In the days following the seizure of the Chornobyl exclusion zone by Russian forces, the Ukrainian nuclear regulator stated that a research reactor in Kyiv and a nuclear installation in Kharkiv have either been shut down or are operating safely. Meanwhile, Ukrainian nuclear power plants remain in operation. Ukraine gets half its electricity from nuclear power and has four nuclear stations, with a total of fifteen reactors, in operation. The problem is that two of those stations, the South Ukraine Nuclear Power Plant, with three units, and the Zaporizhzhia Nuclear Power Plant, with six units, are located north of the Crimea, within the area of the Russian assault.

Russian troops had approached Enerhodar, the city where the Zaporizhzhia plant is located, but the citizens refused to let them in, putting roadblocks and heavy trucks at the entrance to the city and staging a mass demonstration with Ukrainian banners. The Russian military backed off, not daring to storm a nuclear town. According to the city's mayor, Dmytro Orlov, the Russian officers asked city officials to let them in just to take a selfie against the background of the nuclear power plant and report back to Moscow that they had taken control of the facility. The mayor refused. As of 3 March, the plant and the city remained under Ukrainian control. It is anyone's guess what might happen next. Even if the personnel shuts down the reactors in case of military conflict reaching the vicinity of the plant, the reactors can still go into meltdown if the plant loses its electrical supply from outside sources—a distinct possibility in conditions of warfare and airstrikes.

The situation might spin quickly out of control, whatever the intentions of participants in the war. Back in 1986, when one of the units of the South Ukraine Nuclear Power Plant went offline, a power grid operator in Kyiv ordered the personnel of the Chornobyl nuclear power plant to keep reactor no. 4 going even though it was already in shutdown mode. The operator needed additional electricity to offset the loss at the South Ukraine plant. Unbeknown to him, this decision became a major contributing factor to the Chornobyl disaster. Ukraine, Europe, and the world at large might now face a similar situation, with a chain of events leading to another, much greater nuclear catastrophe. Russia should stop its aggression before this war goes nuclear not only metaphorically but also physically.

March 2023

16. Who Is in Charge?

*Interview conducted by
Meghan Kruger, The Washington Post*

Meghan Kruger (MK): *Who is in charge of Chornobyl now? Do we know?*

Serhii Plokhy (SP): Now, it's under the control of the Russian military. The Ukrainians are saying that they've kept the original plant personnel there, that they're hostages, that there was supposed to be a shift change, but it didn't take place. People can't communicate with their families; they're not able to get in touch with their superiors in Kyiv.

MK: *How problematic is it to have people who are not familiar with a specific nuclear plant running it? Can Russia just supply its own staff?*

SP: Local knowledge is extremely important. You have to know the state of things—you can't just parachute somebody in. And that is especially true of the new confinement system [a multibillion-dollar hangar installed in 2016 to replace the failing "sarcophagus" that previously enclosed the damaged plant—ed.]. It's a new technology; you have to know what you're doing.

MK: *How likely is it that fighting around Chornobyl could cause an accident? Or is the greater risk from someone working at the plant who doesn't know what he's doing?*

SP: The danger comes from military actions around that area. Missiles don't necessarily fly in the direction that people want them to fly. Even if no one wants to aim in the direction of the reactors, there are large stores of nuclear fuel there. That might do more damage. And the Ukrainians claim that they are intercepting Russian missiles. Who can control where the wreckage goes? It's a war zone.

MK: *Are there other radiological dangers besides Chornobyl that people should worry about?*

SP: People should be alarmed. At the Zaporizhzhia nuclear power plant, there are six reactors; it's one of the largest plants in Europe. It's exactly in the path of Russian troops moving northward from the Crimea. According to reports, there are Russian troops near the gates of the town where the plant is located—Enerhodar. The situation we have today is: the Russian plan was about blitzkrieg, winning the war in one or two days. But that didn't happen; they turned out to be much less effective in fighting the Ukrainian military than they assumed. They're now shelling the city of Kharkiv, in eastern Ukraine, and residential areas as well. The big concern is that the Russians will become much more indiscriminate in what they're doing... That's when you get into really morbid outcomes. The war has to be ended now, if only to avoid the threat of fifteen new Chornobyls.

MK: *How hard is it to trigger a cataclysmic accident at a nuclear plant today? Are there protections in place now that could help prevent a Chornobyl-type catastrophe?*

SP: You don't need a bomb dropped on a nuclear facility to have a major disaster. Chornobyl shows that a combination of design issues and mistakes can explode a nuclear plant under peaceful conditions. Fukushima showed that the only thing needed for a meltdown is to cut off electricity. You don't need planes, you don't need bombs—just cut off electricity, which can happen as a result of military action, without anyone wanting to damage a nuclear power plant. And then you'll get Fukushima. They have backup generators, but the question is, how long can they last? War and nuclear energy are not the right combination.

16. Who Is in Charge?

MK: *If there were to be a nuclear accident, what would the response look like?*

SP: Well, the International Atomic Energy Agency will express its concern. It's unlikely that they would actually condemn Russia; the agency can't even spell or pronounce the word "Russia," like any other agency that depends on a paycheck from China or Russia. Then they'll try to talk to the warring sides about what to do.

March 2022

17. Nuclear Terrorism

Interview conducted by
Tobin Harshaw, *Bloomberg*

Tobin Harshaw (TH): *The latest news is that the Chornobyl plant is no longer transmitting data to the International Atomic Energy Agency, and that electricity at the site has been cut off. How much of a concern is that?*

Serhii Plokhy (SP): The concern is enormous, and the threat of a nuclear accident is very real. The emergency generators can work only for 48 hours, and after that there will be no electricity to keep the equipment going. In the new 1.5-billion Euro confinement over the damaged fourth unit of the station, electricity is needed to keep pressure in the facility lower than in the atmosphere, not allowing radioactive particles to get out of the structure. But the biggest concern is the spent-fuel facility, which contains 200 fuel assemblies. Electricity is required to keep the assemblies from overheating. Overheated assemblies are a particular threat, as they can start to disintegrate and release enormous amounts of radiation into the atmosphere.

TH: *Those of us who watched the miniseries* Chernobyl *are terrified of conjectures that the containment structure might be imperiled. Were you concerned? How dangerous is it that an exhausted skeleton crew of Ukrainian POWs is now overseeing the ruins?*

SP: The Ukrainian personnel at the Chornobyl facility are indeed prisoners of war. They are being kept in virtual captivity, are not allowed to communicate with their superiors or loved ones, have no medicine and little food, which they are saving, as no one knows what comes next. They are doing their best, working in shifts to keep the equipment functioning and radiation levels under control. With the recent damage done to the power supply by military action in the area, a lot depends on their professionalism. But they are under enormous stress, and if that is not a recipe for nuclear disaster, I do not know what is.

TH: *More generally, how stable is the facility now, in terms of a potential disaster in either war or peacetime? Is the "new safe confinement" that covered the old sarcophagus a lasting solution?*

SP: Yes, it is a lasting solution—the structure should be good for another hundred years or so. But there is one caveat: there should be no fighting in the area, no shelling, no disruption of electricity supply, etc. The facility prevents the "escape" of radiation from the damaged reactor but does nothing to deal with the source of that radiation—the remains of fuel and radioactive debris in the damaged reactor. The removal of that source of radiation is a task for the next few decades, provided that the current war ends, and the Ukrainian nuclear regulatory authorities restore their control over the facility and the exclusion zone as a whole.

TH: *When the Russians were seizing the Zaporizhzhia plant, the largest in Europe, Zelensky warned in a video message that an explosion there could spell the "end of Europe." Was that hyperbole?*

SP: The continuing occupation of the Zaporizhzhia nuclear power plant can lead to a nuclear disaster that might dwarf the one in Chornobyl. The reactors have been shut down by the Ukrainian personnel, but it takes a long time for their active zones to cool. If the war continues, the supply of electricity can be cut, as happened at Chornobyl. What will follow is well known from the story of Fukushima: there, four reactors either experienced a partial meltdown or their containment structures exploded for lack of electricity to pump water and cool the reactors. In Fukushima, the prevailing direction of winds was toward the ocean. There is no ocean around Ukraine, just European landmass. So, yes, the end of Europe as we know it was and still is a distinct possibility.

TH: *Why have the Russians apparently made taking these plants a high priority? To scare the West?*

SP: The Chornobyl nuclear power plant was on the path of Russian troops proceeding from the Belarusian border to Kyiv—the shortest route available to the aggressors—and they used it, raising radioactive dust in the exclusion zone as their tanks and equipment moved toward the Ukrainian capital. The Zaporizhzhia nuclear power plant happened to be on the route of Russian forces making their way from the Crimea, annexed in 2014, toward central Ukraine, but they could easily have bypassed it. The point was indeed to scare Ukraine and the world. We are dealing here with nuclear terrorism.

TH: *Apparently people are stockpiling against disaster: Bloomberg News reports that the price of a bottle of 180 potassium iodine pills on Amazon has more than doubled since the beginning of the year. Is this sort of precaution smart or silly?*

SP: Ukrainians survived the Chornobyl disaster, so for them the threat of another Chornobyl is not something purely theoretical. The new nuclear crisis is happening literally in their backyards—the Zaporizhzhia nuclear power plant is located next to Enerhodar, a city of more than 50,000 inhabitants. Under the circumstances, it would be silly not to take precautions. Media outlets are posting instructions on what to do in case of a nuclear emergency.

TH: *Finally, you grew up mostly in Ukraine. What are your hopes and fears right now about the war?*

SP: My hope is that it ends soon, and that Ukrainian sovereignty and territorial integrity, along with basic principles of international order, are restored. My fear is that the war may drag on for a long, long time. Out of that fear comes another hope for international action, not just solidarity, which would not allow that to happen.

March 2022

18. Between a Rock and a Hard Place

The president of the European Commission, Ursula von der Leyen, once called "climate neutrality," or net zero greenhouse emissions, a European destiny. But should one follow that destiny? The answer came on 2 February 2022, when the European Commission presented a proposal that labeled nuclear energy and gas environmentally sustainable or, in other words, "green" economic activities that should help the European Union to achieve net zero emissions by the year 2050.

This new status for nuclear energy had been advocated by France, backed by a number of East European members of the European Union, and opposed by Germany and some of its Central and West European allies. In France, nuclear energy accounts for more than 70 percent of energy production, while Germany is close to abandoning nuclear reactors—2022 was supposed to be the last year of its nuclear phaseout. Thus Germany got its way on the use of natural gas, one-third of which it was importing from Russia. The European Commission proposal placed natural gas in the same basket as nuclear energy—environmentally sustainable economic activities that would allow the EU to reach its goal of net zero emissions by mid-century.

The final decision on which "green" activities will be allowed to battle greenhouse gases is supposed to be made by the European Commission before the end of this year, releasing a flood of Euro-denominated investment into industries identified as "green" in the battle against climate change. But, within a few weeks after the announcement, two potentially green industries, natural gas and nuclear energy, found themselves under attack. Surprisingly—or perhaps not, given that the new "green deal" satisfied the main EU stakeholders, Germany and France, to different degrees—the assault came not from within but from outside the European Union, and in the form not of political but real warfare.

On 24 February, Russia, the main supplier of natural gas to Germany and provider of 40 percent of the EU's natural gas, launched an unprovoked attack on the sovereign state of Ukraine. With a Russian army of more than 150,000 on that country's borders, no one gave it much of a fighting chance. Both Moscow and Washington predicted the collapse of the Ukrainian government within days. But the Ukrainians refused to surrender and fought back. The United States and Europe agreed to impose an unprecedented set of sanctions on Russia, among them Germany's decision to halt construction of the 11 billion Nord Stream 2 pipeline, which was all but ready for operation and would have made Germany and the EU even more dependent on Russian gas.

There is growing pressure on the EU leaders to embrace nuclear energy. The International Atomic Energy Agency has released a ten-point plan to reduce the EU's reliance on Russian hydrocarbons, including the recommissioning of reactors taken offline for maintenance and postponement of shutting down five reactors. Given the impact of Russia's war on Ukraine and, by extension, the rest of Europe and the West in general, would it not make sense to invest in nuclear energy? The problem with this argument is that the war, which put the continuing supply of Russian natural gas in question, also delivered a major blow to the future of nuclear energy.

***

The start of the all-out Russian invasion dramatically shifted the focus of discussions about nuclear energy. On 24 February, the first day of the invasion, the Russians took over the Chornobyl nuclear power plant and exclusion zone. On 4 March, under cover of darkness, Russian forces attacked the Zaporizhzhia plant, , which was protected by a small detachment of Ukrainian guardsmen who fought back. The operators began the lengthy process of shutting down the reactors by reducing their power levels. The public-address system transmitted a message to the attackers: "Stop shooting at a dangerous nuclear facility. Stop shooting immediately! You threaten the security of the whole world!" It had no effect. Shelling continued, setting one of the buildings of the nuclear complex on fire. Thanks only to the heroism of the firefighters, the fire was extinguished. But the Russian military succeeded in taking control of the plant, took its personnel hostage, and placed them under the command of a Russian military officer.

The war in Ukraine suddenly went nuclear in a way that no one expected. The Russian military authorities were violating safety rules by setting off mines and bombs unexploded during the battle in close proximity to the reactors. The military takeover of the plant placed the personnel under enormous stress, making mistakes more likely. It was personnel errors that had contributed to the Chornobyl accident back in 1986. President Volodymyr Zelensky of Ukraine declared the military takeover of the Zaporizhzhia plant an act of nuclear terrorism. The director of the IAEA, Rafael Mariano Grossi, issued his own statement: "Firing shells in the area of a nuclear power plant violates the fundamental principle that the physical integrity of nuclear facilities must be maintained and kept safe at all times."

Judging by the IAEA statement, Grossi once again avoided direct reference to Russia. But the US representative to the UN, Ambassador Linda Thomas-Greenfield, was much more straightforward. "Russia's attack last night put Europe's largest nuclear power plant at grave risk. It was incredibly reckless and dangerous," she declared in her statement at the UN Security Council emergency meeting, demanding that Russia "abide by international humanitarian law, which prohibits intentionally targeting civilians and civilian infrastructure."

In its statement on the Russian takeover of the Chornobyl facilities, the Ukrainian Nuclear Regulatory Inspectorate accused Moscow of violating Article 56 of the first additional protocol of the 1949 Geneva Conventions on the conduct of war. The article states that "nuclear electrical generating stations shall not be made the object of attack, even where these objects are military objectives, if such attack may cause the release of dangerous forces and consequent severe losses among the civilian population."

Although that sounds very clear and unambiguous, the protocol does in fact permit attacks on a nuclear facility if they do not cause the release of radiation. Moreover, the same article removes any protection from a nuclear power plant if it "provides electric power in regular, significant and direct support of military operations and if such attack is the only feasible way to terminate such support." Thus, a nuclear power plant that supplies electricity to the power grid used by the army defending the nuclear plant can become a legitimate target under international law.

The protocol was open for signing and ratification in June 1977, although neither the US nor Russia currently subscribe to it. The next decade and a half saw massive military attacks on nuclear reactors, beginning in September 1980 with Iran's bombing of the Al Tuwaitha nuclear complex in Iraq. The two countries were engaged in bitter warfare, but the attack was encouraged and facilitated by the Israelis, who were determined to stop the development of Iraq's nuclear arms program.

In June 1981, Israeli airplanes penetrated Iraq's airspace and destroyed the Osirak nuclear research facility. Iraq responded with six bombings of Iran's Bushehr nuclear plant, the strikes taking place between 1984 and 1987. The United States went on to bomb three Iraqi reactors and other nuclear facilities in 1991. Meanwhile, Iraq fired Scud missiles at Israel's Dimona nuclear reactor. Sixteen years later, in 2007, Israel attacked a Syrian reactor under construction. There was nothing in international law to prevent such attacks.

The additional protocol of 1977, no matter how imperfect, applied only to civilian reactors. Such facilities also came under attack, but not by state actors. In 1973, fighters of the Maoist People's Revolutionary Army captured Argentina's Atucha I Nuclear Power Plant, then still under construction, without doing any damage. In 1982, the Koeberg Nuclear Power Station in South Africa was attacked by militants of the African National Congress, who detonated four mines, destroying considerable infrastructure. Nuclear power plants were also considered as targets by 9/11 terrorists, but no operating civilian nuclear plant had ever been attacked until March 2022.

18. Between a Rock and a Hard Place

* * *

The seizure of the Zaporizhzhia nuclear power plant in Ukraine is the first takeover of a nuclear facility by a state actor and its military forces. They acted in violation not only of the additional protocols of the 1949 Geneva Convention but also of Rule 42 of the International Humanitarian Law, which prohibits attacks on nuclear facilities. The 2001 Russian Federation regulation on the application of that rule states that nuclear power stations "shall not become the object of attack even when they are military objectives, if attacking them may result in the abovementioned consequences." The consequences in question are the release of radiation and the death of civilians.

The Board of Governors of the IAEA, which, among other things, oversees the security of nuclear facilities, adopted a resolution calling on Russia "immediately to cease all actions at and against nuclear facilities in Ukraine." The resolution was ignored, and there was little that the IAEA could do about it. Kyiv's call to establish a 30-kilometer no-fight and no-flight zone around the nuclear facilities fell on deaf ears, too. In fact, things got worse as the Russians, according to the Ukrainian side, deliberately targeted and damaged a nuclear research reactor at the Kharkiv Institute of Physics and Technology—the cradle of the Soviet nuclear research program in the 1930s.

The Russian takeover of the Chornobyl exclusion zone and its facilities, along with the attack on and occupation of the Zaporizhzhia nuclear power plant, highlights a vulnerability of nuclear energy production that has been largely ignored until now—the possibility of an accident or multiple accidents caused by warfare. At Chornobyl, the electricity needed to cool spent fuel was cut in the course of warfare in 2022, raising concerns about fuel elements getting overheated and releasing radiation into the atmosphere. The damage done to the power lines left the water pumps unable to function and the super cool reactor without water, which could have led to a meltdown of the kind that happened at Fukushima.

In early April, as the fortunes of war changed, Russian troops in the Chornobyl zone withdrew to avoid encirclement. What the Ukrainians found at the site afterwards suggested that the story of the Chornobyl contamination was far from over. Before leaving the station, the Russian soldiers had dug trenches in the highly radioactive Red Forest and had stolen more than one hundred radioactive elements from the Chornobyl facilities. While some of the soldiers soon ended up in hospital, the radioactive elements that they stole remain unaccounted for.

* * *

The world turned out to be completely unprepared for Russian nuclear blackmail. Not only is the IAEA unequipped to deal with the threat posed to the safety of nuclear reactors by a country that is a permanent member of the UN Security Council, but there is little in the body of international law that gives it a basis for action.

At present, we lack effective legal instruments that could stop Russia from targeting Ukrainian nuclear sites. There are no international treaties dealing specifically with military attacks on nuclear power plants. While treaties and conventions are no panacea against criminal behavior in the international arena, they could clarify responsibility for attacks on nuclear power plants, as the current legal regime fails to do. This is a rude awakening for the world in general and proponents of nuclear energy in particular. Unless nuclear reactors are legally protected from attack in wartime, there can be no serious consideration of nuclear energy as a solution to the problem of climate change, no matter how many times it is declared "green," as the European Commission has recently done.

The accidents at nuclear power plants, of which Chornobyl and Fukushima are the most notorious, are the main reason why the public is at best reluctant to embrace nuclear energy as a solution to the climate change crisis. The war in Ukraine delivers one more blow to the nuclear energy option, pointing to the vulnerability of reactors in conditions of conventional warfare and the inability of the international order to do anything to prevent another nuclear catastrophe, this time caused by deliberate military attack. If the worst happens in Ukraine in the coming weeks and months, producing another Chornobyl or multiple meltdowns of the Fukushima type, the impact will be felt not only in Ukraine but in the rest of Europe as well.

Back in the 1950s, when President Dwight Eisenhower initiated the Atoms for Peace program and the International Atomic Energy Agency was created, there was a vision that peaceful uses of nuclear energy would stop the proliferation of nuclear weapons, with Atoms for Peace defeating Atoms for War. That never happened. Instead, Atoms for Peace provided technological know-how to those who wanted to build Atoms for War, and now conventional warfare can turn Atoms for Peace reactors into dirty bombs.

If that is the kind of risk that must be taken to attain "climate neutrality," the question is whether humankind will be around to enjoy its benefits. We should definitely invest in the safety of existing nuclear reactors by putting in place legislation and mechanisms protecting them not only from natural disasters but also from manmade ones such as war. Beyond that, new investment should go into renewables and technologies of the twenty-first century instead of the morally discredited technologies of the previous one.

2023

19. Atoms for Peace and Atoms for War

Answers to questions from
LatePost

LatePost (LP): *You have written three books about nuclear energy and accidents associated with it (*Chernobyl, Nuclear Folly, *and* Atoms and Ashes*). How did you start researching those topics? Why are you so interested in the subject? Could you tell me about the history of your research on nuclear energy?*

Serhii Plokhy (SP): I lived in Ukraine when the Chornobyl disaster happened, and, like almost everyone there, was affected by it. Our children stayed indoors, and my colleagues and students were drafted into the army and sent to the Chornobyl exclusion zone as cleanup workers. So I always wanted to know what happened, who was responsible, and why we knew so little about the fallout. Once I realized that I could consult Soviet archives on the history of the accident, I decided to research that topic and look for answers to the questions I always had. That put me on the path of researching the history of the Nuclear Age.

LP: *What do you think about the intrinsic connections and differences among these three books? Is there a pattern to your work on the subject? In the process of research and writing, what significant changes have occurred in your understanding of nuclear energy?*

SP: Two of my books, *Chernobyl* and *Atoms and Ashes*, deal with "atoms for peace," accidents that happened mostly at civilian nuclear facilities. *Nuclear Folly* deals with "atoms for war," or nuclear weapons. We often think about nuclear energy and the nuclear industry as separate fields, but I realized in the course of my research that they are not. The same people worked on military and civilian projects, and governments often dealt with nuclear fallout in the same way. All the reactors we have today are variants of those created for military purposes.

LP: *It seems that you will be writing another book on this subject. Could you talk about what issues you want to explore? What will the content be? What will be the connections and differences between that book and your previous works?*

SP: Yes, indeed. Although I would like to move on and write about other subjects, the nuclear theme will not let go of me, partly because it keeps popping up in the news again and again. My next book will deal with the Russian takeover of the Chornobyl nuclear power plant in February and March 2022. This is the first case in history of a military force taking control of a nuclear site on foreign territory—in other words, the first time that a nuclear site was engulfed by war. It turned out that the international community could not respond adequately to the crisis through the IAEA and other institutions. We have 440 reactors in the world today, and none of them was designed to withstand a military attack. The Russian takeover of Chornobyl caught the world unprepared.

LP: *The Chinese version of* Atoms and Ashes *is about to be published. One major feeling I had after reading it is that, although people cannot determine when the next nuclear accident will happen, it will definitely occur. Could you explain why nuclear accidents will definitely happen in the future? What can we do now to reduce the problems and risks caused by nuclear accidents?*

SP: Scientists and engineers keep learning from every new accident, but accidents, including catastrophic ones, keep happening, surprising experts and the public every time. One reason for this is that nuclear reactors work by implementing the most complex means of boiling water, so to speak, invented to date. Accidents happen in complex technological systems because it is impossible to anticipate everything that can go wrong; hence they are known as "normal accidents." They happen no matter what. There are also factors pertaining to the economics of nuclear energy production. It is a business, so designers, construction crews, and operators tend to cut corners in order to save money. Those "savings" come at a cost. Currently, with the nuclear industry facing competition from renewables, pressure to cut costs is increasing, and so is the possibility of nuclear accidents.

LP: *At the end of* Atoms and Ashes, *you quote Gregory Jaczko's words: "the autumn years of nuclear power." Do you think that this technology should be gradually abandoned or phased out? Why?*

SP: As I mentioned earlier, nuclear power production is the most complex and dangerous way of boiling water. It is a twentieth-century technology, and we should look for alternatives. With regard to Jaczko's words, I think they have special meaning when it comes to the aging fleet of nuclear reactors, many of them built using outdated technologies. As the nuclear industry faces ever greater economic pressure and government funds are redirected to the support of renewables, we cannot compromise the safety of already existing reactors. Before investing in new reactors, we should at least make sure that the old ones are safe.

LP: Atoms and Ashes *presents two completely different attitudes toward nuclear energy: the public generally opposes it, while governments often support it. Why do you think this gap exists? How can the public ensure that the government does not abuse nuclear energy? How can the government be held accountable to the public when a nuclear accident occurs?*

SP: The public is concerned about its own safety and does not trust governments, which have a record of covering up nuclear and other disasters. Governments, on the other hand, are preoccupied predominantly with economic growth and prioritize it over safety. Tensions between government and public on that matter are very much present in today's Japan. It is one of the consequences of the Fukushima accident, which has been regarded as a result of excessively close relations between government and industry. Unless governments find a way to engage the public as a partner with regard to the nuclear industry, distrust will continue.

19. Atoms for Peace and Atoms for War

LP: *A book review claimed that you exaggerated the dangers of nuclear power and downplayed conventional harm caused by other energy sources. "Since Chornobyl, fatalities caused by civilian nuclear power have fallen essentially to zero." This statement is similar to Bill Gates's argument: "Nuclear power kills far, far fewer people than cars do." Do you have any response to these criticisms and statements?*

SP: The trick is that we do not know what the human toll of Chornobyl has been. People die from cancer and other diseases caused by exposure to low levels of radiation decades after a nuclear accident, and we have never had a comprehensive examination of the health consequences of such accidents on the same level as we had after Hiroshima and Nagasaki. So comparisons with car accidents, in which the results are immediately obvious, are not appropriate. Besides, car crashes do not leave zones of more than a thousand square miles uninhabitable, as was the case in Chornobyl, and do not require multi-billion-dollar shelters over the sites of accidents such as that one.

LP: *Christopher Nolan, the director of the film* Oppenheimer, *said that, when he first started writing the screenplay, his son told him, "No one cares about nuclear weapons anymore." But, two years later, his son was no longer saying that. I'm curious, have you seen the movie? What are your feelings? The film mainly discusses Oppenheimer's moral anxieties about nuclear weapons and showcases scientists' various positions on this issue. Do you have any thoughts? I remember that* Atoms and Ashes *also compared the views of J. Robert Oppenheimer, Edward Teller, and Andrei Sakharov on nuclear weapons.*

SP: It is a very powerful movie, and it could not have come at a better time. We are already involved in a new nuclear arms race, and the question of what is moral and what is not in such a context is being asked once again. Oppenheimer built the first atomic bomb and, despite the opposition voiced by many of his colleagues, supported the government's decision to use it. His hope was that, once people saw the enormous power released by the bomb, it would not be used again. To a degree, his gamble worked.

The use of nuclear weapons became taboo in international relations, and we should keep it that way.

LP: *In relation to this, you reconsidered the 1962 Cuban missile crisis in* Nuclear Folly. *Do you think there is still a risk of nuclear crises in the future? What lessons and experiences can we learn from history to prevent the occurrence of nuclear crises?*

SP: Yes, of course. As long as nuclear weapons exist, so does the risk of nuclear war. It is easy to misjudge the other side, and incomplete information and error in judgment can easily lead to a nuclear confrontation. My biggest discovery during my work on that book was related to the fact that neither Nikita Khrushchev nor John F. Kennedy could control the crisis after a certain point. A nuclear escalation is easy to start but very difficult to stop, as commanders on the ground start making decisions of their own. Accidents that can lead to a nuclear strike do happen irrespective of the wishes of the principal actors.

LP: *In August of this year, Japan began to discharge treated wastewater from the Fukushima nuclear power plant into the ocean. This action has been met with opposition among Chinese people, and the Chinese government has also suspended the import of seafood from Japan. I'm curious, how do you view this event? Are the concerns of the Chinese people justified?*

SP: As far as I know, concern has been expressed not only by the Chinese people and government but also by the Japanese public. No one is happy with the situation, and rightly so. The wastewater crisis reminds us once again that decisions to build nuclear power plants are made by national governments, but the consequences of nuclear accidents are international. That was the case with Chornobyl and is the case with Fukushima. If the international community pays the price for decisions made by national governments, then it must have a say in their decision-making processes.

LP: *When the Russo-Ukrainian war broke out in February 2022, you were concerned that Ukraine's nuclear power plants could be damaged in the course of the war, leading to a nuclear disaster. Nineteen months have now passed. Are you still worried about the* *possible occurrence of a nuclear disaster during the war? What might be the consequences? What can people do now to prevent such consequences? As you wrote in* The Spectator, *"It is high time to start a new movement calling for an international treaty banning the weaponization of nuclear sites."*

SP: Yes, I am still concerned. Chornobyl is now back under Ukrainian control, but Zaporizhzhia, the largest nuclear power plant in Europe, is not. It remains close to the front lines of the war, but efforts of the international community to introduce a no-fight zone around the station have produced no results. Back in March 2022, the Russian capture of the station with the use of tanks and missiles resulted in human casualties, and one of the buildings caught fire, endangering the safety of the plant. The same can happen again, with unpredictable consequences.

LP: *As a historian, you published a highly relevant book this year,* The Russo-Ukrainian War. *You see this war as part of a long-term process of imperial disintegration. Could you talk about why empires disintegrate? Is this related to the trend of national identity that you emphasize, which is stronger than the trend toward liberal democracy? How do you define "empire"? Niall Ferguson, for instance, previously referred to the United States as an empire, which sparked a lot of controversy.*

SP: There are numerous definitions of empire. I use the term in the most traditional way, having in mind the largest European and Eurasian empires of the modern era, among which the Russian Empire was one of the most prominent. It fell apart in 1918, was stitched back together by the Bolsheviks in 1922 under the name of the Soviet Union, and then fell apart again in 1991. We all hoped that the heir to one of the largest imperial states would disintegrate without a major war. We were wrong. The war was simply postponed. We know how such wars end: with the victory of national-liberation movements and the withdrawal of empires. There are expectations that this war will not differ from similar wars of the past. The key questions are: when it will end, and at what price?

LP: *How do you think the Russo-Ukrainian war will end? What are the possibilities? What has changed, and what has not changed because of this war?*

SP: It is already clear that Ukraine will survive as an independent state and a distinct nation. It is also clear that Russia is paying a huge political and economic price for its imperial adventure. There are also changes in the international arena, with the revival of the trans-Atlantic alliance and Russia's economic reorientation from Europe toward Asia. I expect those trends to continue.

LP: *Overall, do you think that nuclear technology contributes more to war or to peace? Why?*

SP: With the successful test of the hydrogen bomb in 1954, nuclear technology produced a weapon that endangered the entire world but also helped to maintain global peace by making war between nuclear superpowers unthinkable. We got very lucky during the Cold War: despite all the nuclear brinkmanship, we had governments and leaders who managed to avoid confrontation or, as was the case with Kennedy and Khrushchev, to step back from the brink of nuclear war. We should learn from their experience to keep our luck going.

LP: *What state and setting are you in when answering these questions? During the period before and after the interview, have you done or will you do anything important or interesting that you can share?*

SP: It is a long weekend in the United States. Tomorrow, we resume our classes at Harvard. One of the courses I will be teaching this semester is on the Yalta Conference of 1945. We examine the origins of the Cold War. There are lessons to be learned about that period by the new generation of students and decision makers. We all have a lot of work ahead.

October 2023

20. Nuclear Plants Could Become Dirty Bombs

Russia's invasion of Ukraine came as a shock and reminded the world of the worst moments in its history. Not since the end of the Second World War has Europe seen a conflict of such proportions, destruction, and human suffering.

The war has also brought back fears of nuclear destruction. Vladimir Putin's decision to increase the readiness of Russian nuclear forces in its first days, and veiled nuclear threats from Russian officials, provoked a direct response from Joe Biden. In May 2023, he promised "severe consequences" for "any use of nuclear weapons in this conflict on any scale." But the war has already brought a different kind of nuclear danger. It happened when Russia's forces took over the site of the Chornobyl nuclear power plant on the first day of the war and shelled and captured Zaporizhzhia, the largest nuclear power station in Europe with its six reactors, in early March 2022.

Muted responses, including from the International Atomic Energy Agency (IAEA), which has responsibility for the security of the world's approximately 440 nuclear reactors (of which 15 are located in Ukraine), point to an inability to deal with the dangers posed by conventional warfare at nuclear sites. The IAEA's early statements failed even to call Russia the aggressor or condemn its actions. The problem goes beyond one agency, however. No commercial nuclear reactors, as opposed to those that produce plutonium, have been built to withstand military attack. No protocols or regulations have ever been created to deal with the possibility of warfare at a nuclear power plant, and no body of international law, including conventions and agreements relating to conduct in war, adequately deals with the possibility.

The first additional protocol of the Geneva Conventions on conduct in war comes from 1977. It treats nuclear power plants on a par with dams and dykes and withholds protection from them if a plant "provides electric power in regular, significant and direct support of military operations and if such attack is the only feasible way to terminate such support." It is too easy today to make a credible case for the legality of any attack on a nuclear reactor. This is a dangerous situation. Today, nine countries possess nuclear weapons; 33 countries use nuclear reactors to produce electrical energy. Nuclear energy accounts for the production of 10 percent of global electricity. There are growing hopes that a new generation of reactors will help to curb the use of fossil fuels and so tackle climate change.

Yet the war in Ukraine has raised new questions about the future of nuclear energy. To the dangers of nuclear accidents and unresolved issues over spent nuclear fuel, add one more problem: the possibility that nuclear reactors operating today could become dirty bombs in a war. Ukraine demonstrates how such a scenario could come to pass. For the first time, operational civilian plants have been attacked by ground forces. (In the past, only plants under construction and those producing plutonium have been targeted.) It was pure luck that the shells fired by the Russian National Guard, who have little or no combat experience, did not hit any of the reactors at the Zaporizhzhia station. Thankfully, they set alight a training center instead. Operating the reactor under normal circumstances is a difficult task; operating it amid fighting on the station's site could have been a disaster. The professionalism of the reactor's operators deserves praise.

At Chornobyl, the question of how nuclear waste should be dealt with emerged in frightening circumstances. The most dangerous moment of Russia's five-week period of control came with a power outage as a result of shelling. Electricity is needed for the control systems of the shelter that encases the station's damaged fourth reactor. It also powers the pumps that bring water to the cooling pond containing spent-fuel assemblies from Chornobyl's last reactor (it was shut down in December 2000). More than two decades on, the assemblies are still too hot to be left without coolant—they can rupture and release radioactive material. (Spent-fuel storage also poses a challenge at nuclear plants around the world.) Only the use of emergency generators, and the fact that there was enough diesel to power them, saved Chornobyl from a new nuclear accident.

The war is ongoing, and Russian cruise missiles continue to fly over Ukraine's remaining three nuclear power stations. A glitch in a targeting system or a hit by Ukrainian anti-aircraft defenses could lead to damage. No one knows how to deal with such a scenario, and few are considering it. The threat posed to nuclear plants in Ukraine raises uncomfortable questions about whether we should continue building them in the future, and the degree to which we can turn to nuclear energy as a means of mitigating climate change. These questions deserve serious consideration. But one answer seems to be obvious even now: we should not build new nuclear plants unless we can find a way to protect existing ones in war.

It is time for governments to wake up to the new kind of nuclear threat. Mr. Biden should warn Russia about the consequences of damaging nuclear sites as starkly as he has done over the use of nuclear weapons. We should ban fighting on and around nuclear sites as soon as possible and protect the hundreds of nuclear reactors in existence—and the dozens under construction—from the effects of war. The IAEA should lead the way and host a conference to discuss related legal and institutional questions. The need is urgent. Exposure to radiation in Ukraine or elsewhere will harm attackers, defenders, and civilians in equal measure.

June 2023

21. Hiroshima Diary

This weekend, the leaders of the G-7 countries meet in Hiroshima to discuss the most urgent issues facing the world today. The Russian aggression against Ukraine and the ban on the use of the nuclear weapons are among the key items on the summit's agenda. When I visited Hiroshima last month, the war in Ukraine and nuclear issues were also at the top of my personal list of concerns. At the site of the Hiroshima Peace Memorial, also known as the Atomic Dome, a visitor can hardly avoid being taken aback or even shocked by the contrast between the stark skeleton of a magnificent building destroyed by the nuclear explosion of 1945 and the beauty of its surroundings. When I was there recently, the lawn was resplendent with the colors of spring—green leaves on the bushes and blossoming red, pink, and white roses. Beyond the park is a prosperous modern city bursting with life.

A Japanese television reporter who accompanied me to the dome spoke about visiting American students who reflected on the horror of the atomic blast but noted that at least the bomb had exploded in the middle of the park, with few people around. The sad irony is that there was no park on that spot in Hiroshima when the bomb was dropped on 6 August 1945. The Industrial Exhibition Hall—the future Atomic Dome—stood approximately 160 meters away from the epicenter of the explosion. More than 140,000 people were killed by the blast and radiation.

As I listened to the story, my thoughts went back to Chornobyl, the site of another nuclear disaster that I had visited a few years earlier. The comparison could not have been more striking. At Chornobyl, nature also revived, but the people did not return.

The nearby city of Prypiat is still a ghost town decades after the explosion and will probably remain in that condition for generations to come. While the immediate destructive impact of nuclear bombs and the high levels of radiation they release are extremely damaging in the short run, nuclear accidents and their low doses of radiation turn out to have more lasting effects.

Hiroshima and Chornobyl came together in my mind because, after Russia's all-out invasion of Ukraine in February 2022, Chornobyl became the world's most recognized symbol not only of nuclear accidents but also of the weaponization of nuclear energy in wartime. The Russo-Ukrainian war managed to do something that World War II could not, turning atoms for peace into atoms for war. An attacker can now use nuclear power not only to produce destruction on the scale of Hiroshima and Nagasaki but also to make the sites of nuclear explosions uninhabitable for decades if not centuries, as happened at Chornobyl.

On 24 February 2022, the first day of the Russo-Ukrainian war, Russian forces captured the Chornobyl nuclear site, took the personnel of the plant hostage, and forced the same shift to work around the clock with no relief for twenty-five long days. They did not allow Ukrainian repair crews to come to the area and restore the power lines supplying the plant with electricity required to keep the nuclear facilities safe. The exhaustion of the plant's staff and the lack of power to operate the cooling ponds containing spent nuclear fuel might very well have caused another nuclear accident at Chornobyl.

The Ukrainian armed forces drove the Russian invaders out of the Chornobyl nuclear zone in late March 2022, but Russian contingents besieged another Ukrainian nuclear power plant—Europe's largest—southwest of Zaporizhzhia. There, the Russians employed heavy equipment and missiles during a struggle for the plant in March 2022. The administrative building suffered the greatest damage, but a training facility much closer to one of the station's six reactors also caught fire.

Around the time I was visiting Hiroshima, Rafael Mariano Grossi, the director general of the International Atomic Energy Agency (IAEA), issued his 154th statement on the condition of nuclear power plants in Ukraine. Its text was particularly alarming.

Grossi reported that, on visiting the plant three weeks earlier, he had seen military preparations taking place nearby. And during the previous week, IAEA personnel whom the Russians allowed to remain at the station had heard shelling on a daily basis. That was especially dangerous, as the station relied on a single power line to supply the electricity required to cool its reactors. If it had been damaged, emergency generators would not have managed to provide backup electricity indefinitely, and meltdowns of the kind that took place at the Fukushima nuclear power plant might have followed.

Grossi's earlier attempts to implement the IAEA Board of Governors' resolution demanding that Russian forces leave the plant had produced no results. Russia declared that the nuclear power plant was its property and entrusted its operation to Rosatom, the Russian nuclear monopoly. Grossi and the international community then relied on Rosatom's good will to gain access to the station and implement IAEA recommendations on avoiding disaster. With a Ukrainian counteroffensive expected in the region next month, it is anyone's guess what may happen to the station and its lone power line.

As I returned from the Hiroshima Atomic Dome to my hotel, I thought that the only way to save the world from future disasters like those at Hiroshima and Chornobyl is to make the capture of nuclear power plants—there are more than 440 in the world today—as much a taboo as the use of nuclear weapons.

Governments are unlikely to initiate such measures of their own accord: they would require strong public pressure, which proved effective in bringing about a treaty to ban atmospheric testing of nuclear weapons in the 1960s. The Ban the Bomb movement of the sixties made that landmark treaty possible and helped to secure numerous treaties on the nonproliferation and control of nuclear weapons. It is high time to start a new movement calling for an international treaty banning the weaponization of nuclear sites.

May 2023

V. The Western Alliance

22. Magical Thinking

Interview conducted by
Oliver Gehrs, *Fluter*

Oliver Gehrs (OG): *Ukraine? For a long time, many people were hardly interested in this country. Yet its location and history make it enormously important to Europe. Where exactly is your home country located: in the middle of Europe, as many people in Ukraine say, or rather on the eastern edge?*

Serhii Plokhy (SP): Europe should always be understood as an intellectual space. In the eighteenth century, the idea emerged that Europe extended to the Urals, and the Russian colonies beyond it in Siberia were in Asia. In this sense, Ukraine is located almost exactly in the center of Europe. Culturally, too, there has been a close connection between Ukraine and Europe for centuries.

OG: *The name Ukraine means "borderland." What are these borders?*

SP: Historically, Ukraine is a kind of contact zone between Eastern and Western Christianity, Judaism and Islam. For a long time, it was divided between Austria-Hungary, Poland-Lithuania, the Russian Empire, and the Ottoman Empire. This means that a great many cultural influences came together. Looking back from today's viewpoint, it is apparent that Western influences have been most important in the formation of Ukrainian identity.

OG: *But still it looks as if there is a pro-European western part of Ukraine and an eastern part leaning toward Russia.*

SP: The mere fact that two languages are spoken, Ukrainian and Russian, does not mean that there is not a common identity characterized by a desire for democracy, freedom, and stable political institutions. Russia also misjudged this, believing that its tanks and soldiers would be cheered by Russian-speaking people in the Donbas. Instead, there were also many who opposed them with Ukrainian flags. The elections of 2014 and 2019 marked the first time that the country was no longer divided between east and west. Previously, the east had often voted for pro-Russian parties. Now, because of the war, the country is even more united. But that doesn't prevent it from being pluralistic in terms of languages or even religion. Volodymyr Zelensky, for example, is the only Jewish president outside Israel.

OG: *The word "nation" has a negative connotation for many Germans. Do we therefore sometimes lack understanding for the Ukrainian aspiration to be one?*

SP: I remember German reunification, when my German colleagues told me that it would not be about German identity and nation. I had to smile in response. Thinking nationally doesn't necessarily have anything to do with Nazis. In the case of Ukraine, we are seeing a nation being formed around values such as freedom of speech and democracy and defending those values against a power that does not want to be a nation but an empire. Ukraine is a country in which democracy survived after 1990, but also in 2004 and 2013, when Russia tried to install an authoritarian regime. All this resulted in violent protests on the Maidan in Kyiv.

OG: *Is Ukraine just moving more toward the West or Europe toward the East?*

SP: After World War II, countries such as the Federal Republic of Germany turned strongly toward the West, and then, after the fall of the Berlin Wall, so did the countries of the former Eastern bloc, such as Poland or the Baltic states. They saw an opportunity to escape Russian influence and joined alliances such as the European Union and NATO. Ukraine suddenly found itself in a gray area between East and West. But Ukraine also tried to distance itself from Russia as much as possible and freely determine its own destiny.

OG: *What went wrong then?*

SP: Among other things, the West had the same concerns as it does today. Ukraine was seen as historically close to Russia, and the West did not want to irritate Russia. The Russian president at the time, Boris Yeltsin, was not to be toppled by Russian nationalists. If you look for reasons why Ukraine is not a member of NATO, one answer over and over again is that the West did not want to worsen its relations with Russia.

OG: *So has the West not been supportive enough of Ukraine's democratic movements? How, then, has democracy been able to survive?*

SP: Because of the people. Ukrainian civil society proved its strength during the Orange Revolution of 2004, when it defended its right to vote and stopped the advance of authoritarianism. Democracy in Ukraine has already survived the most difficult period of the 1990s, when it collapsed in Russia, Belarus, and most post-Soviet republics.

OG: *Have Western countries paid too little attention to Ukraine and too much to Russia?*

SP: Absolutely, especially Germany. This also goes back to the *Ostpolitik* of the 1970s under Willy Brandt. At that time, the division of Europe into East and West was accepted, and the focus was on change through rapprochement. Another catchphrase was "change through trade": countries started to buy oil and gas from Russia. At that time, there was a belief that good business would keep the peace. And, when the Wall came down, it was seen as confirmation of that. But yesterday's recipes don't have to be today's. The mistake was not to change this policy when Russia became more aggressive and openly imperialistic. The Russian war in Chechnya in 1994, and later in Georgia—all this did not influence Western policy. On the contrary, the more aggressive Russia became, the more trade relations were expanded, and, with income from gas and oil, Russia was further upgraded. That peace and prosperity could be maintained in this way was magical thinking.

OG: *In 1994, Ukraine gave up its nuclear weapons and transferred them to Russia. In retrospect, was that a mistake?*

SP: Above all, it was a broken promise. With the so-called Budapest Memorandum, Ukraine gave up the nuclear weapons that had been stored there since the Soviet era and were, after all, the third-largest arsenal in the world. The United States, Great Britain, China, and France preferred that everything remain in the hands of one power, Russia. In return, Ukraine received security assurances from the Western powers, which promised to intervene if its integrity and sovereignty were threatened. That promise was broken when Russia annexed the Crimea in 2014 to little response. Yet there had been discussions in Russia's parliament about annexing the Crimea as early as 1994, at the time of the agreement. One could have guessed then what happened later. Against this background, when you see how the Ukrainian president has to beg for weapons today, it is shameful. In my view, the countries that promised security at the time now have a responsibility to supply weapons.

OG: *What about Germany's responsibility?*

SP: Germany has a special responsibility because, after all, many Nazi crimes were committed on Ukrainian territory. After all, Hitler did not attack Russia but the Soviet Union, which did not consist only of Russia. If you look for the countries most victimized by the Nazis during the Second World War in proportion to their population, you will find not Russia but Poland, Belarus, and Ukraine.

OG: *Do you think that Germany should support Ukraine because of its history?*

SP: I don't want to say that history is the only reason, but it is very important. When people say now that they can't supply tanks because German tanks have been in Russia before, that is historically questionable: if you look at the map and the numbers, Ukraine was victimized far more than Russia. That is not clear to many in Germany.

OG: *The concerns of the post-Soviet states are getting more attention than ever. Is the political center of Europe shifting eastward right now?*

SP: There's a saying in the US: War is God's way of teaching Americans geography. I'm afraid that's also true of many countries in Europe right now. The zones of political ambiguity are becoming fewer, and many things are being made clearer. For example, that Russia's goal is to conquer Ukraine and destroy the nation. Only proximity to the EU and NATO can save Ukraine from this. So, yes: to the extent that Ukraine is trending westward, the center of Europe is now moving farther eastward.

OG: *Criticism of Ukraine is often ignited by the existence of far-right movements and a cult of the nationalist Stepan Bandera who was involved in mass shootings during World War II.*

SP: Before 2014, Bandera was a kind of folk hero for part of the population, especially in western Ukraine. Then, after the war began, he was increasingly perceived by many as a fighter for independence. Most Ukrainians who treat Bandera's memory sympathetically today in the face of the Russian attack do not identify themselves with the radical nationalism of the 1930s. I am not saying that there is no problem with right-wing extremism, but it is no greater than in other countries and does not lend itself to defaming Ukraine as a country of "Nazis," as Russian propaganda does. The far-right parties have not been in parliament since 2014 because they did not clear the five-percent hurdle.

OG: *Nevertheless, the question again: to what extent is Bandera responsible for the massacres of Polish civilians and the ethnic cleansing in what is now western Ukraine?*

SP: Bandera spent most of the war in a Nazi concentration camp for declaring Ukrainian independence in June 1941. I am sure that he knew little about what was happening in Ukraine in 1943–44 and had no influence on it.

OG: *EU accession was also repeatedly postponed because of corruption in the country. Do you see any changes there?*

SP: Many people voted for the actor Zelensky because they were fed up with corrupt politicians. He also promised to bring peace and fight corruption. In fact, we now see a president who is not using his position to become the richest person in the country, unlike some of his predecessors or Putin in Russia. There were also laws adopted before the war to limit the power of oligarchs. Then, with the war, there came a time when there was a kind of agreement to take care of survival first and foremost and postpone other things. That is over. Journalists are no longer quiet but investigating all the time. And the president is distancing himself from officials who tolerate corruption in the ministries. Let's see how effective that will be. But it's an approach that has not been seen since 1991.

OG: *What could Ukraine look like after the war?*

SP: United as never before. Chances are that Ukraine will emerge stronger as a nation. Then it will be a matter of further integration into the Western structures—NATO and the EU. The price of all this is very high, and the only way to reduce it is to help Ukraine defend itself. The country is on the front line of a global conflict between democracy and freedom on one side and autocracy and dictatorship on the other.

OG: *And what will happen if Ukraine loses the war?*

SP: Quite simply, look to Belarus.

March 2023

23. Germany and Ukraine

*Interview conducted by
Katja Hoyer, Zeitgeist*

Katja Hoyer (KH): *I think we share a belief that it is important to understand history in order to understand the present. The German-Ukrainian relationship has come under a lot of scrutiny recently because of the Russo-Ukrainian war, but it goes back a long way. So let us have a look at some of the history between the two countries, starting with the first formal Ukrainian state established at the end of the First World War. Following the Russian Revolution in 1917, Ukraine declared itself independent of Russia, to which Russia responded with military aggression. At that point, Ukraine looked to Germany for help. Can you tell us a bit more about that? How did the cause of Ukrainian independence become intertwined with Germany's response to it?*

Serhii Plokhy (SP): This has to be seen in the context of World War I. In 1918, the last year of the war, a number of independent states emerged on the border of the Russian Empire, and one of them was Ukraine. Initially there had been a desire for a form of federation of which both Russia and Ukraine would be constituent parts. But Lenin's Russia waged war on Ukraine, putting it in desperate need of allies. The most natural ally seemed to be Germany, since it was at war with Russia. So the issue became part of peace negotiations, in which only an independent state could take part. Thus the name "Germany" is writ large on the history of the first declaration of Ukrainian independence in 1918.

KH: *What did Germany and Ukraine each get out of this relationship? Why did they seem more attractive to each other than Russia did?*

SP: Ukraine already had a reputation as the "breadbasket of Europe." German commanders were interested in the food supplies that Ukraine could provide. Ukraine in turn needed military assistance against Bolshevik aggression. The relationship was not trouble-free. The Germans didn't like the socialist-leaning Ukrainian government, so it was removed, and a more conservative one under Pavlo Skoropadsky was installed. German occupation, while unwelcome, provided stability and a space for the establishment of Ukrainian institutions. There was a flurry of such activity in 1918. For example, the Ukrainian Academy of Sciences, a number of universities, and the National Library were established. The main desire was to be independent of Russia, and that was what the German military could provide.

KH: *But this arrangement was not very long-lived...*

SP: No, the Ukrainian socialist leaders who had been removed from power launched an uprising against the Skoropadsky regime, which was no longer backed by Germany once it removed its troops at the end of World War I. Skoropadsky went into exile in Germany, from where he continued to promote the idea of an independent but multiethnic Ukraine that could be a home not just for Ukrainians but also for minorities such as Russians, Jews, and others. That remained an important idea.

KH: *When the Soviet Union was set up in 1922, much of Ukraine became part of it.*

SP: Yes, but Ukrainian territory was divided between four countries after World War I. The largest part joined the Soviet Union as the Ukrainian Soviet Socialist Republic. Other parts of Ukraine went to Poland, Romania, and Czechoslovakia, and the dynamic was different in each state. In Soviet Ukraine, after the Holodomor—the Great Ukrainian Famine of 1932–33—the political elite had no autonomy whatever. Meanwhile, the western parts of Ukraine in the other countries saw a rise of radical nationalism. Those movements

23. Germany and Ukraine

looked to Germany and Italy for ideological models to follow and for political alliances. Germany in turn was keen to weaponize radical nationalism in the countries it sought to conquer and break up, particularly Poland and Czechoslovakia in 1939.

KH: *Was it not a concern that Hitler's vision of* Lebensraum *(living space) for his German state in Eastern Europe also included Ukraine? His interests were hardly aligned with those of the radical Ukrainian nationalists.*

SP: That's right. The Ukrainian nationalists and the German Nazi regime were on a collision course. Hitler wanted to take Ukrainian land, resettle and colonize it while expelling indigenous populations. The nationalists wanted to create an independent Ukrainian state. Those aims clashed. For instance, one of the radical nationalist groups, led by Stepan Bandera, declared an independent Ukraine when the Nazis entered Lwów, now Lviv in western Ukraine, in 1941. But they were soon rounded up and arrested. Bandera and others were sent to the Sachsenhausen concentration camp. Whatever alliance existed between the Nazis and the Ukrainian nationalists broke down. They had very different visions: the Germans wanted *Lebensraum*; Bandera and the radical nationalists wanted an independent Ukrainian state.

KH: *Ukraine ended up becoming one of the main battlegrounds of the war. It's always struck me as odd that some Germans today argue against sending weapons to a state fighting Russian aggression because Germany did terrible things to the Russian people during the Second World War. There seems to be a lesser degree of empathy and understanding when it comes to the bloodshed caused by Hitler's war in Eastern Europe, including Ukraine.*

SP: Yes, a lot of Germany's guilt feelings are directed toward Russia. But, if you look at the casualties of World War II, Poland is at the top of the list of countries that suffered most in proportion to its population. Belarus and Ukraine are next. Ukraine was also a place where the Holocaust took on a very specific image, one associated with the massacre at Babyn Yar, in which more than 33,000 Jewish residents of Kyiv were murdered. These are the countries that suffered most from the genocidal politics of the

Nazi regime. Timothy Snyder talks about that, but I don't know how much of it makes an impression in Germany.

KH: *And something else often forgotten outside Ukraine is that the fighting continued even as the Germans were beginning to retreat.*

SP: Yes. When the Red Army returned in 1943–44, it immediately began to wage war against the radical nationalists who by then had acquired an armed force, the Ukrainian Insurgent Army. There was only limited cooperation with the Germans, but they released Bandera in September 1944 in the hope that he would galvanize the fight against the Soviet Union.

KH: *Bandera is a complex character who continues to be the subject of intense controversy. When the former Ukrainian ambassador to Germany, now deputy foreign minister of Ukraine, Andriy Melnyk, expressed admiration for Bandera, he caused international outrage and was recalled to Kyiv shortly afterwards. How is he seen in Ukraine today?*

SP: For many, Bandera is a symbol of Ukrainian independence, and that image functions quite independently of Bandera as a historical figure. The real Bandera actually spent a lot of time in Polish and German prisons. Even though the Ukrainian Insurgent Army continued to fight the Soviets after the war, Bandera never returned to Ukraine. He stayed in Germany, in the American occupation zone. The assassination of Bandera by a KGB agent in Munich in 1959 sealed his reputation as a national hero. The controversy you see today concerns Bandera as a symbol rather than a historical figure. In the current Russo-Ukrainian war, Bandera and the Ukrainian Insurgent Army have reemerged as symbols of resistance and independence. It's the closest historical parallel to the present-day struggle against Russian aggression. Like so many historical myths, that of Bandera is flexible, allowing people to project their hopes and fears onto it.

KH: *Like Bandera, many Ukrainian nationalists ended up in the American zone of occupation after Germany was defeated and split into sectors allocated to each of the victorious Allies. Why was that?*

SP: The point was to be as far away from Soviet control as possible. Even if you ended up in a divided city such as Vienna or Berlin, the chances of being kidnapped by the Soviet authorities were very high. There was, for instance, the story of Wilhelm von Habsburg, who was closely associated with the Ukrainian cause. He was kidnapped in Austria and eventually died in prison in the Soviet Union. So the farther one could get from the Soviet zone of occupation, the better, and the American zone was considered the best bet, although it wasn't entirely safe either.

KH: *Once these occupation zones fossilized into two separate German states from 1949 onward, did they build or maintain relations with Ukraine as such, or was this done solely through relations with the Soviet Union?*

SP: East Germany wasn't in a position to formulate its own foreign policy, and Ukraine even less so, but the Soviet Union encouraged relations among its dependencies, "friendships of people" across the borders within their bloc. But even that was controlled. Travel between countries behind the Iron Curtain was by no means easy, but there was communication nonetheless.

KH: *You were born in 1957 in the Soviet Union and began your academic career in Ukraine at the University of Dnipropetrovsk [now Dnipro—ed.]. Did you come across any exchanges with East Germany during that time?*

SP: Yes, I was affiliated with a department that specialized in German studies, which really meant working on East Germany. It may sound strange today, given that the Stasi became the symbol of East Germany, but my boss in the department wrote a couple of books on the multiparty system under socialism. And he was writing about East Germany! But for us, it was unthinkable that you could have anything other than the Communist Party. For us, East Germany was a strange country—much more buttoned-up, and in some ways more communist than Ukraine. On the other hand, it remained part of Central Europe, and even its strange multiparty system survived and became a subject of study in Ukraine.

KH: *And were there official or diplomatic connections, too?*

SP: There was an East German consulate in Kyiv, but Ukraine was part of the Soviet Union. One of the first East German students to arrive in Dnipropetrovsk came to study Russian. Today, it would be seen as an insult if someone went to Ukraine to study Russian. But that's how these things worked in the 1980s.

KH: *When people traveled the other way, was this possible only for work and study, or were there also private trips and holidays to Germany?*

SP: It was certainly unthinkable to travel to West Germany. East Germany was difficult but possible. A friend of mine traveled there as a tourist. He went to Berlin.

KH: *And what did he make of it?*

SP: To most of us, East Germany was a well-ordered police state as opposed to the Soviet Union, which was a poorly ordered police state.

KH: *Given that there were interactions between East Germans and Ukrainians but very little contact with West Germany, did this temporary dualism have consequences for German-Ukrainian relations?*

SP: Not from a Ukrainian perspective. There is now only one Germany, but Ukrainian perceptions of it are still changing. For the generation of my parents, who endured German occupation in World War II, the image was extremely negative, and nothing could be done about that. But in my generation, there was a perspective that the Germans were out there, out in the world, closer than we were to the center of global change, and that applied even to East Germans. Equally, there was a strange perception that any German, anyone from the West really, who came to Ukraine must be a communist.

KH: *Really?*

SP: I remember that I once had a conference, and a couple of people from Germany attended. When they came to visit my dacha,

23. Germany and Ukraine

a neighbor heard them speak in a foreign language and asked who they were. I said that they were my colleagues, professors from Germany. My neighbor replied: "Say hello to the German comrades!" Many people thought that only communist Germans could visit the Soviet Union. So the image stuck.

KH: *Did that change in the 1990s, after the fall of the Soviet Union?*

SP: Yes, in the 1990s there were great expectations that Germany would become a major player in Eastern Europe and an ally to Ukraine. There was widespread belief that the German language would become important.

KH: *Why do you think that was?*

SP: As is often the case, expectations for the future are based on certain realities of the past, even the distant past. As we know, however, history rhymes but does not repeat itself. Ukrainian expectations concerning Germany's role in Ukraine never came true.

KH: *Quite the opposite in this case. When the Soviet Union was falling apart, Germany opposed Ukrainian independence to begin with. Why did Ukrainian and German visions for Eastern Europe diverge so much in the early 1990s?*

SP: Germany was preoccupied with its own unification, becoming one country again, and it was also troubled by that process. I think that different ideas of nationalism were at the root of that problem. Germany was still coming to terms with its own past before 1945, with Nazism. Its policies were dominated by the thought of not repeating the horrible years of the 1930s and 40s. In that context, nationalism of any kind was a dirty word.

KH: *But Germany itself was busy restoring and celebrating its national unity...*

SP: I remember meeting colleagues from West Germany at a conference around the time of reunification, and they were really determined to convince me and other Ukrainians that the reunification of Germany was not about nationalism. Of course, my question to them was: "If it's not about nationalism, then what is it about?" You want cultural boundaries to coincide with political boundaries. What is that if not nationalism?

KH: *Apart from these cultural and historical dimensions, were there practical and political considerations behind Germany's reluctance to support the cause of Ukrainian independence?*

SP: Yes, and they were as powerful as the cultural and historical ones. Russian consent was needed not only for German unification itself but also when it came to the removal of troops from German soil. The Germans had to be on good terms with both Gorbachev and Yeltsin. Ukraine and the rest of Eastern Europe were secondary concerns. In terms of security policy, there was also a big question around the integration of East Germany into NATO. It was the same in Poland, which made an informal deal with Yeltsin: Poland would not interfere in Ukrainian affairs unless there was a major crisis, and, in exchange, Russia would not oppose Poland's accession to NATO. These were important security objectives, and security was all about Russia.

KH: *And this established a pattern for Germany's security policy going forward…*

SP: Yes, it really came to the fore at the Bucharest NATO summit in 2008, where Germany and France were strongly opposed to Ukraine and Georgia making meaningful steps toward NATO membership, which I see as the start of a policy of appeasement. When Russia waged war against Georgia immediately after the summit, Germany emerged as a mediator. And as US-Russia relations became strained, Germany under Angela Merkel continued in that role, as an intermediary between the West and Russia, following a model of appeasement.

KH: *Was this a planned, coherent strategy, or did Germany respond to each critical moment as it saw fit at the time?*

SP: There was an idea that you could make Russia more peaceful through closer economic ties. The motto was, "Let's make peace while making money." This goes back to West Germany's *Ostpolitik* of the 1970s, which brought more Russian gas and oil

23. Germany and Ukraine

to Germany. That economic tie was expected to help democratize Russia and make it more peaceful. It became a magic formula that was assumed to have succeeded when the Soviet Union collapsed and Russia transformed itself.

KH: *So it was continued into the 1990s and 2000s...*

SP: Yes, the gas pipelines Nord Stream 1 and Nord Stream 2 came along, following Russian aggression against Georgia and the annexation of the Crimea, respectively. Germany was negotiator-in-chief between the West and an increasingly aggressive Russia. Merkel, being from East Germany, was seen as an expert on Russia. But in essence Germany's policies were the same as they had been in the 1970s, despite the fact that the world had changed dramatically. The Moscow of the 1970s was essentially interested in preserving the status quo, maintaining the boundaries it had created after the Second World War. The Moscow of the 2000s, on the other hand, was a revisionist power that sought to change and expand its boundaries. Berlin either didn't notice this change or chose not to act on it.

KH: *The rude awakening came in February 2022, when Russia invaded Ukraine. The new German chancellor, Olaf Scholz, announced a* Zeitenwende, *a turning point, in German foreign and security policy. But, at the beginning of the war, German-Ukrainian relations plummeted to a new low.*

SP: Initially Olaf Scholz was very big on rhetoric but very short on helping Ukraine in the first critical weeks and months of the war. Germany was once again very concerned, for historical and political reasons, about sending any meaningful military equipment to Ukraine. Vitali Klitschko, who I understand is quite popular in Germany because of his former boxing career, was deriding Germany for offering to send helmets. "What next," he asked, "are they going to send us pillows?" In that atmosphere, the German president, Frank-Walter Steinmeier, who had become something of a symbol of Germany's more recent *Ostpolitik* enacted during his time as foreign minister, had to abandon plans to visit Kyiv when it became clear that he would not be welcome there. But that was a short-lived crisis, and those things are behind us.

KH: *I'm glad you are so optimistic about German-Ukrainian relations going forward. And that also leads me to my final question. It seems that Germany has gradually come to terms with the idea of sending weapons and military equipment to Ukraine and has now emerged as one of the biggest supporters of its war efforts. Are we witnessing a* Zeitenwende *in the German-Ukrainian relationship?*

SP: I certainly don't see that there is a way back from Germany's engagement with Ukraine as a key country in the newly emerging Eastern Europe. Germany saw its previous policies fail. By 1991, Germany's *Ostpolitik* seemed to have produced the end of history. By 2022, it had produced the end of peace. There is no way back. And then there are the changes in Germany itself. The war has changed Germany's understanding of its role in Europe and the world. Germany is beginning to understand that it needs to play a much more active role, and that change is there to stay. But that means confronting its own history, which is a complex process. It means nothing less than rethinking Germany's image in this new world.

KH: *That's a great point on which to end this conversation. Given that war continues to rage in Ukraine, relations between Germany and Ukraine will continue to play a major role. As we have seen, the history of those relations has been full of trauma, expectations, and conflict. But a clearer understanding of history is an important step toward doing better in the future.*

August 2023

24. Why the Delays?

I long planned to go to Ukraine to see my relatives, deliver an address at the leading university, and launch a Ukrainian translation of my book on the Russo-Ukrainian war. I had little choice over the timing of the visit—it had to take place around the start of the new Ukrainian academic year but before Labor Day and the start of the first week of classes at Harvard where I teach.

I had more control over the itinerary. Ukrainian airspace is closed because of the war, making it impossible to fly to Kyiv or any other city. The most popular route to Ukraine now goes through Poland. I arranged to fly from Boston to Munich and then to Krakow, continuing by train to Przemyśl on the Polish-Ukrainian border. From there, a train was supposed to take me to Zaporizhzhia, my hometown and the heart of the current Ukrainian counteroffensive in the south of the country. Then I would go on to Dnipro (formerly Dnipropetrovsk), where I had studied and begun my academic career, and where some of my relatives lived. My journey would end in Kyiv, where the translation of my book was to be launched, and professors and students were ready to welcome me to give a talk as a newly minted honorary professor at Ukraine's oldest university, the Kyiv Mohyla Academy, founded in 1632.

My original plan was to arrive in Ukraine in time to celebrate the thirty-second anniversary of Ukrainian independence on 24 August. But a colleague told me: "You would spend the whole day in a bomb shelter. The Russians will be sending 'birthday gifts' in the form of missiles and kamikaze drone attacks." I knew what she meant. In 2022, on Ukraine's Independence Day, the Russians attacked the cities of Zaporizhzhia, Dnipro, Kharkiv, Mykolaiv and their environs. In the town of Chaplyne, east of Zaporizhzhia, they hit the railway station, setting train wagons on fire, killing 25 people and wounding more than 30. Among the dead were children aged 6 and 11. I revised my itinerary to leave the United States on 24 August, planning to arrive in Ukraine on the night of 25 August one day after the anniversary.

My sister in Zaporizhzhia told me over the phone, before I boarded the plane, that there had been no attacks on our hometown that day. But, in the early hours of 24 August, the Russians had fired rockets at the city of Dnipro, 85 km to the north, and the next point on my itinerary. They hit several targets, including the bus station. Fortunately, the station was deserted in the early morning, but three people were wounded in the city and eleven buildings damaged. I saw the damaged parts of the bus station and the pile of debris in front of it when I arrived on the morning of 28 August, four days after the attack. I had used the station countless times when traveling between the two cities. Unable to imagine a missile attack on that familiar station, I stared at it in disbelief. Another attack might come any time, with little if any warning.

A relative who picked me up at the bus station said that, in that part of Ukraine, sirens generally sound after the attack, not before it. I heard a similar warning from my sister during my stay with her, as one siren followed another. We are being attacked from the Tokmak region, she told me, so missiles would arrive in less than a minute—not enough time to sound a warning. In Zaporizhzhia, all stores and banks would close when the initial alerts of missile attacks began to sound, but, by this point in the war, some remained open, including a wine store where I got some excellent Portuguese wine for a festive table.

"You can't put your life on hold indefinitely," I heard more than once during my stay. And, certainly, one could not run to the shelter every night, as I learned on my own. My sister gave up on that idea long ago and sleeps in her bedroom. Her daughter does likewise when she comes to visit from a somewhat safer city in central Ukraine, but she tries to stay away from the windows—they go first in an explosion, and flying glass causes a lot of damage. It can kill. My relatives in Dnipro sleep in their

24. Why the Delays?

hallway, taking advantage of the so-called rule of two walls—hallways have no windows, and their ceilings collapse last in case of a direct hit.

Last autumn, a Russian missile hit a market across the street from the building where my relatives live. When my cousin left the safety of the hallway and rushed to the bedroom, where she had left her mobile phone charging, the bedroom ceiling started to collapse. She managed to get out unhurt, phone in hand. Since then, she's been much stricter about staying in the hallway. The damaged ceiling is still there—I saw it. There is no point in repairing it, explained my cousin, as there could be another hit at any moment. She and her husband live not far from the headquarters of the Ukrainian Security Service—an important target for the Russian missile men. They have managed to hit buildings on both sides of the headquarters, but not the command center itself.

At an early dinner with my relatives in a restaurant on the Dnieper River embankment, we discuss the war—their experiences during the course of it and the international politics that determine it. One question that everyone asks me, a visitor from the United States, is why the Americans and their Western allies are dragging their feet, supplying the Ukrainian armed forces with the absolute minimum required to hold the line but not to counterattack successfully and move the front line away from cities like Zaporizhzhia, Dnipro, and President Zelensky's hometown of Kryvyi Rih. Numerous theories about the influence of Russian money and corrupt American and Western politicians were proposed and discussed at the table. "We are paying for those delays with our people's blood," says the wife of one of my cousins.

I have no good answers to such questions. No NATO army has ever launched a major offensive without overwhelming air superiority or, rather, complete control of the airspace involved. Why Western commentators expected the Ukrainians to succeed without supplying the requisite jet fighters and played ridiculous games of finger-pointing with regard to tanks, is impossible to explain to the people of Ukraine. The same applies to expressions of disappointment over the slow progress of the offensive voiced by some unnamed Western officials and far-from-anonymous pundits. At the train station, I could not help noticing a number of young amputees. The number of Ukrainian soldiers who have lost their limbs to Russian mines skyrocketed during the counteroffensive, crossing the 50,000 mark.

There, in Dnipro, sitting at that table, I represented the entire West, showing the flag, defending some indefensible actions, taking credit for the generosity of others, and trying to reassure people I have known for most of my life that we in the West will not abandon Ukraine in the war that is saving us all from future aggressions. I explain that the delays are due not to corruption but to American and European concern about crossing imagined red lines in Vladimir Putin's mind, thereby avoiding escalation and possible use of nuclear weapons. If that is the case, says one of my relatives, why would the West not just surrender to Putin right away? Why drag it out?

I say something in response, but I know that he is right: the best way to encourage a bully is to succumb to his threats. The conversation moves on to family topics, including the story of a family member who found refuge in Britain along with her ten-year-old daughter. There, I feel on firmer ground. The West is doing a lot to support Ukraine. It is just that everyone here needs this nightmare to end and see the Russians kicked out of Ukraine. Whether my words produce the desired calming effect on my interlocutors or not, their words and actions certainly have that effect on me. My friends and relatives—seemingly in concert with everyone else in Ukraine—have learned to live and fight back under impossible wartime conditions. They keep calm and carry on.

I arrived in Kyiv in time for the most severe attack on the city in more than half a year. As I moved into my dorm room at the Kyiv Mohyla Academy, a custodian told me that it helps to keep the windows open. Otherwise, a blast wave can break the glass. I did as advised. On 30 August I woke up moments after 5:00 a.m. to the sound of a huge explosion. It felt like thunder, but there were no thunderclaps. I thought to myself: I am in Kyiv; it must be a blast. So it was. When I checked the news on my iPhone, an air raid alert was on. I had slept through it and, as it turned out, through a couple of other blasts as well. The one that woke me up was the strongest and closest. Kyiv was under attack by drones and missiles launched from Tu-95 strategic bombers.

In the next hour, news about the attack began to appear on social media. "I am OK. They are extinguishing a fire next to my building," wrote a friend on Facebook. Mayor Vitali Klitschko was commenting on developments, and all the emergency services were helping people. It was then that I realized how lucky I was. First, American-supplied Patriots had probably shot down all the missiles. Second, the explosions caused by debris from the destroyed missiles had fallen relatively far from the area where I was staying. Several buildings had been damaged, two people killed and three injured in the city itself. In a village not far from Kyiv some houses had been damaged, but, thank God, there had been no casualties.

That day in Kyiv, there were no signs of panic, just hatred for the aggressors and calm determination to keep going. Life was proceeding as usual, and people were attending to their business. Later that day, I met with an official from the general prosecutor's office who was investigating ecological crimes committed by the Russian aggressors, ranging from the occupation of Chornobyl to the destruction of the Kakhovka Dam. As our conversation moved away from Chornobyl—the main subject of my interest and the reason for the meeting—the prosecutor reached for his iPhone and showed me a video of buildings in a village near Kyiv damaged earlier that morning. His home turned out to be located on a street parallel to the one destroyed by the attack, and he might easily have been among the victims. But he was not, and there he was in his office, doing his job.

Nor were there any signs of panic two days later, on 1 September, when President Serhiy Kvit of the Kyiv Mohyla Academy welcomed me as I arrived to deliver my address. There were 750 new students in the auditorium, and Professor Kvit told them that, in case of an air raid alert, everyone was to proceed to the shelter. They all knew how to behave. The freshmen had graduated from Ukrainian schools where interrupting classes to take shelter had become a norm. Thankfully, there was no alert that morning. My lecture went as planned, and the meeting continued for more than two hours, as there was no end to the lineup of students who wanted to comment and ask questions—some of the most intellectually informed and mature questions that I had dealt with since the start of the war. The young people of Ukraine are looking to the years ahead with concern but also with determination. They asked how I imagined the Ukrainians of the future. I told them that I did not have to resort to imagination: those Ukrainians were in front of me.

Book sales in Ukraine are increasing, I learned from the publisher with whom we had launched the Ukrainian translation of my *Russo-Ukrainian War* the previous day. A year earlier, he had wondered whether the invasion would put an end to his business. He and his family had left Kharkiv in March to avoid a possible occupation, but they were back in May, enduring the bombardment of the city and resuming their publishing activities. Luckily, their huge book warehouse near Kharkiv was not hit. Now he was looking toward the future with optimism just as, I knew, were the students I had met and others buying books in war-torn Ukraine.

On the evening of 1 September I boarded the train to Przemyśl, taking with me some of the contagious Ukrainian determination and optimism. That train, like every other one I took on the trip, left on time and reached its destination on time, even though sirens were audible as I passed through some stations. The same applied to the Polish trains. Meanwhile, my Lufthansa flight from Krakow to Munich was late, making it problematic to catch the connecting flight from Munich to Boston. I made it only because the Boston flight was even more delayed than the one to Munich.

The difference between the Ukrainian trains, which left and arrived on time, often under missile attacks, and the chronically delayed Western airliners could not have been more striking. My most nerve-wracking experiences—whether I would reach the next destination or not—all happened outside Ukraine. While I survived the delays in airline schedules, I knew that many Ukrainians, especially those in the armed forces, had not survived the delays in the supply of Western armaments, many of them long promised but never delivered. The number of

24. Why the Delays?

portraits of professors and students who have died in this war—portraits marked with black ribbons—is constantly growing on the memory walls in my alma mater, Dnipro University, which I visited on my trip, and in the Kyiv Mohyla Academy, where I delivered my talk.

I left Ukraine with one question foremost in my mind: why the delays? I could find no answer when people asked me the same question in Ukraine, or when I thought about it while rushing through Munich airport to catch my connecting flight. I caught the flight, but I did not arrive at an answer.

December 2023

25. Worrying Signs

Interview conducted by
Manuel Cudel, *Midi Libre*

Manuel Cudel (MC): *The highly anticipated Ukrainian counteroffensive failed to break through Russian defenses in 2023. What is the situation on the ground today, and what are the prospects?*

Serhii Plokhy (SP): We are in a situation greatly reminiscent of the trench warfare of World War I, the difference being the use of drones and electronic warfare. According to the Ukrainian military commander, General Valerii Zaluzhny, it would be difficult to turn the tide of the war without superiority in electronic means of waging war—the weapons of the twenty-first century.

MC: *Could the war reach a turning point in 2024?*

SP: The first turning point in the war was April 2022, after Ukraine defeated Russian troops in the battle for Kyiv and the West decided that it was worthwhile to support Ukraine. After that, Ukraine achieved a number of successes on the battlefield, from the Kharkiv counteroffensives to the liberation of Kherson. Now we have reached another turning point: with the front line static, will the West continue to support Ukraine? The ultimate outcome of the war depends on the answer to that question, and the year 2024 may be decisive in that regard.

MC: *Russian industry still produces weapons despite Western sanctions; Putin also wants to strengthen his army and has*

25. Worrying Signs

announced a "new phase" in the war. How do you analyze it? Can Russia regain the advantage?

SP: Putin started to prepare his army, industry, and country for a long war soon after his blitzkrieg failed in the first months of the invasion. Both Ukraine and the West had been slow to think long-term and increase the production of weapons and munitions. Putin will try to take advantage of that lag in the new year. It will be a difficult year for Ukraine and its allies.

MC: *Could the entry of F-16 fighters supplied to Kyiv change the situation?*

SP: I am not a military expert, but those who are believe that it can help Ukraine to achieve parity in the air and protect the skies over Ukrainian cities, although it will probably be insufficient to ensure the success of a major counteroffensive.

MC: *The unity around Volodymyr Zelensky seems to be cracking because of criticism from Ukrainian officials, notably the mayor of Kyiv, an exhausted army that has suffered heavy losses, a population sometimes discouraged, and Western support now weakened, particularly in the US Congress. Are these signs worrying for Kyiv, in your opinion?*

SP: The signs are worrying not only for Kyiv but also for European capitals and Washington. Europe is in the middle of the largest war in Europe since 1945. Its outcome will determine the future of international relations for the foreseeable future. Neither Ukraine nor the West can afford to lose a war of such proportions.

MC: *Could Zelensky be pushed toward the negotiating table, at the risk of giving up the 17 percent of Ukraine's territory occupied by Russia, or will he try to reconquer all that territory, including the Crimea?*

SP: If that happens, it will not be the end of the war. Ukrainians know that from the experience of the Minsk agreements of 2014–15. The current Russian leadership does not recognize the right of Ukraine to exist as a separate nation; hence their talk about Russians and Ukrainians being the same people. Territorial concessions might bring an armistice but not peace.

MC: *Ukraine is continuing its path toward membership in Europe. Does its future lie within the European Union and NATO?*

SP: Yes, that is what Ukrainians are fighting for. This war has shown that independent Ukraine can have a future only in European and Euro-Atlantic structures. Otherwise, there will be no independence, and possibly no Ukraine.

January 2024

26. The War That Neither Ukraine nor the West Can Afford to Lose

The war between Russia and Ukraine can continue indefinitely unless the West realizes that what's at stake isn't just the fate of Ukraine but the future of the West itself.

As the New Year arrived in Ukraine with a Russian missile attack on Kyiv early in the morning of 1 January 2023, there were two main questions on the minds of policymakers around the world. The first pertained to the fate of the continuing Russian winter offensive, while the second concerned the results of the planned Ukrainian spring counteroffensive.

The answer to the first question came in May, when Yevgeny Prigozhin withdrew his Wagner Group troops from the ruins of Bakhmut. Taking control of Bakhmut had come at a high price to Wagner, with perhaps 20,000 soldiers killed, most of them convicts recruited by Prigozhin from Russian prisons. That was the only significant success of the offensive. Bakhmut was to remain under Russian control, but Prigozhin rebelled when the Kremlin decided that it didn't need his services and ordered him to integrate his troops into the regular Russian army. The mutiny revealed fissures between the Russian political and military leadership, which didn't rush to protect the regime. The Kremlin eventually assassinated Prigozhin, but the military brass's dissatisfaction with Putin's handling of the war suggested possible trouble in the future.

The Counteroffensive

The failure of the Russian offensive opened the door to Ukraine's June counteroffensive. Despite some optimistic predictions, the destruction of the Russian Army-controlled section of the Kakhovka Dam on the Dnieper River effectively dashed Ukrainian hopes of using it as a bridge to cross the Dnieper and sever the supply lines connecting Russian troops in the south of Ukraine with their logistical hubs in the Crimea.

As a result, the situation on the mainland reached a stalemate. Less than 200 square miles changed hands from the beginning of the year. Russia managed to stabilize the front line by bringing at least 300,000 additional soldiers and officers into the Russian Army. Ukraine, as well as being outnumbered 3 to 1 in terms of manpower, lacked superiority and often even parity in firepower. While the Ukrainians had received tanks, fighting vehicles and anti-aircraft missile batteries, they didn't receive the F-16 fighters they had requested, nor the US ATACMS long-range guided missiles. Delays in supply were caused by various reasons, including disagreements between NATO commanders and their Ukrainian counterparts on the required weaponry and timing, quarrels between the allies on who should supply what (notably the public dispute between the US and Germany regarding supply of Leopard and Abrams tanks), and White House concerns about crossing Putin's red lines and provoking a nuclear war.

No End in Sight

But efforts to prevent the war from escalating no doubt will contribute to lengthening it, likely through 2024 and beyond. What's more, the battles of 2024 will be fought amid a political event—the US presidential election—that will be as important to the future of the war as any individual offensive. The US remains the largest Western supplier of weapons to Ukraine and is second only to the European Union in financial assistance to Kyiv. The political uncertainty in the US will greatly affect the country's ability to provide Ukraine with crucial military aid.

Ukraine is likely to face a shortage of munitions at some point in the coming year. Yet it takes time for Ukraine's Western partners to increase the production of munitions. The US has already doubled the production of some artillery shells, but there is a long way to go to meet the demands of the Ukrainian front. Meantime, the European Union is unlikely to meet its pledge to supply one million shells to Ukraine. The surprise Hamas attack on Israel and the possible start of a larger Middle Eastern war could further exacerbate Ukraine's munitions situation. To be sure, Russia also faces challenges in terms of munition supplies but has been able to fill the gap with the help of North Korea, which supplied Moscow with one million shells. Beyond that, Putin has been effective in circumventing Western sanctions, stabilizing Russia's economy, and mobilizing its industry for wartime needs.

Land for Peace?

As 2023 comes to an end, there are more calls for a cease-fire and eventual "land for peace" settlement. However, such an outcome won't provide either stable or lasting peace in the region. While Ukraine has been engaged with its allies in discussing the "peace formula," the Kremlin insists on achieving all of its original goals, including the so-called denazification of Ukraine, which is a code word for the destruction of Ukraine's political and intellectual elites.

Ukraine can't lose this war, because the very existence of the Ukrainian state and nation depends on its outcome. And ending it with an armistice resulting in the loss of people and territories and without NATO membership is tantamount to losing the war. Ukraine has been in that position before, in 2014–15, when the Minsk agreements never brought peace but provided Russia with the ability to build a stronger army and come back in force a few years later. The Russian policies targeting Ukrainian activists, kidnapping children, and replacing Ukrainian school curricula with Russian ones would lead to the eradication of anything politically and culturally Ukrainian in the occupied territories.

A loss for Ukraine would also be tantamount to a major loss for the United States and its allies. Russian victory would result in

Moscow strengthening its grip on the post-Soviet space, restoring its positions in the Caucasus, where Armenia has indicated its interest in strengthening its relations with the West, and in Central Asia, where Kazakhstan uses its ties with China to counterbalance Russian power in the region. Even more important, Russia's success in Ukraine would increase a threat to NATO's eastern flank—in particular, the Baltic states and Poland. Outside Europe, it would embolden Moscow's allies Iran and North Korea and provide China with a template for a military solution of the Taiwan dispute. In all those cases, US and NATO troops could find themselves in the midst of a military conflict of the sort that Ukraine is fighting today without direct NATO involvement.

In many ways, the biggest disadvantage for the West is the striking difference between the ways in which the war is viewed in Russia and the West. While the Kremlin perceives it as a life- and-death struggle with the US and its allies, whipping up anti-Western hysteria in the Russian media to mobilize the population and resources to wage such a war, Western governments imagine this war largely as a conflict between Ukraine and Russia, debating the degree to which they should help Ukraine without antagonizing Russia too much.

What the Western perspective misses is that the key question on the global agenda is the future of the West itself. At stake in this war isn't just the fate of Ukraine but also the security of the West, the stability of the international order, and the future of democracy as a global force. The outcomes of wars of such magnitude shape the future for generations to come. Even if much of the West doesn't yet recognize it, this war is no exception.

December 2023

27. The Trump Card

Interview conducted by
Jens Uthoff for *TAZ* (*Die Tageszeitung*)

Jens Uthoff (JU): Mr. Plokhy, how did your Ukrainian friends and relatives react to Donald Trump's election victory?

Serhii Plokhy (SP): The dominant concern is how and whether the United States will support Ukraine in the future. Trump's second term comes with a good deal of uncertainty. There is still hope that there may be a turn for the better for Ukraine.

JU: Why?

SP: Trump supplied weapons to Ukraine during his first term. I think he did not want to be seen as responsible for further possible losses in Ukraine after the annexation of the Crimea. And candidate Trump did not further torpedo the passage of the huge $60 billion aid package for Ukraine in the spring of 2024. We do not know what to expect; we do not know whether we will live to see this Trump.

JU: Joe Biden has launched a kind of "final offensive" shortly before the end of his term in office…

SP: Yes, Biden's Ukraine policy worked well during the first two years of Russia's war of aggression. But it no longer worked in 2024 because there were significant delays in the delivery of weapons that had already been promised or restrictions on the use of weapons that had been delivered. Now, after the presidential election, the Biden administration has suddenly lifted the restrictions, and Ukraine has been able to use ATACMS missiles.

JU: *What do you think about that?*

SP: Protecting and defending Ukraine is a very important part of Biden's political legacy. He doesn't want to be remembered as the president who didn't give Ukraine what it needed to defend itself. But this also shows that the reasons for all the delays in arms deliveries were made up beforehand.

JU: *How likely do you think it is that the conflict will be "frozen" and that there will be peace with massive concessions on the part of Ukraine after Trump's inauguration?*

SP: It seems that the plan of the next US administration is to freeze the war on the current front line and propose that Ukraine will not join NATO for a period of perhaps 15–20 years. The question is whether this can be implemented. Russia's stated goal is to fully control the Zaporizhzhia, Kherson, Luhansk, and Donetsk oblasts. That has not yet been achieved. This is the least on which Putin would insist, and the question is how long his ambitions will be limited to those four oblasts. The Trump administration's potential plans are not very realistic.

JU: *Do you also mean the plan of the designated US special envoy for Ukraine and Russia, Keith Kellogg?*

SP: Yes. The plan coauthored by Kellogg last May calls for a ceasefire that would delay Ukraine's accession to NATO and provide security guarantees for the country. Kellogg is opposed to large-scale military aid for Ukraine and the involvement of US troops in military conflicts. He has a plan to force Ukraine to the negotiating table but no clear means of getting Putin to agree to his terms.

JU: *What does the nomination of Keith Kellogg mean?*

SP: We now know exactly what Trump thinks about ending the war. Instead of general statements about ending it by means of a negotiated settlement, we now know the details.

27. The Trump Card

JU: *The future US Vice President J. D. Vance has outlined a similarly disadvantageous peace for Ukraine, with territorial losses, a demilitarized zone, and a renunciation of NATO membership.*

SP: That would be fatal not only for Ukraine but also for Europe as a whole. If Ukraine receives no prospect of NATO membership, it is almost guaranteed that this conflict will fall back on Europe as an even bigger war. We have seen what followed the peace plan for Georgia and the Minsk agreements. Vance's plan is also bad for the USA because it endangers America's leadership role in the world as well as its economic and political standing. All this could encourage China to act more aggressively, in Taiwan for example. Putin would be rewarded with this kind of peace for what Russia has done in Ukraine. There would be no stop signal, and he would carry on. But Russia will not cease until it is stopped. That can only be done with a militarily and economically strong Ukraine, not with a piece of paper signed in Brussels or Washington. I think that a quick end to the war and Trump's promise to end it within 24 hours is absurd anyway.

JU: *Why?*

SP: Take the Korean War in the early 1950s. It took two to three years to achieve peace and a partition of Korea. That required a change of leadership in Moscow and Washington, the death of Stalin, and the election of President Eisenhower. If you look at the end of the Vietnam War, it took two American administrations under President Johnson and five years under President Nixon to achieve a withdrawal of US troops. A plan for negotiations is not the same as the start of negotiations. And what the final result will be is a completely different matter. I therefore consider it impossible to make any serious predictions at the moment.

JU: *The talk-show host Pete Hegseth, who is to become Secretary of Defense, did not consider support for Ukraine important in the past. Marco Rubio is to become Secretary of State and is considered an advocate of a negotiated solution, as is the designated National Security Advisor, Mike Waltz. What does the Trump II cabinet stand for?*

SP: During his first term, Trump still relied on people with more expertise. He depended on generals and retired generals when it came to security or military policy. Now he is mainly looking for loyalists and considering positions for which they might be suitable. It will be a much more Trumpian and unpredictable government than the first. Retired General Keith Kellogg, who was already Chief of Staff of the National Security Council in Trump's first cabinet, seems to be the exception. But it is unclear what all this means for Ukraine.

JU: *For Ukraine, does everything really depend on the USA? What can or must the EU do if the USA refuses to support Ukraine?*

SP: Although I'm sure that I won't make myself popular with this view, Trump was right when he said during his first presidency that the situation in Ukraine was more worrisome for Europe than for the US and that Europe was not fully living up to its contribution to NATO. The large EU states, such as Germany and France, should really present themselves as potential mediators and not just sit at the table as spectators. And the EU should at some point be able to defend itself and Ukraine. The EU should be not only an economic power but also a military one. Out of self-interest.

JU: *Emmanuel Macron called for that back in 2017. Did Germany come to understand it too late?*

SP: Yes. And I think that there was a vacuum after Angela Merkel's departure. Chancellor Olaf Scholz did not want to take the position of European leader after the start of Russia's war of aggression. Macron took up that position quite convincingly.

JU: *At the beginning of the week, Scholz made a surprise trip to Ukraine...*

SP: Given his refusal to supply Ukraine with Taurus missiles and criticism of his fruitless phone call with Putin, Scholz is under pressure. He must show that he continues to support Ukraine. Hence the visit, which was more about symbolism than substance.

JU: *What role will the elections in Germany play?*

27. The Trump Card

SP: Wherever Germany goes, so does Europe. It is extremely important that Germany stay on course when it comes to Ukraine. If the CDU were to form a government in Germany, that would certainly mean stability for Ukraine. The stronger the populist parties become, the worse it will be for Ukraine.

JU: *You have been teaching at Harvard for many years. Now, Linda McMahon, a woman from show business, will be Secretary of Education, and, even though education is a state-run matter, her policies would affect schools across the country. Are you also worried about the universities under Trump II?*

SP: In this second term, it will be important for universities to defend the autonomy of scholarship and academic freedom. Whenever this is undermined, I become very worried.

JU: *Are you thinking about leaving the USA?*

SP: Many of my colleagues are thinking about it. But I believe that American democracy is strong enough to survive. A democracy with such a long tradition will not be eliminated even though Trump has won the election. As you see, I am trying to remain optimistic.

December 2024

VI. Making Sense of War

28. Writing History as It Happens

Interview conducted by
Maria Ramirez, *El Diario*

Maria Ramirez (MR): *How has this year [2022—ed.] been for you?*

Serhii Plokhy (SP): It has been a very stressful year, but, surprisingly, it ends with more optimism than there was at the beginning, in the first days of the war. Despite the fact that the war brought much destruction, death, and more than eight million displaced people, there is hope that it will not end with just *any* peace, but that there will be a *just* peace. The number of Ukrainians who believed in victory in March 2022 exceeded 80 percent. It is now [in February 2023—ed.] over 95 percent. It's amazing. The biggest surprise of this war, apart from Putin's attack, which is brutal and, in many ways, counterintuitive, has been the resistance of the Ukrainian people. Like other observers, I am surprised.

MR: *Now you are writing a book on the origins of the war. What is it like for a historian to write about something that is still happening?*

SP: That's the question I was asking myself, whether I wanted to write the book or not. And my original answer was that I couldn't, because, as a historian, I can't write about the world today. But then people kept asking me for interviews and feedback. And I thought that maybe I could somehow influence events. I realized that I probably had concrete knowledge to talk about the war that others did not. From interviews like this one, I gained confidence that, despite being a historian, I could still do something when history is part of current events and helps to explain them.

MR: *What is the main element in the origin of the war?*

SP: I see this war as a continuation of a story well known to Europeans, the story of the disintegration of empires. As we know, that process can last a long time. When you look at the current war and Putin's rhetoric, it actually goes back not to Soviet times but to those of imperial Russia, when there was a belief that Russians and Ukrainians were the same people, or that Ukrainians were a branch of the Russians. Even in Putin's rhetoric and justification of the war, you see these signs of empire. This war continues the story of the disintegration of empires.

MR: *In Western Europe, some speak of NATO enlargement as a factor in the origin of the war, but in your book* The Gates of Europe *what counts above all is Ukraine's desire to join the European Union.*

SP: It is very important to note that this war did not start in 2022. It began in February 2014, when Russian special forces seized the Crimean Parliament and Autonomous Government buildings, and the Crimea was annexed. And the trigger for that war was not Ukraine's desire to join NATO or even the European Union. The trigger was Ukraine's insistence on signing an Association Agreement with the European Union, not even the candidate status it now has. That was enough for Putin to risk relations with the West and begin the annexation of Ukrainian territories. He recognized that, if Ukraine were to sign the Association Agreement with the European Union, as it did, then it would not join his Eurasian Union.

On the Russian side, the war was always about restoring and controlling post-imperial and post-Soviet space and holding other countries hostage, as we now see in Belarus. The war was part of the same plan to integrate Ukraine into a Russian-led union. People talk about the consequences of this war for Europe, but imagine if not only Belarus but also Ukraine were subject to the same military occupation and control from Moscow. What would that mean for Poland? What would that mean even for Germany? For

28. Writing History as It Happens

Central and Eastern Europe and Europe as a whole? So that is what is at stake today if we go beyond the issues of democracy and values, which are very important. Just looking at the geopolitical map of Europe, that is what's at stake in Ukraine. The trigger for the war was not Ukraine's desire to join NATO but its insistence on signing the Association Agreement with the European Union.

MR: *Your book* The Gates of Europe *ends with the idea that Europe is risking its future. Is there more awareness of this?*

SP: At the time, that sounded like an exaggeration—I wrote The Gates of Europe after the start of the war in 2014 and published it in 2015 (in English). I left those sentences in the text because, as a historian, I believed that what was happening was extremely important. And now that statement no longer sounds exaggerated. Which may be another proof that historians can add some value to the understanding of our present and future.

MR: *Your book now reads like a rebuttal of Putin's speeches on medieval history or World War II. Did you see his aggression coming?*

SP: In 2005, I published Unmaking Imperial Russia about the historian Mykhailo Hrushevsky who was also the first leader of Ukraine in 1918 and wrote the first modern history of Ukraine. I knew the history of imperialism and nationalism very well. Putin claimed that Russians and Ukrainians are the same people and repeated that claim a couple of times before my book was published in 2015. And I recognized that right away. There are shades of the imperial analogy: it wasn't as pronounced as it is today, but it was already there. Putin couldn't predict the future, but his claim was not just a sentence that someone wrote for him: it was part of his deep belief.

What is being decided in this war is not only the future of Russian control over post-imperial space but also the future of Russian identity itself. As long as the Russians aren't sure who they are, as long as they don't think that Ukrainians and Belarusians are distinct peoples, they cannot understand their own identity in post-imperial terms. So this is a war about Russia's imperial aspirations, but mostly it's about the decolonization of Ukraine and the Russians' idea of themselves.

MR: *When you were a student and professor in Ukraine, did you experience this denial of history?*

SP: I began my studies as a historian and my academic career in Ukraine when it was part of the Soviet Union. The Soviet narrative was the model. It was an imperial model, but the Soviet communist regime made some concessions to the non-Russian nationalities. Ukrainians were recognized as a separate nation. The Ukrainian language was taught in school. Of course, everything was very Russocentric—political, cultural, academic life. But it was not denied that there was a separate Ukrainian nation or that it had a history of its own. I could not speak publicly about imperialism or Ukrainian nationalist ideas, but there was a compromise that Putin now rejects. In the same speeches or articles in which he claims that Ukrainians do not exist as a separate nation, Putin attacks the communists—Lenin and even Stalin—for making concessions to Ukrainians and others. He spurns that Soviet communist-era compromise in favor of the old pre-1917 imperial narrative.

MR: *What is the biggest misunderstanding you have encountered in the West about the history of Ukraine?*

SP: The misunderstandings correspond to two key propaganda themes employed by Russia today. Clearly, someone in Russia was smart enough to figure out what those misunderstandings were and use them for propaganda warfare. The first theme, as Putin has said several times, is that Ukraine is not even a real state but part of Russia. And this was certainly said with the expectation that it would be welcomed in the West, which had little knowledge of Ukraine. Because Ukraine, like most countries in the world today, has not been an empire since medieval times, it was late to make its appearance on the political map. Its history was therefore a clean slate for most people outside Ukraine, in Europe, in the West, and in the Global South.

And the second propaganda theme claims that Ukraine is a country of nationalists and anti-Semites, as Putin says in order to justify the war. Ukraine has had a difficult history of relations with its neighbors, such as the Poles and Russians, and minorities such as the Jews and Crimean Tatars. No doubt. But Ukraine was also, in many ways, historically a multiethnic land where people not only fought but also learned to live together. And that is Ukraine today. Its survival indicates that the history of Ukraine does not consist only of dark pages. Ukraine today has the only president of Jewish origin outside Israel. Ukraine has a functionally bilingual society in which people can switch from one language to another. There are some regional differences, but it has the largest language exchange I have seen anywhere in the world. And the world is realizing this only now—better late than never. Of course, it's sad that Ukraine is coming to world attention as a result of war and suffering; that it has to show extraordinary resilience. But that is not unique either: sometimes we learn about the world through very tragic events.

MR: *Do you think that the focus on Russia over the years has helped Putin, especially in Europe?*

SP: For a long time, Russia had a lot of sympathy in the West. Whatever came from Russia certainly got much more attention than anything that came from Ukraine, Kazakhstan, or any of the Soviet republics. And there was a reluctance even to take account of developments that were already obvious, such as Russia's war on Georgia and the subsequent annexation of the Crimea. Only the all-out war of 2022 truly called all those narratives and attitudes toward Russia into question. People began to criticize what they had previously ignored—aggression, violation of accepted rules, the collapse of Russian democracy, and the rise of an authoritarian regime in that country. Some changed their views for ideological reasons.

In Europe, anti-Americanism has been one of the key factors obscuring developments in Russia. It's not that people didn't sympathize with Ukraine or Georgia, or that they favored Russian aggression, but anything that challenged the United States was seen as somehow good. Others allowed financial benefits to obscure their judgment. And most were too busy with their daily lives, as happens in all countries. All this made Europe blind to what was happening on its eastern flank until it became truly impossible to ignore reality.

MR: *Have you found any key that can lead us to understand how this war ends?*

SP: Churchill once said that democracy is the worst form of government except for all the others. And I've reached the conclusion that historians are the worst forecasters of the future except for everyone else. A historical framework helps one think about long-term rather than short-term consequences of the war. And the long-term consequences are all too clear. We know what happens to empires: they fall apart. We know what happens to old colonial peripheries: they emerge as independent states. And we know what happens to old imperial powers: they reinvent themselves.

I don't see that this war is going to lead to a process different from those familiar to us in European and world history. It is clear today, as it was not a year ago, that Ukraine will survive and remain an independent state. That was a question in February and March of last year. It is a pretty safe bet to say that Ukraine will continue its integration into European institutions and security structures like NATO and the European Union. It already has EU candidate status and is basically fighting with NATO weapons. So Ukraine is more integrated into NATO with regard to current weaponry than any major country, because the Ukrainians have more experience fighting with all those weapons than, say, the Spanish or the French.

It is now a safe bet that Ukraine will survive, remain independent, and join the European Union—much safer than it was before the start of the war. Russia will come out of this conflict substantially weakened. And there's already a major realignment taking place in the world with the return of the Western trans-Atlantic alliance in a form different from the one prevailing for the past thirty years. Thus, a number of historically important developments are already clear. What we don't know and probably cannot predict is exactly when the war will end, where the borders will be drawn, and how permanent the peace will be. I don't have instruments to predict that, but, from a slightly broader historical perspective, I think that the key outcome of this war is already apparent: Putin miscalculated, this war is bad news for his regime, and Russia will come out of the conflict severely weakened.

28. Writing History as It Happens

MR: *What do you think of the idea that Ukraine can attain a status like that of South Korea, as the historian Stephen Kotkin suggested in an interview a few days ago?*

SP: It's possible. Looking at the likely outcome of the war in March or April, when it was already clear that Kyiv would not fall, a status like that of divided Germany seemed possible and is certainly still possible today. But there is also a very likely scenario that Ukraine will regain control of all its territory. Today, I read a very interesting statement by Aleksei Navalny, the imprisoned leader of the Russian opposition. Before his imprisonment and before the war, he claimed that the Crimean issue was resolved and that it would stay in Russia. He now says that, after the war, Russia and Ukraine must remain within their internationally recognized borders. Previously, even Russia's opposition leaders accepted the annexation of the Crimea, but the war has changed that. Now the opposition to the Russian regime accepts the internationally recognized borders of Ukraine. We do not know how the war will end. But the scenario of a status like that of divided Korea or Germany, which was probably the only one that existed in March or April, is now not so obvious and not the only possible one.

MR: *As an expert, are you concerned about the nuclear facilities in Zaporizhzhia or even Chornobyl?*

SP: Yes, I'm worried. During the Russian occupation of Chornobyl, there were scary times when the electricity supply was cut off and a Fukushima-type accident was possible. Fortunately, it didn't happen. The most worrisome site today is the Zaporizhzhia nuclear power plant, the largest in Europe. It has six reactors that Russia took over as a result of military action, with the use of weapons causing a fire in one of the buildings. Still under Russian occupation, it is being used as a shield for Russian artillery firing on Ukrainian positions. This war has also confronted us with a new reality when it comes to nuclear power. No reactor in the world was ever designed to withstand military attack. Never before has a nuclear installation been taken over by a foreign army or state, and that raises serious questions about our global future in terms of energy.

Wars will most likely continue in a world with more than 400 nuclear reactors, which can become dirty bombs in the hands of terrorists and other regimes. I think that we still don't get it, just as people refused to see what was happening when Russia invaded Georgia and seized the Crimea. We are now in a different era. We need to rethink our attitude toward the safety of nuclear reactors and of nuclear energy in general. This debate is clouded by the fact that the greatest problem this winter was how to survive without Russian gas in Eastern and Central Europe. One response was to rely more on nuclear power. So we are in a highly complex situation.

MR: *How will your new book end?*

SP: It covers the first year of the war. The conclusion is open, because much of the future will depend on us. Without a doubt, the most positive thing I can say is that we have the power to change the future.

MR: *You will have to write an epilogue.*

SP: I am sure that new chapters will be added: Ukrainians are now writing them by their actions.

February 2023

29. Not Since World War II

Interview conducted by
Petro Dolhanov, *Ukraina Moderna*

Petro Dolhanov (PD): *You begin your latest book,* The Russo-Ukrainian War, *with an account of how you found out that the war had started and how your colleagues overseas reacted. Did you and your fellow historians believe that a great war was possible in Europe?*

Serhii Plokhy (SP): Before the start of the Russo-Ukrainian war in 2014, Timothy Snyder predicted its likelihood. Right before the full-scale military invasion, the role of "prophets" passed from historians to the US and UK administrations and intelligence agencies. The possibility of a full-scale war was discussed both privately and publicly, but people somehow did not believe that events would take such a turn. Today, when we look at the mood before the beginning of the full-scale war, it is clear that we (I, for one) were seeing certain signs of its inevitability but didn't want to believe them.

I think there was a general notion that the world we had known since the fall of the Berlin Wall, a phenomenon that Francis Fukuyama called "the end of history," remained unchanged. Humanity seemed to have reached a stage of development where the page of history describing unprovoked wars and great wars in general had been turned. At least, one wanted to believe that it was true. As for me, I predicted that a war was possible, but everything pointed to a continuation of the 2014–15 hostilities in eastern

Ukraine. That is why this great war was a big shock. In examining these events in my book, I trace how the war approached and what increased the chances of its happening. But, until the war actually began, for the most part, many of us did not see anything or simply refused to see.

PD: *In your book, you seek to pinpoint the causes of the current war in the history of nineteenth- and twentieth-century Russian imperialism. How does this approach help you understand the war's events and the continuity of Russian imperialism?*

SP: This is one of the approaches that I apply. Of course, I also look at the preconditions and factors that were at play after 1991. But the imperial, colonial framework is the most important one. In other words, I look at this war in the context of many others that accompanied imperial collapses. I look at it not just in the context of the fall of the Soviet Union (although this is the closest and crucial context) but also from the perspective of the collapse of the Russian Empire, which began in 1917 during the First World War. This contextual framework is the broadest. It helps me immensely not only to understand some elements of this war but also to carry out a comparative analysis of similar wars in the world in the last two hundred years.

One of the reasons to apply this framework is found in Putin's own speeches, because he actually justifies the war by referring to elements of Russian imperialist ideology and historiography. The argument that Russians and Ukrainians are one people, that is, that Ukrainians are not a separate people, dates back to the historiography of imperial Russia in the nineteenth and early twentieth centuries. Many of Putin's other ideas can be traced to this period, which not only justifies the application of the imperial framework but also goes a long way toward explaining Russia's motives for this war and understanding its causes.

PD: *How do current approaches to interpreting history affect the construction of the Russian imperial paradigm?*

SP: Take another look at Putin's articles and speeches, and you'll see that he is not using new finds, discoveries, and interpretations within the framework of history but old approaches dating to the times of the Russian Empire. They do not resonate in the Western world in any significant way. Meanwhile, the negation of any versions of national history, which are to be found in the Western intellectual milieu, helps not so much to restore imperial narratives as to spark interest in empire and, in a way, to legitimize it. I would not say that some kind of historiographic debate is taking place along those lines and that Putin's ideas in this regard are being perceived in a better light. But, on the other hand, we have an overt attack on national narratives, whatever they may be. That attack comes both from Russia (the old imperial Russian interpretation) and from the West (the new post-national paradigm).

PD: *What role can an obsession with the history of the Second World War and the distortion of the history of Nazism and the Holocaust play in constructing the Russian imperial paradigm?*

SP: The Russian side utilizes not only imperial narratives but also Soviet ones. I am talking about the portrayal of Ukraine as an "anti-Semitic" country that needs to be freed from "Nazi" control. Until 24 February 2022, these statements resonated with narratives popular in the West. However, with the beginning of the full-scale invasion, what became apparent was the obvious absurdity of such accusations against probably the only state in the world (excluding Israel) where the democratically elected president was of Jewish origin. The topic of genocide was voiced by Putin both before and during the full-scale war, when he declared that a "genocide" was taking place against his imaginary "people of the Donbas." In other words, the themes of anti-Semitism, nationalism, and genocide became part of the propaganda accompanying this war. In this case, I am talking more about politics than about the work of historians or intellectuals.

PD: *Do you think that there was a certain turning point, missed by most Western countries, in Russia's imperial policies, starting from the 1990s? Did Russia have a chance to set out on a different, more democratic path of development and construction of a national state (not an empire)?*

SP: In the late 1980s and early 1990s, Russia was a kind of beacon of democracy and democratic development in the Soviet Union, especially in comparison with republics that were more conservative at the time. I mean not just the countries of Central Asia but also Belarus and Ukraine, where the old party apparatus held power for a very long period. From this standpoint, there were great hopes regarding Russia's rapid democratic transformation. Boris Yeltsin and his milieu positioned themselves as representatives of the democratic wing and possessed a certain collection of ideas about creating a new Russian political nation. These chances for transformation dissipated over the next few years, perhaps even months.

Looking back from today's perspective, it is evident that those expectations were unrealistic and illusory. They were based on the idea that history is of little value and that communism had captured essentially democratic societies and countries, making them temporarily totalitarian. Take away communism, and democracy would return and blossom. In other words, this model comes from Eastern Europe at the time (now Central Europe) and was applied to Russia and the USSR. Today, it is unmistakably apparent that miracles do not happen, and that a history of existence without democratic traditions and institutions is a crucial factor that does not contribute to the building of democracy. From this perspective, the theory of a certain watershed moment that was supposedly overlooked seems doubtful.

I am more skeptical about such declarations today, although I don't deny the idea that Russia may change. But I reject the possibility of rapid revolutionary transformations; they will take place very gradually. If we look at certain iconic moments, it is difficult to find a more symbolic event in this history than tanks shelling the Russian parliament in the fall of 1993 on orders from Yeltsin, who had defended that same parliament under the banner of democracy two years earlier.

PD: *Is Russia's development beyond the imperial paradigm possible?*

SP: I am convinced that a quick change of the social system is impossible, but I believe that Russia, like any other society, may be transformed and is transforming itself. Transformation does not happen in a short span of time. A real transformation of social

29. Not Since World War II

relations takes longer. The only exception is that of countries occupied for many years, such as Japan and West Germany. But countries left to their own devices in the wake of defeats, such as Germany after the First World War and Russia as the center of the Soviet Union after it lost the Cold War, set out on the path of revanchism.

PD: *What scenarios for ending the war do you see?*

SP: The most likely scenario, which emerged after the first few weeks of the war, is that Ukraine survives and continues to develop as a separate state and independent nation. Furthermore, Ukraine will continue along its path toward integration into Western structures. This process has already begun and has accelerated with the war. In the medium- and long-term perspective, Ukrainian statehood and national self-awareness will be preserved and strengthened.

This is the most likely scenario. Moreover, it fits best into the broad conceptual framework that we discussed earlier, which I use in my book. In other words, this is a framework of imperial and colonial wars. It is generally known that such wars end with the collapse of empires and the creation, legitimization, and strengthening of states that emerge from their ruins. If we look at the current political map of the world, we realize that most of today's states did not yet exist in 1914. This is the general direction of historical processes over the last two hundred years.

PD: *How has the Russo-Ukrainian war affected the Western democracies and their geopolitical strategies?*

SP: In my opinion, Western democracies are on the same trajectory as they were in the 1930s. For a long time, a policy of appeasement was pursued; we can see absolute parallels with the policy of the 1930s. At the time, Western states perceived the *Anschluss* of Austria as a semi-legitimate measure; in our own day, they took a similar view of Putin's annexation of the Crimea. This approach makes it possible to delay war and offer concessions to aggressors, hoping that a larger conflict will not occur. But, at a certain stage, there comes a turning point. In the 1930s, it came when Adolf Hitler and German tanks entered Prague. In the case of Ukraine, that did not happen, thank God; Russian tanks did not enter Kyiv. But they came close, and that moment became something of a turning point.

This led to the rebuilding of connections that had existed during the Cold War. The so-called trans-Atlantic alliance between the United States and Europe, which experienced a severe crisis after the Cold War and especially during the Trump presidency, was revitalized. By the end of last summer, Germany and France, which had tried initially to act as intermediaries above the battle, fully joined this coalition on the level of discourse as well as financially, militarily, and ideologically. Today, this coalition is stronger than it was during the Cold War because it now includes the countries of the former Eastern Europe and the Baltic republics, which were once part of the Soviet Union. The unity that the West is demonstrating today pertains not only to policies toward Russia but also toward China, and this, too, is a phenomenon with certain elements of unity from the Cold War era.

PD: *What might the new world order look like after the conclusion of the Russo-Ukrainian war?*

SP: At one time, Yevgeny Primakov, an adviser to Mikhail Gorbachev and, later, prime minister of the Russian Federation, noted that, when the Cold War ended, a unipolar, Americentric world emerged. This state of affairs did not please Russia. The Russian model became that of a multipolar world, and the goal of achieving it remains operative to the present day. Sergei Lavrov raised this issue not long ago during a meeting with African leaders. According to a plan formulated by the Russian political elites, Russia should become one of the poles of the contemporary world. They realized that Russia could become such a pole and compete with the European Union and China only if it restored the resources of the former Soviet Union. It is therefore extremely important for Russia to control Ukraine, the second-largest former Soviet republic in terms of economy and population. For this reason, one of the dimensions of this war is Russia's struggle for a multipolar world in which it is one of the poles and controls the post-Soviet space as its sphere of influence in the form of the Eurasian Union.

That did not happen, and Russia is much weaker today than at the beginning of the war. The attempted putsch that we recently observed is in no way a sign of the country's strength. In fact, what happened was a disseverance, at least for a while, from the idea that Russia could truly be one of the poles of power in a multipolar world. Instead, it is becoming increasingly dependent on China. Right now, the latter is truly one of the poles of the bipolar economic world, and it is assuming greater importance as a political and military power. So this war, which began with the idea of a multipolar world, is nudging humanity toward the bipolar division of the Cold War. The revival of the Euro-Atlantic alliance attests to the strengthening of the Western pole, and the war against Ukraine is clearly contributing to Russia's rapprochement with China.

PD: *How has this war affected your reinterpretation of the past? Has it changed something in your approach to historical interpretation?*

SP: I decided that I had to write about this war a few weeks after it began, but, in doing so, I was using certain approaches that I had formulated even before it started. This war has clearly given me a much better understanding of many processes and phenomena connected with the history of the twentieth century. Right now, I am looking at some of my earlier works. The words I wrote seem correct, but a complete understanding of events and processes, including emotional understanding, is coming only now. In other words, I have a fuller picture of how the Second World War was fought by the Soviet Union and the Red Army and of the attitude prevailing in Russian and Soviet political culture toward the value of human life, including the lives of its own soldiers, to say nothing of the civilian population. All doubts as to the crimes of the Red Army against the civilian population not only of Germany but also of Eastern Europe and Ukraine have disappeared.

Moreover, I now look a bit differently at my predecessors who created the Ukrainian diaspora and Ukrainian studies in the West. I now have a better understanding of the trauma of war and refugee status. So the history of the twentieth century has become more understandable, and emotionally closer, to me.

PD: *What role can historians play in wartime conditions? What advice would you give them?*

SP: War shifts accents, and many things become more intelligible. Not since the Second World War has any war been so morally clear-cut not only for Ukrainians but also for the world as a whole. In the context of moral choice, it offers a very specific understanding of who the aggressor is and who the victim, who is on the side of democracy and who supports authoritarianism. The source of threats and death becomes patently clear. This cannot fail to leave a mark on the choice of topic and how academics write about war and peace. That is a political plus. But, when we talk about writing the history of war, inevitable simplification—black-and-white polarity—also emerges. So there will be a clear turn, particularly in Ukrainian historiography, regarding the choice of topics and approaches, regarding the language of writing. I mean not only the choice of language (Ukrainian, Russian, or English) but also the increasingly categorical nature of many conclusions.

As for historiography in general, I think that certain changes will take place in Ukraine and elsewhere. The Second World War was a privileged research period among Ukrainian historians. It would be difficult to find another five- or six-year period, like 1939–45, that received so much attention and had so many publications devoted to it. But I think that the bulk of questions connected with the new war will be at the forefront from now on. More attention will be paid to economic and social history during wartime, and so on. Foreign policy and crimes will be researched, as well as the impact of war on society. What is happening right now is also the formation of a new quality of Ukrainian society and identity and the reappraisal of ideas about global security. However, we still cannot fully research the phenomena and processes taking place before our very eyes. We do not possess adequate instruments for this; even sociologists say that measuring public opinion in wartime does not meet certain standards. But there is a lot of work for historians now and in the future.

PD: *What are your predictions about the decolonization of academic study of Eastern Europe as a result of the war?*

SP: The decolonization of narratives is the main topic of the next meeting of the Association for Slavic, East European, and Eurasian Studies, which will take place in the United States. When we talk about decolonization, we mean Russian or Russocentric studies and approaches. In this sense, Russian, Soviet, and East European studies are trying to catch up with processes that took place after the decolonization of the 1960s in the historical narratives of the Western empires, British and French. This process entails rewriting the histories of the empires "from below," from the perspective of peoples and social groups on the lower rungs of the hierarchy. I think that this process will only gain momentum.

Considerable attention was devoted to the nationalities in the Russian Empire and the Soviet Union after 1991. But that body of research viewed various national and cultural groups and their movements mainly from the perspective of the center, because the main focus was still the study, for example, of Soviet nationality policy as a whole. Therefore, the rewriting of Soviet or Russian imperial history from the perspective of Ukrainians, Georgians, and other ethnic and religious groups should be taking place right now. I believe it will gain strength because this trend is in unison with what is going on in the historiography of other imperial and post-imperial territories.

This makes certain demands of Ukrainian studies. The decentralization and decommunization of Russian or Eurasian studies requires bolstering the perspectives of non-imperial groups, of whom Ukrainians are among the largest. The success of decentralization or decolonization will also depend on the extent to which Ukrainian historians are integrated into these processes and participate in such discussions. It is also crucial for Ukraine to develop a new perspective on what empire and the Soviet Union mean to us, where the national communism of the 1920s and 1930s is positioned, and what to do with it. In other words, there are many questions, and we have to take a fresh look at them, including in the context of the current war.

As for certain structural changes, I think that a lot will depend on the specific country. In Germany, the question of which departments universities should have is decided on the governmental level, which provides financing. However, in the United States and Canada, much depends on the number of students and their enrollment in certain courses. Depending on this, teaching and research positions are allotted. Therefore, we have the task of restoring what existed earlier and has practically vanished today, namely Slavic departments, which were turned into Russian departments or integrated into departments of Modern Languages and Cultures, and the like. Whether this can be implemented will depend not only on the quality of the discussion and arguments within the expert milieu but also on how many students in North America register for courses that are not Russian or Russocentric. Today, these processes have begun in the form of discussions among professionals and in the pages of journals. It is hard to imagine how this could have happened without the impetus provided by the war.

PD: *Could you briefly summarize the main idea of your latest book? Are there plans to publish it in Ukrainian? If so, approximately when can Ukrainian readers expect to see it?*

SP: Most of our conversation has been a discussion of the ideas raised in the book. In terms of chronology, it covers a longer period. The first chapter deals with the collapse of empires. I discuss Russo-Ukrainian relations, starting from the Kyivan Rus′ period and ending with the dissolution of the Soviet Union. However, the discussion of preconditions of the war focuses mainly on the post-Soviet period from 1991 to 2014. The next section deals with the unacknowledged war of 2014–22. Then there is a chapter about the events of the war after the full-scale invasion. I end with two chapters devoted to the external political effects of the war. These are the revival of trans-Atlantic cooperation, the significant weakening of Russian positions in the world, and the development of relations with China. The book ends with an epilogue about the war as an international factor propelling us toward a bipolar world. There are plans to publish the book in Ukraine; the translation is almost ready. It is supposed to come out before the Lviv Book Forum.

September 2023

30. Turning Back the Clock of History

Review of Mark Galeotti, *Putin's Wars: From Chechnya to Ukraine* (Osprey Publishing, 2022); Owen Matthews, *Overreach: The Inside Story of Putin's War against Ukraine* (Mudlark, 2022); and Luke Harding, *Invasion: Russia's Bloody War and Ukraine's Fight for Survival* (Vintage Books, 2022)

In December 2021, I accepted an invitation from the former prime minister of Ukraine, Oleksii Honcharuk, to attend a conference that he had co-organized at Stanford. I wanted to hear firsthand what Honcharuk, who had headed Volodymyr Zelensky's first government, thought about the chances of a major war between Russia and Ukraine—a subject that had been dominating the media for weeks.

Honcharuk assured me that there would be no war, at least not in the next few months. With Joe Biden focusing the world's attention on Vladimir Putin's preparations to strike, he explained, the timing was not good for Moscow. In 2014, Russia's annexation of the Crimea had come as a surprise. This time, everyone was ready—the Ukrainians with their new army and the West solidly committed to punishing Russia with heavy economic penalties. Putin would have to wait it out. Honcharuk's argument seemed plausible. But common sense is not necessarily a reliable guide to predicting the future.

On 21 February 2022, three days before the invasion, Putin formally recognized the independence of the two puppet states that Russia had created in 2014 when it occupied part of Ukraine's eastern Donbas region. He also laid claim to Ukraine as a whole. "Since time immemorial, the people living in the southwest of what has historically been Russian land have called themselves Russians and Orthodox Christians," he asserted in his speech, going on to argue that Ukraine was an artificial creation of Vladimir Lenin and the Bolsheviks. Putin was determined to turn the clock of history all the way back to the Russian Empire, whose rulers had posited the existence of a tripartite nation consisting of Great Russians, Little Russians (Ukrainians), and White Russians (Belarusians). This would be his principal contribution to a project that had begun, in effect, immediately following the collapse of the USSR in December 1991, with Moscow moving swiftly to reestablish control of the post-Soviet space. In the wake of 1991, the Kremlin had set about modernizing the remains of the Soviet army in order to achieve its foreign and domestic political objectives.

* * *

The First Chechen War, launched by Boris Yeltsin in 1994 to crush the Chechen drive for independence, inaugurated this new era of post-Soviet warfare. The Second Chechen War, which began in 1999, opened the door to Putin's election as president and launched what Mark Galeotti, in *Putin's Wars: From Chechnya to Ukraine*, calls the "Wars of Russian Assertion." Packing his narrative with detail and analysis, Galeotti argues that, in Russia, more than in many other countries, the armed forces became "a symbol of national pride and power." For Putin, Russia's military is "not just a guarantee of its security" but also the means of making Russia "a credible international power again."

The Chechen wars were followed by the use of military force outside the borders of the Russian Federation, in the form of the invasion of Georgia in 2008 and the seizure of the Crimea in spring 2014, which immediately revealed itself as a prelude to the hybrid warfare launched in the Donbas a few weeks later. Putin's goal in Georgia and Ukraine was to stop those countries' drift toward the West, but in both cases his actions had the opposite effect. When Ukraine sought closer integration with the Western democracies, Putin abandoned what Galeotti calls "his usual cautious approach" and attempted an all-out invasion and partial occupation of the country.

Galeotti advances a number of reasons for Putin's decision, including his Covid isolation and possible illness, which may have made him feel as if his "personal clock was ticking faster than he had once assumed." In the author's view, Putin did not have to invade in order to win his "political war" against Ukraine: the credible threat of invasion sufficed to drive away Western investors, making Ukraine's European aspirations all but moot. But the master of the Kremlin miscalculated. Galeotti rightly suggests that Putin planned a "police action," not a war, which he then tried to fight in his own way by dismissing the opinions of the military brass. The invasion, Galeotti says, was "not the generals' war." One can almost feel Putin's disappointment when Galeotti observes that "arguably, 20 years of high-spending military reform was wasted in 20 days."

In *Overreach: The Inside Story of Putin's War against Ukraine*, Owen Matthews explains how Russia's attempts to reform its military were destroyed by the political hubris of the man who initiated and promoted that reform. Based on the author's intimate knowledge of Russia and its political life, this is the best available account of the country's road to war. The list of prominent Russians interviewed in the years leading to all-out conflict includes Putin's spokesman Dmitry Peskov, who is thanked for "chats in his Kremlin office and over dinner that have been tours de force of adamantine defiance of reality," and Sergei Kirienko, who is not only first deputy chief of staff of the presidential administration but also responsible for running the occupied territories in Ukraine.

Matthews is convinced, and claims repeatedly, that the Kremlin's war on Ukraine is first and foremost a war against the West. He argues that the underlying motive for the invasion is the same as the one behind the poisoning and subsequent imprisonment of Putin's main political opponent, Aleksei Navalny: to protect Putin's regime from what the president and his circle of former KGB operatives regard as Western encroachments. Thus, for Matthews, the most productive question is not why Putin unleashed an all-out war against Ukraine but why he did not do so earlier. His answer is that, given the botched American withdrawal from Afghanistan and Angela Merkel's departure from the political scene, Putin considered the moment opportune for curbing Western influence in Ukraine. Indeed, Russia had a war chest of

$650 billion—oil and gas money stashed away by Putin for just such an offensive—and now was the time to strike.

Matthews begins the countdown to invasion with the one and only meeting between Putin and Zelensky, arranged and attended by the leaders of France and Germany in Paris in December 2019. Zelensky made no concessions to Putin, despite earlier promises by Ukrainian representatives. Under pressure from his domestic opposition, the Ukrainian president refused to remove his troops from the frontline in the Donbas, to allow elections in the Donbas before Russian soldiers had left the region, or to change the constitution in such a way as to give the Donbas veto power over Ukrainian foreign policy.

Soon after the failed summit, Putin fired Vladislav Surkov, his point man in Donbas affairs. It was then, argues Matthews, that the Kremlin began its slide toward military confrontation. Isolated by the Covid epidemic, Putin had time to study imperial Russian history and write his own disquisition on Russo-Ukrainian relations. The role of security officials such as Nikolai Patrushev, who retained direct access to the president, increased tremendously.

In the spring of 2021 Putin moved his troops to the borders of Ukraine in an effort to blackmail Zelensky and the West into allowing the Trojan horse of the Donbas puppet states to enter the Ukrainian constitutional fortress. The threat failed, but, with American policy in disarray after the retreat from Kabul, the Kremlin decided to achieve its goals in Ukraine by military means. Matthews designates Putin's security men as the main hawks—Patrushev, the secretary of the security council, and Aleksandr Bortnikov, the head of the FSB, or internal counterintelligence and secret police. By early December, the defense minister, Sergei Shoigu, and the military brass had sped up their planning for the war.

When Putin called a meeting of the security council on 21 February 2022, in order to discuss the alleged "independence" of the Donbas puppet republics, Patrushev, Bortnikov, and Shoigu were probably the only members who knew that his real plan was to go to war. The rest suspected what was going on and simply hoped for the best. Describing the atmosphere at the meeting, Matthews quotes Galeotti: "King Lear meets James Bond's Ernst Stavro Blofeld." The invasion began three days later.

If Matthews presents the best current analysis of the countdown to war, Luke Harding provides unparalleled coverage of the invasion as experienced on the Ukrainian side. Harding was in Kyiv when the attack began and has visited Ukraine repeatedly since then. He vividly describes the atmosphere on the streets in the early hours of the war and tracks changes in the public mood as the Russians withdrew from Kyiv while battles continued in eastern and southern Ukraine. His account covers developments up to September 2022.

No figure better reflected, embodied and articulated the transformation of Ukrainian society by the war than the country's president, Volodymyr Zelensky, whose patriotic credentials were unclear and often challenged by the opposition during his first two and a half years in office. A few weeks before the Russian attack, he gave a joint press conference with the then British prime minister, Boris Johnson. Harding, who was invited as a member of the press, finds the Ukrainian president to have been "somewhat behind the curve of history—struggling to respond to developments, and to the mighty storm bearing down upon him." While Johnson spoke of "imminent" Russian aggression, Zelensky called it "possible." That was the line he took with visiting foreign dignitaries and his own people.

Despite the talk of imminent invasion in Washington and London, Kyiv did not mobilize its army reserves until Russian tanks crossed the border and Russian missiles awakened Zelensky and his family at the presidential quarters outside Kyiv on 24 February. But, having publicly downplayed the possibility of war, he quickly became an inspirational symbol of Ukrainian resistance once the invasion began. The new Zelensky was born with the sound of those first explosions. He had shown courage earlier, but now it took on added purpose and significance. If his talent as an actor had allowed him to gauge the mood of his audience to attain the presidency, he could now draw on it not just to provoke laughter or calm frayed nerves but to make Ukrainians discover their inner strength. He became what Harding, quoting the *Guardian* columnist Jonathan Freedland, calls "Churchill with an iPhone."

In effect, Zelensky's story reflects that of the Ukrainian people who dreamed of peace but were forced into war by Russian aggression. Their resolve to fight back was not crushed but solidified by the invaders' atrocities, such as the cold-blooded killing of Volodymyr, a young resident of Bucha. His apparent mistake was to give three Russian soldiers his phone when they demanded one. It is not clear what the Russians found there, but they took Volodymyr away, tortured him, broke his arm, and demanded that he tell them where the "Nazis" were. Their actions were gruesome evidence of the effectiveness of Putin's propaganda about waging war against "Nazis"—this in a country with the only Jewish head of state outside Israel, and one of the few post-Soviet nations with a working democracy.

There were no Nazis in Bucha, and Volodymyr kept telling his captors that he knew nothing. They took him for further interrogation. His aunt, Natasha, got a glimpse of him after he was tortured but then lost track of him. She would find his body in a nearby cellar after Ukrainian forces liberated Bucha. Harding, who interviewed Natasha soon after, quotes her: "They made him kneel and shot him in the side of the head, through the ear."

Ukrainians have been fighting and dying not only to save their lives but also to defend their democratic ideals. "Freedom is our religion" was the message on a poster that covered a burned building on Kyiv's Maidan Square after the Revolution of Dignity in 2014. Harding's interviews show that the phrase was no mere slogan. "A leitmotif of Ukrainian literature, historiography, and philosophy is opposition to the centralized idea of state and universe," Harding quotes Volodymyr Yermolenko, a leading public intellectual in Kyiv, as saying. Olena Chebeliuk, a history teacher from Lviv, tells the author: "We don't like dictators here... If he tries to make a dictatorship in Ukraine, he will fail."

The war destroyed whatever sense of East Slavic unity and national brotherhood still existed in Ukraine. It also turned the most pro-Russian of Ukrainians into the Kremlin's sworn enemies. Before the war, Oleksandr Vilkul, the military governor of Zelensky's hometown, Kryvyi Rih, was one of the leaders of what many considered a pro-Russian opposition to the president. Yet, despite being offered a prominent position in a Russian-backed government, he refused appeals to support the invasion. Instead, he led his fellow citizens in their fight against the invaders. "They believe in Lenin, victory in the Second World War, and the nuclear arsenal," he says of the Russians, adding that he always knew

Russia to have been dangerous but did not expect it to become a "crazy monster." Asked about the outcome of the war, Vilkul is confident of Ukraine's victory. He tells Harding: "Like Hitler, Putin will destroy his own country."

Galeotti, Matthews, and Harding give their own answers to the question of how the war is likely to end. Galeotti divides Putin's long incumbency into two parts—the successful decade of the 2000s and the disastrous period after 2010, characterized by the squandering of what he achieved during his previous two terms in office. He acknowledges the damage that the war has done to Russia but hopes that its new generation of leaders will be more pragmatic, if no less nationalistic, than the current one. Matthews seems less optimistic, suggesting that the war "opened a Pandora's box of alternative futures for Russia that were much more scary than Putin's regime had ever been." He envisions two scenarios for Ukraine: a negotiated settlement or endless warfare. Harding, taking a historical perspective, sounds the most optimistic. "Ukraine had not won the war—or not yet," he writes, adding that, in the words of the country's national anthem, it "had not yet perished" either. According to Harding, Ukraine has become a "proven state."

Through the current war, Ukraine has indeed established its right to existence and shown that it is here to stay, regardless of how much longer the current regime survives in the Kremlin and what kind of rulers succeed it. What this means in historical perspective is that a war fueled by the Kremlin's misreading of the Russian and Ukrainian past, and its own desire to regain the great-power status of Soviet times, is destined to end in victory for Ukraine as an independent state and the defeat of Russia as an imperial one. This is not just the best-case outcome of the war but also its most realistic one.

The main question is when that will happen and at what cost. To hasten the outcome and minimize the damage means staying the course and helping Ukraine to prevail. This in turn will help Russia to free itself from the hubris of the empire that it once was but is now a chimera that holds it in its thrall.

February 2023

31. The Zelensky Effect

Review of Olga Onuch and Henry E. Hale,
The Zelensky Effect (Oxford University Press, 2023)

In a recent interview with Volodymyr Zelensky on "My Next Guest Needs No Introduction," David Letterman asked the Ukrainian president about the source of his country's fighting spirit. Letterman also suggested that he already knew the answer: that it came from Zelensky himself. The president demurred, instead praising the courage of Ukrainians in military uniform defending their country.

The basis of Zelensky's personal courage and the solidarity of Ukrainians resisting unprovoked Russian aggression are among the key themes of Olga Onuch and Henry E. Hale's deeply researched and well-argued book *The Zelensky Effect*. They locate the roots of Zelensky's ability to captivate and mobilize the imagination of his fellow citizens in the rise of Ukrainian civic identity. "This is not simply Zelensky's doing," the authors write, adding that the Ukrainian president is "a product of a Ukrainian culture steeped in the same sense of civic national belonging and duty that he advocates, advances and now symbolizes."

The Zelensky effect, as the authors define it, is the manifestation of Ukrainian civic identity since the start of the all-out war, though its origins are far older. Looking for the sources of Ukraine's inclusive national identity, which crosses linguistic, ethnic, and religious lines, Onuch and Hale follow the life story of Zelensky and his generation from the final decades of the USSR to the current war. The results of that history were succinctly expressed in the words "I'm Ukrainian" printed on the hoodie that Zelensky wore on "My Next Guest." But it's even clearer in the language he used in that interview, responding to questions in Ukrainian but slipping in a few Russian words when telling a Jewish joke from Odesa. As Onuch and Hale explain, the rise of independent Ukraine in the early 1990s helped to overcome the obstacles that had long divided Ukrainians and Russians from each other and from their Jewish and Crimean Tatar fellow citizens.

Zelensky, who today represents the entire Ukrainian nation, was long regarded by supporters and opponents alike as a representative of Ukraine's Russian-speaking east, a region whose inhabitants had stood apart from the struggle for democracy and sovereignty embodied by the revolutions of 2004 and 2014. But Russia's annexation of the Crimea and its attack on the Donbas in 2014 changed Zelensky and Ukraine itself. A comedian who made a name for himself in Russia before becoming known in Ukraine, Zelensky left political news to others. But, in 2014, he turned political, reacting to the annexation of the Crimea with pointed barbs and sarcasm. Zelensky and his cohort, politically inactive up to that point, adopted the big-tent Ukrainian civic identity that Onuch and Hale regard as a result of decades of civic activism.

The vision of a multiethnic and multicultural Ukrainian nation was initially formulated in the middle of World War I by Mykhailo Hrushevsky, the first scholar to make a persuasive historical case that Russia and Ukraine were separate entities. Hrushevsky envisioned the rise of a free Ukraine as the result of common efforts of Ukrainians, Jews, Russians, and Poles. Jews, as fellow victims of Russian imperial rule, were at the top of Hrushevsky's hierarchy of friends of Ukrainian freedom. He also welcomed Russians and Poles who wanted to support the cause, promising Ukrainian support and cultural autonomy in return.

In 1917, Hrushevsky's vision of a multiethnic and multicultural Ukraine served as the political foundation of the first modern Ukrainian state, known as the Ukrainian People's Republic. It did not survive the Bolshevik invasions of 1918 and 1919, which brought civil strife and violence, often directed against minorities. To pacify Ukraine, however, Vladimir Lenin eventually made concessions to the Ukrainian cause that Vladimir Putin now finds unforgivable. The Ukrainians were recognized as a distinct people, and their language and culture received state support in the Ukrainian Soviet Socialist Republic, one of the founding polities of the Soviet Union. Joseph Stalin reneged on many of those concessions, pushing a Russification agenda that produced a new category of citizens, Russian-speaking Ukrainians, consisting largely of Ukrainian peasants who moved to the cities where they lost their language but not their identity.

In December 1991, when Ukrainians went to the polls to vote on the future of their republic, the results were astounding: more than 92 percent chose independence, with huge majorities registered not only in all regions of Ukraine but also among all ethnic groups. Jews demonstrated slightly greater support for independence than did ethnic Russians. A week after the Ukrainian referendum, the Soviet Union was dissolved by the leaders of Russia, Ukraine, and Belarus. Independence created a new country that faced the difficult task of reconciling its borders with the politically, culturally, and linguistically diverse population that it inherited from the USSR. At the time, some observers wrote of two Ukraines: the largely Ukrainian-speaking and Europe-oriented west and the Russian-speaking and Russia-oriented east. Those were the divisions that Russia tried to exploit in 2014, annexing the Crimea and starting a hybrid war in the Donbas that succeeded in some Russian-speaking areas but failed in others.

That was the juncture at which Zelensky and his generation of Russian-speaking citizens from Ukraine's east and south joined the battle to preserve the Ukrainian nation and state. When Putin ordered his armies into Ukraine in February 2022, the new Ukraine embodied by Zelensky fought back. Zelensky was both product and architect of Ukraine's new sense of identity. That identity has grown stronger over the course of the war, helping to ensure Ukraine's survival as an independent nation-state after Putin's Russia confronted it with an existential challenge. In their conclusion, Onuch and Hale write that "Ukrainian civic identity was what had produced not only Zelensky, but 44 million Zelenskys."

March 2023

32. The Sources of Russian Conduct

Review of Sergey Radchenko, To Run the World: The Kremlin's Cold War Bid for Global Power (Cambridge University Press, 2024)

"At bottom of Kremlin's neurotic view of world affairs is traditional and instinctive Russian sense of insecurity," wrote George Kennan in his "Long Telegram" of February 1946, which has been considered the first intellectual salvo of the Cold War. According to Kennan, the Kremlin was burdened with two types of insecurity. During their early history, Russian agriculturalists had found it difficult to defend themselves against their nomadic neighbors. Later, it was mostly their elites who suffered from a sense of inferiority to the West. "Russian rulers have invariably sensed that their rule was relatively archaic in form, fragile and artificial in its psychological foundation, unable to stand comparison or contact with political systems of Western countries," suggested Kennan.

    Kennan was writing at the very start of the Cold War. He developed his views in the article "The Sources of Soviet Conduct," published in July 1947 under the pseudonym "X." Now, more than 75 years after the appearance of Kennan's writings and 35 years after the end of the Cold War, a prominent historian of the Cold War, Sergey Radchenko, picks up where Kennan left off. In his latest book, *To Run the World: The Kremlin's Cold War Bid for Global Power*, Radchenko offers his take on the sources of Soviet conduct. He does so with the benefit of hindsight, deep knowledge of the history of the Cold War, and acknowledgment of the threats posed by the new Cold War that involves the United States, China, and Russia. In his analysis, Radchenko brings to life some of the key participants in the original Cold War, making clear their beliefs, ideas, and positions, as well as restraints on their power to implement their desired policies. The book is exceptionally well researched, even better argued, and beautifully written.

As the title suggests, this is first and foremost a book about Soviet thinking and action on the world stage. An important feature of the book less obvious from the title is Radchenko's conscious and highly successful attempt to go beyond the bipolarity paradigm, in which Soviet thinking was defined by Kennan and others through competition with the United States alone. He brings China into the picture as well: more often than not, its role in the Cold War was obscured in historical narratives, but China now looms large in discussions of the new Cold War, which helps to reevaluate Beijing's role in the original Cold War. Having written a number of important works on the non-Western Cold War, Radchenko carries out his analysis with exemplary confidence, expertise, and primary source knowledge.

While Radchenko asks basically the same key question as Kennan, he diverges from the views expressed by the dean of American Cold War geopolitics more than he follows them. If, according to Kennan, "the political personality of Soviet power" was "the product of ideology and circumstances," Radchenko refuses to place ideology in the center of his analysis. According to him, "the sources of Soviet ambitions are not specifically Soviet, but both precede and postdate the Soviet Union, overlapping with the Cold War." Radchenko claims that it is almost impossible to separate ideology from "the quest for security (in the benign version) or outright imperialism (more commonly accepted)." But he moves closer to Kennan when he writes: "At some level the Soviets felt very insecure about whether or not they really were America's equals."

Radchenko identifies the interplay between the Soviet Union's great-power ambition to shape the world and its search for legitimacy as the key driver of that country's behavior in the international arena during the Cold War. Legitimacy from the West "was attainable through recognition either as a partner or as an adversary," he writes, noting that communist and anti-imperial

32. The Sources of Russian Conduct

forces were alternative sources of legitimacy. This is another radical departure from Kennan, who focused exclusively on Russia's relations with the West.

What does this new approach allow us to understand about the Cold War that we did not know before, and how can that help us understand Putin's Russia? Let's begin where Radchenko does, with the Big Three negotiations at Yalta. Stalin was seeking not just security but also legitimacy, emphasizes Radchenko. The Soviet dictator achieved his Far Eastern goals at Yalta and got pretty much what he wanted in Europe at Potsdam. He backed off in Iran and Turkey, failing to obtain Western consent to keep his sphere of influence in northern Iran and establish military bases in the Black Sea straits. He did not insist on acquiring the former Italian colonies in Africa. But he refused to bow to American nuclear power, matching the US atomic project with his own.

Africa, denied to Stalin by the West, became a target for his successor, Nikita Khrushchev. What was the reason? Radchenko suggests that decolonization produced opportunities unavailable to Stalin. One can argue with that proposition: after all, the British lost India, the Dutch parted with Indonesia, the French got involved in a bloody war in Indochina, and the Americans withdrew from the Philippines, all on Stalin's watch. For Radchenko, however, the key argument concerns ambitions, not opportunities. Khrushchev's ambition was to be recognized for his contribution to the anti-colonial movement. "Such recognition translated into legitimacy," writes Radchenko. This time, it came not from the West but from the communist and anti-colonialist camp, in which China played a key role.

The Cuban missile crisis, arguably the most dangerous moment of the Cold War, became a platform for Khrushchev to realize his dual ambition—to make the USSR the equal of the United States, even though it possessed too few ballistic missiles to present a serious threat to American territory, and of China, whose leader, Mao Zedong, challenged Khrushchev's leadership in the communist and anti-imperial movement. Khrushchev's gamble did not pay off. He managed to secure Cuba for the communist bloc but was perceived as a loser both at home and abroad. His removal of Soviet nuclear arms from Cuba became part of a public deal, while the Americans' withdrawal of their missiles from Turkey remained secret.

If Khrushchev tried only one strategy, that of challenging Washington, to achieve recognition and legitimacy from both the United States and the communist and anti-colonial forces, Brezhnev diversified his tactics. He was determined to acquire legitimacy from the United States more as a partner than an adversary in the field of nuclear arms control even as he continued to challenge the United States in the former colonial world. The Soviet nuclear strategy, which had almost produced a nuclear war over Cuba, was now divorced from its anti-colonial policy. By the late 1960s, the more likely scenario became nuclear war with China rather than with the United States.

Radchenko is reluctant to offer conclusive answers regarding the sources of Soviet policy under Gorbachev, but he demonstrates very well how Gorbachev tried to satisfy his craving for recognition as "the prophet of a new world order" by positioning the Soviet Union as America's partner not only in the realm of nuclear arms but also in the Third World. Ultimately, he failed to win recognition as an equal but succeeded in positioning the USSR as a partner, albeit a junior one, of the West in general and the United States in particular. This status came with partial delegitimization at home and almost complete delegitimization in the anti-imperial camp. Those processes led to and accompanied the end of the Cold War.

Yeltsin's and especially Putin's foreign policy became in many ways an attempt to rebuild Russia's great-power status, which was lost by the end of the Cold War. Craving Western recognition, Yeltsin offered the United States partnership in the denuclearization project in the post-Soviet space and continued Gorbachev's policy on control of nuclear weapons. Putin offered Moscow's partnership in the "war on terror." What he wanted in return was Western acknowledgment of Russia's right to intervene politically, economically, and militarily in the post-Soviet space. It was more a return to Stalin's spheres-of-influence approach than to Khrushchev's and Brezhnev's search for superpower equality on the global stage. Wisely, the West never provided such recognition or legitimacy, making Putin complain about "double standards" as

32. The Sources of Russian Conduct

he abandoned the partnership model for an adversarial one in relations with the West.

In his speech on the annexation of the Crimea in March 2014, Putin justified the first annexation of European territory since World War II by referring to the independence of Kosovo, enhanced by the West to stop a genocide. "We keep hearing from the United States and Western Europe that Kosovo is some special case," argued Putin. "What makes it so special in the eyes of our colleagues? It turns out that it is the fact that the conflict in Kosovo resulted in so many human casualties. Is this a legal argument? This is not even double standards; this is amazing, primitive, blunt cynicism." With the start of the Russo-Ukrainian war in 2014, Putin moved from a partnership to an adversary strategy of seeking recognition. This strategy very much defines the current foreign policy of Russia.

To Run the World helps to explain why Russia's grasping for great-power status often looks so irrational. The Kremlin repeatedly punches above its weight and strikes militarily before it is ready economically or strategically. Its outsize ambitions, inherited from the Russian Empire and often challenged by the West, which learned in the twentieth century to treat Russia as not only culturally but also ideologically alien, are often responsible for such behavior. With no sign that Russia's great-power ambitions are waning, the book still offers a silver lining of sorts. The policies that Russia's ambitions produce and inform can change. After failing to gain legitimacy as an adversary, Russia tends to pursue the same goal as a partner. Russia's war on Ukraine failed to provide legitimacy in the West and positioned it as a weak junior partner of China in the East. Russia will have to change its strategy in the future. For that to happen, the West needs to show resolve, as Truman did in the 1950s, Kennedy in the 1960s, and Reagan in the 1980s.

June 2024

33. Decolonizing the Past

Conference presentation
at the University of Alberta, Edmonton

Russia's all-out war on Ukraine and, more important, Ukraine's heroic resistance to it are having a major impact on the international agendas of governments and reshaping the agendas of academic and cultural institutions and communities. The field of history is one of those most affected by the changes that the war is producing, and it is essential to have a thoughtful discussion of the challenges and opportunities facing that field today. What I would like to offer here is an agenda for such a discussion focusing on historians' relations with the larger community, the field of Russian, East European, and Eurasian studies and, last but not least, our colleagues in Ukraine.

Let me begin by going back to the months and weeks before the start of the Russian invasion of Ukraine and the beginning of the all-out war in February 2022. At that time, I, like quite a few members of this panel and, I assume, some people in the audience as well, participated again and again in webinar sessions on the war, answering questions about when it might break out and what to expect.

Most of those panels were dominated by experts on Russia. When military affairs were discussed, the participants were exclusively experts on the Russian army. The impression one got from such webinars was that Ukrainian society and, in particular, the Ukrainian armed forces did not exist. There is now general awareness that both—society and the army—existed then and exist today. In the United States today, both academic and non-academic observers are asking: How did we miss it? And why didn't we expect Ukrainian resistance on such a scale?

How did the Western expert community miss the existence of the Ukrainian armed forces? Following general recognition that there had been major misjudgments of Ukraine's capacity to fight back, it slowly emerged that the military experts had done what they usually do—they counted tanks and artillery. That was a good beginning, but there was a gap when it came to assessing the morale of troops and understanding Ukrainian politics and society. This is now a more or less mainstream view, creating an opportunity for people with expert knowledge of the field to contribute to the discussion about the origins and nature of the Russo-Ukrainian war.

There is now a demand for expertise on Ukraine and, most interestingly and perhaps counterintuitively, most of the questions are being addressed not necessarily to military experts or political scientists but to historians. The interest now shown in the important work of Timothy Snyder and Anne Applebaum is indicative of that. How did Ukraine, Russia, and the world get into this war? What will come next? There has been a feeling that only historians can provide an explanatory framework for the war, and questions of this sort—important, essential questions—are being asked of historians more than of other experts in the field. This public spotlight imposes a particular responsibility on us, on our field, and creates an opportunity that, as we know, will not last forever. This is the moment when our voices can be heard—voices of historians in particular. This is the time for us to educate our colleagues in different disciplines and the public at large and, in so doing, influence the debate on Ukraine.

Now let us consider the challenges facing us as practitioners because of this new, perhaps unexpected attention focused on the country that we study and the field we represent. Those challenges first manifested themselves before the start of the all-out war with the publication of Vladimir Putin's essay "On the Historical Unity of Russians and Ukrainians." I can tell you from personal experience and from my discussions with colleagues both in North America and in Ukraine that the overall response was to call that essay not history but pseudohistory. The question was how to engage with pseudohistory and debunk it without legitimizing it.

It is easy to lend a sort of legitimacy to an argument if you engage with it. Accordingly, the overwhelming reaction of professional historians was, "Just ignore it." What came out a few months later was that Putin's "essay" was not just an exercise in bad history or misuse of history but preparation for the largest war in Europe since 1945. The questions for us and our field are as follows: How do we deal with such challenges in the future? How do you counter bizarre and outdated arguments from the other side? This is the first issue that I would like to place on the agenda.

The second question deals with challenges from Western academia, of which we are an integral part. In the first weeks of the war, a number of academic organizations in the United States organized online marathons in which experts in the field, broadly defined, were asked to comment in one way or another on research of theirs somehow related to the war and help explain the situation. First of all, it was a very moving manifestation of goodwill on the part of the field as a whole—that is, the scholars affiliated with the Association for Slavic, East European and Eurasian Studies (ASEEES). Second, it provided a very clear understanding of what the field looked like.

Experts on Ukraine per se were a minority, with the majority comprised of individuals mostly engaged in Russian and Eurasian studies trying very hard to contribute to an academic effort that they considered politically and morally important. But the best that we got, in most cases, was a perspective from the center. There might be a discussion of nationalities, dealing in part with Ukraine, but people were referencing their work, which was Russocentric, as was most of the expert discussion on the prospect of all-out war before it began.

Those in the Ukrainian field took notice. Some protested, others lobbied, and, in November 2022, the ASEEES initiated a number of panels on decentering and decolonizing the field. That also became the main theme of the ASEEES Convention planned for November 2023. If this was not a call to action addressed to practitioners in the field of Ukrainian studies to offer their expertise and try to reform a field traditionally centered on Russian studies,

33. Decolonizing the Past

then I do not know what else might represent such a call. Our discussion is taking place ahead of the 2023 ASEEES Convention, which gives us an opportunity to exchange opinions. The question, then, is as follows: Now is the moment to influence the situation. What do we have to offer?

Let me suggest a number of possible answers. Obviously, experts at the Canadian Institute of Ukrainian Studies and the Harvard Ukrainian Research Institute have been working on some form of decolonization of either Russian or Eurasian studies since the inception of both institutions. We can demonstrate that we have much to offer just by reminding people about the body of work accomplished in the past two or three decades. Bringing it to the fore is crucial, because the average attention span of an academic field is relatively short: we tend to focus on books and articles that appeared two to three years ago, and then we all move on. There are new publications appearing all the time, so drawing attention to the work of our predecessors is very important.

Another task is to use our expertise in Ukrainian studies to reimagine and reform the Russo-centric field as a whole. Most of the time, our ASEEES-defined field is imagined within the sphere of the Russian Empire or the Soviet Union—not exclusively, but in most of the existing research. Histories of Russia as an empire are already out there, but they are written from the perspective of the center. The same is often true of histories of the USSR. Not that the topic of nationalities does not get attention—that changed after 1991—but most research on the history of the Soviet Union is done from its center and on the basis of the central archives, or else we deal with relatively isolated histories of individual republics or national groups.

I personally know just one work of the kind that I am advocating here, and it has not yet been published. It is a dissertation written by Erin Hutchinson under Terry Martin's supervision on the rise of cultural nationalism and writers in the Soviet Union. She reads five languages of the former Soviet Union, so her work includes Ukraine, Russia, Moldova, and Armenia. This is the first such work that truly deals with Soviet history from below, more specifically from the level of the republics, focusing on the multiethnic character of the Soviet Union. The task of decentering imperial histories and integrating national ones is nevertheless still ahead of us.

What is also very clear when it comes to the field of Russian and Eurasian history is that it pretty much missed its turn to engage in decolonization of the sort that took place in the historiographies of other European empires in the course of the last half-century. In British and French history, those processes were bolstered by the decolonization drives of the 1960s. A major change occurred in the Russian/East European/Eurasian field after the fall of the Soviet Union in 1991, but the field remained rather old-fashioned and out of touch with what was happening elsewhere, especially in European history.

There is much that we, as experts in Ukrainian history, can do to help transform the broader field in which we work, but for that to happen we have to be engaged and should not understand decolonization as an opportunity for self-gratification and an invitation to build taller walls and stronger fortifications between Ukrainian history and Soviet or Russian history. The same applies to the history of the Ottoman Empire and the Middle East, Austria-Hungary and Central Europe, Poland, and Eastern and North European history. Historians of Ukraine have something significant to contribute to the rethinking of all those fields. It is important to think about decolonization not just as taking on the old Russian narrative but also as taking advantage of the broader opportunities that the history of Ukraine offers us.

Now, what about Ukrainian studies per se, narrowly defined? Or is it only our colleagues in other fields who must change and decolonize? I think that there is a demand to reassess our field as well; the demand that Volodymyr Kravchenko was talking about in his opening remarks, an impulse that really comes from transformational changes on the ground, in Ukraine. Olga Andriewsky was talking about the decolonization that seems to me to be happening on the front line of today's war, which is itself an important factor.

This brings me to the third theme and set of questions related to the processes taking place in Ukraine. The historians, authorities, and public there are engaged in a massive effort of decolonization involving the removal of monuments and changing of place-names. Which of the political and cultural figures whose names are attached to localities in Ukraine can stay, and which ones should go? Whose names should replace them? These are questions that people on the ground in Ukraine are trying to answer, bearing in mind not only the past but also the present and future. For us, the "Pushkinopad" in Ukraine should rank equally with the "Leninopad" of previous years as a stimulus to look again at Ukraine as part of the Russian Empire and the Soviet Union in order to distinguish imperial elements from Soviet ones in Ukrainian history, as well as to identify the long-term impact of imperial history on the development of today's Ukraine.

As we respond to processes taking place in Ukraine, we face the challenge of communicating with fields that have already embraced postcolonial approaches. What is happening in Ukraine has often been defined as an anti-colonial war from the perspective of Ukraine, and as an imperial or colonial war from the perspective of Russia. What our colleagues in Ukraine want to talk and write about today is often defined by anti-colonial paradigms. What our colleagues in the West are prepared to engage with is postcolonialism. Again, that is a challenge: how can we simultaneously deal with this demand from the field and understand the sort of questions being placed on the agenda in Ukraine?

In conclusion, I offer a few words about our responsibility as historians working in the West toward our colleagues in Ukraine and Ukrainian scholars who have come here as part of the refugee wave generated by the current war. One thing that this war has produced is a massive outflow not just of people in general but also of academics. We know how difficult it is in European and North American universities and academic institutions to find permanent positions, so chances are that most of those who have left Ukraine will not stay abroad, or, if they stay, will not be able to reenter academia. Those who go back to Ukraine will return transformed in many ways, voluntarily or not, by their experiences of living, teaching, studying, and trying to fit into or rebelling against the Western academic environment.

The war has produced and will keep producing a new generation of scholars in Ukraine who will think or want to think differently than they did before. In so doing they will build new bridges between the West, Europe, and Ukraine. That broad group of scholars, whether they stay in Ukraine or find positions abroad, has every opportunity to transform not just the field of Ukrainian studies but also the broader field of Russian, East European, and Eurasian studies. This, then, is a moment of enormous challenges but also of new opportunities. Much in our field will depend on how we respond to those challenges and seize those opportunities as individuals and as institutions.

May 2023

34. We Have to Make the Russians Think Differently

Interview conducted by
Khrystyna Kotsiura for *Hromadske*

Khrystyna Kotsiura (KK): *You often employ the phrase "imperial disintegration" and say that it is now up to Ukraine not only to determine whether we will remain an independent state but also to deimperialize Russia. Will we have sufficient strength and capabilities to accomplish all that?*

Serhii Plokhy (SP): In world history since 1945, there have actually been only exceptional instances of great powers winning wars against mobilized national movements. In this sense, Ukraine has plenty of strength. By defending itself, Ukraine is also shaking the architecture of the Russian sphere of influence when it comes, for example, to Central Asia, Kazakhstan, and Armenia. Since the war is weakening the Russian Federation, dependent territories are distancing themselves from Russia. Moreover, the war is prodding formerly dependent territories, such as Finland, to integrate fully into NATO. We can already see these things. This is the outer perimeter.

With regard to the Russian Federation itself, we see that there has been friction associated with the level of mobilization, which was higher in the national republics. And this war has actually produced an impetus for the Russians themselves when it comes to their attitude toward the regime. In other words, it is contributing if not to destabilizing the regime then to undermining its legitimacy. As a result, an isolated post-Putin Russia will face a very difficult period in which disintegration may become part of the story. It may or may not.

KK: *But war is a crisis, and it is clear that this war cannot continue after Putin because it is not in the interests of many, particularly Russian business.*

SP: There will be changes; there will be some tectonic shocks. And, from this point of view, such countries or parts of Russia, for instance Chechnya, which de facto already function almost as independent countries, may leave Russia, and Russia is Kadyrov's tributary, not vice versa.

I do not believe that these changes will affect the whole of Russia in the long run. It is the Russian territories, or the territories that Russia has managed to fully Russify culturally, that will remain as one country in the long run.

The greatest ideological force in the Russian Federation is nationalism. It will maintain these Russian territories. We need to be alert to the possibility of partial disintegration and to the certainty that Russia will remain our closest neighbor and potentially our most dangerous enemy for the long term.

KK: *My thirteen-year-old daughter asked me: look, the Germans are now a respected nation, everyone respects them, so does this mean that in a few decades, the same will happen to the Russians? I explained to her what Germany had gone through, that the Germans had been paying reparations until recently, and suggested that it was unlikely that Russia would follow this path. But the question remains. How should we live with such a neighbor after the war?*

SP: Negotiations are going on even today. In particular, they are related to the exchange of prisoners of war. That is, some things will remain to be discussed where there are fundamental interests, both ours and Russia's.

Returning to the experience of World War II, I see no prospect that the generation that survives this war will radically change its

34. We Have to Make the Russians Think Differently

attitude toward Russia. For this generation, Russia is an aggressor and a criminal. But new generations will come, and everything will depend above all on what happens to Ukraine and how Russia is transformed. If Ukraine remains democratic and integrates into European structures but Russia does not, then these frictions will continue, to put it mildly, into the following generations.

KK: *But what this war has definitely terminated is the ideology with which Putin started it: that Russians and Ukrainians are "one people." I think that a return to this is unlikely not only in Ukraine but also in Russia.*

SP: For the time being, it is hard for us to say and comprehend what is happening there [in Russia—ed.], but, in historical perspective, the hundreds of thousands of coffins that have come and will come from Ukraine may bear any connotation and any meaning except that Russians and Ukrainians are one people. Sometimes the effect of such things is felt in the long run.

KK: *In your answer to the first question, you said that much will change with Putin's departure. Do you believe that his death may bring about the end of the war?*

SP: I believe that, on a grand scale, this war is absolutely unprofitable for Russia: it is inflicting a great deal of damage on Russian business and Russian representation in the world. I do not believe that this generation of Russians will prefer, say, a vacation in Beijing to a trip to Paris. There will be some kind of rollback and return to rebuilding bridges with Europe because, at their peak, the Russian imperial and modern elites were oriented toward Europe in terms of education and other things.

KK: *After the death of a de facto tyrant or dictatorial leader, there is always a certain selection and struggle among his heirs. And none of them will be strong enough to continue a policy that is so harmful to Russia itself.*

SP: This is the view of a historian. We cannot look into tomorrow; we can only make assumptions. This scenario looks most likely from the viewpoint of Russia's history over the past hundred years. The changes that took place there from Lenin to Stalin and the competition among heirs after Stalin's death exemplify opportunities for totalitarian regimes to change course.

KK: *Sociology shows that Russians still largely support Putin and the war. And there is an opinion that all this is due to strong state propaganda. But is that the only factor? To what extent has imperial historical scholarship in Russia contributed to current Russian support for the war?*

SP: It has contributed to it, of course. Putin is a politician. He tries to make policy based on trends in Russia itself. In a country that existed as an empire for several centuries, losing the Cold War, the collapse of what they considered to be Russia was perceived as a great trauma for the population as a whole. This so-called chauvinistic imperial streak is what helps Russians hold on; it's part of their identity. It doesn't change overnight; it doesn't happen with Boris Yeltsin climbing on a tank and everything suddenly changing. It's a process, and, with the fall of an empire, imperial nations experience what are known as phantom pains. This is a more or less stable reaction of most empires. How is it corrected? It takes place through defeat. That is the only cure for imperialism. And Russia is getting those pains nowadays. Unfortunately, thanks to us.

KK: *Do you follow Russian historians working in exile? And if so, have they begun to comprehend their colonial past and present?*

SP: One of them is Tatiana Tairova-Yakovleva, who is very well known in Ukraine. But her position was clear from the very beginning, so it was not the war that changed her. Journalists reacted more quickly than historians. I wrote a positive review of Mikhail Zygar's book *War and Punishment*. In my opinion, this is the first attempt in several centuries, successful or not, but the first attempt by Russians, the first attempt on behalf of the Russian intelligentsia to take responsibility for what is going on and to revise Russian history from this angle. So there is already this first clear statement from journalists, and, for me, that is a very significant thing. I do not recall anything like it in the intellectual history of Russia over the past two hundred years.

KK: *So "good Russians" do exist?*

SP: Yes, and they have already begun the process of rethinking. And that is our salvation for the long term. We have to make the Russians think differently about themselves and about us. We have to change their perception that Ukrainians are Russians, only somehow spoiled by the Poles, the Austrian General Staff, and all sorts of other things. So that they understand where Russia's borders are, and that Ukraine is not part of them. Until we change their thinking, we are doomed to endless warfare. And the only way to change this is to work with the "good Russians." We simply have no other choice.

KK: *Do you think they can't do it without us?*

SP: They won't if we don't offer them other perspectives and views of some kind.

KK: *You have been living abroad for many years, communicating with various audiences. To what extent has opinion about Ukraine changed? What about the notion that we are not the wicket to Russia but the gateway to Europe?*

SP: I think that this perception has changed among most people. And publications and books on this topic have played a role—it's important; I'm not going to display false modesty.

But perceptions have been changed, of course, mainly by the events that have taken place here [in Ukraine—ed.]. That the country has not fallen, that the country is fighting, that the country is standing. This is a message that cannot be ignored. Interest in Ukraine is not decreasing, and the idea of Ukraine as something other than Russia is growing every day.

KK: *Zelensky has become a superstar around the globe. Do you think that his different background, unconnected with politics, helped prompt the world to start assisting us?*

SP: He has turned out to be a very effective communicator.

KK: *To the outside world?*

SP: Yes, outside. And the fact that he held on and held all this together, which is now being joked about—"because he didn't run away"—is actually very serious. When the top of the pyramid breaks, the whole pyramid falls down.

We know what happened in Afghanistan; we know what happened with Viktor Yanukovych. The stereotype was that you should run away—are you crazy to fight against Russia? What are the chances? Create a government in exile! For various reasons, he refused to do so, which was very important.

His support in Ukraine is now the highest among politicians, despite all sorts of problems. It is clear that he is communicating here, perhaps, less than perfectly, but he is communicating. Now it's somewhat more difficult for him to connect, but, in the early years, he was phenomenal, as evidenced by the mobilization of the world and the money that the world gave Ukraine.

Zelensky has become a brand. And, without such a brand, it's not that nothing would have happened, but it would have been much more difficult.

Textbooks discuss the general assessment. The assessment of his behavior during the war is different from that of his behavior before the war. But the fact that he came and won the presidential election as a candidate for peace, as a "stop shooting" candidate and so on, gave him the political capital to inspire the population of Ukraine as a whole. If such a "stop shooting" candidate says that we need to take up arms and fight, then trust in the proposition that there is no other way out grows significantly. That is, if Zelensky says that Russia is the enemy, there is no doubt about it. It would be much harder for someone like Poroshenko or a candidate of that type to mobilize Ukraine.

KK: *Will Ukraine get an Eisenhower or de Gaulle of its own after the war? We used to joke in the editorial office that de Gaulle lived in London, and now General Valerii Zaluzhny has been sent there. Perhaps this is a twist of fate?*

SP: There is a general trend if the country is democratic. Leaders, no matter how successful, are not usually reelected after a war ends because voters want to forget the war, forget the horror, look at other faces, hear new words, and so on. But leaders born of warfare come back in five to ten years, when memory of the war changes and is heroized. Take Piłsudski in Poland, de Gaulle in

France, Eisenhower in the United States, and so on. This is a trend in democratic countries. If Ukraine remains a democratic country, it may have this kind of thing as well.

KK: *All wars end with the signing of agreements and treaties. What should be in this agreement for us to be sure that Russia will not attack us [Ukraine—ed.] again?*

SP: Two things should be spelled out. First, Ukraine's sovereignty (that Ukraine is independent and sovereign, its entire territory). Second, ironclad guarantees of support from the allies (no restrictions on arms or support so that Ukraine can defend this sovereignty). Everything else can be expressed in different versions, perhaps a temporary solution. But it must be clearly spelled out.

KK: *What are Ukraine's chances of returning to the 1991 borders?*

SP: There are chances. This process can be extended, just as the reunification of Germany took a long time. The reunification of Vietnam also took a certain period of time. With this regime, I foresee political and other perturbations in Russia, and that may happen. So I think that there are chances. But, as a historian, I would like to say that all European countries that gained independence after the Second World War underwent serious territorial changes. Look at Poland in 1921 and Poland in 1945; look at Czechoslovakia. Territorial changes and border shifts are the European norm for the emergence of a new state.

Border shifts are normal. The main thing is sovereignty and independence, along with the ability to maintain them. The Poles today are somehow doing well even without Lviv.

KK: *What has changed most among Ukrainians before the full-scale invasion and after it?*

SP: There is a sense of Ukrainian identity based on the defense of the state and of institutions. Also, as I said before, the idea of "one Russian people" died with the first missiles. That is to say, this exclusive Ukrainian identity is political, not ethnic. The ethnic component is growing, but the identity remains political; it has cemented itself and helped Ukraine survive. And it was a test of whether there is a nation or not, whether there is a state or not.

Anger appeared. And, today, there is fatigue. But, along with fatigue, I don't see a willingness to give up the main thing—sovereignty.

To be sure, Ukraine has become an example for many in the world. The battle of David and Goliath—a smaller country rising up and fighting for its independence. I think that Ukraine's passion will remain.

A great deal will depend on how Ukraine behaves after the war. Whether Ukrainians don't quarrel, whether they don't backslide. The main thing is not to forget what Ukrainians are fighting for today—for democracy and freedom, for individual liberty. And it is also important whether Ukrainians will build a functional, efficient society and economy after the war.

June 2024

References

All previously published texts are reproduced here by permission.

1. "No End to History," originally published in Spanish under the title "El retorno de la historia," *Política Exterior* (Madrid) 204 (November/December 2021): 40–50, https://www.politicaexterior.com/articulo/el-retorno-de-la-historia/. English version published online by the Harvard Ukrainian Research Institute on 30 November 2021, https://huri.harvard.edu/news/return-history-post-soviet-space-thirty-years-after-fall-ussr.

2. "The Collapse of the USSR Is Still Going On," first published as "The disintegration of the Soviet Union is still going on and it is not peaceful," interview conducted by Adam Reichardt, editor-in-chief of *New Eastern Europe* (Krakow), 1 December 2021, https://neweasterneurope.eu/2021/12/01/the-disintegration-of-the-soviet-union-is-still-going-on-and-it-is-not-peaceful/.

3. "Three Decades of Independence" first appeared online under the title "Reflections on the 30th Anniversary of Independence of Ukraine (3 parts)," interview conducted by Nadia McConnell, US-Ukraine Foundation with Dr. Serhii Plokhii, translated by Peter Voitsekhovsky, 24 August, 7 September, and 17 September 2021, https://myemail.constantcontact.com/Thirty-Years-of-Independent-Ukraine--Reflections-and-Projections-by-Dr---Serhii-Plokhii--Part-III.html?soid=1100917358001&aid=GU1fOiS6FoQ.

4. "Books on the War" first appeared as "The Best Books on Ukraine and Russia," interview conducted by Sophie Roell, Editor, *Five Books* (London), 12 February 2022, https://fivebooks.com/best-books/russia-ukraine-serhii-plokhy/.

5. "The Long Shadow," first published in the *Financial Times* (London), 27 January 2022, under the title "The Empire Returns: Russia, Ukraine and the long shadow of the Soviet Union," https://www.ft.com/content/0cbbd590-8e48-4687-a302-e74b6f0c905d.

6. "What Is Happening in Ukraine Is Crucial," interview conducted by Adrien Jaulmes, *Le Figaro* (Paris), 21 January 2022, https://www.lefigaro.fr/international/ce-qui-se-passe-maintenant-en-ukraine-est-crucial-et-aura-des-consequences-pour-les-decennies-a-venir-20220121.
7. "Putin's Revisionist History of Russia and Ukraine," interview conducted by Isaac Chotiner, appeared online in *The New Yorker* on 23 February 2022, https://www.newyorker.com/news/q-and-a/vladimir-putins-revisionist-history-of-russia-and-ukraine.
8. "Did Lenin Create Ukraine?" first published online under the title "Casus Belli: Did Lenin Create Modern Ukraine?" by the Harvard Ukrainian Research Institute, 27 February 2022, https://huri.harvard.edu/news/serhii-plokhii-casus-belli-did-lenin-create-modern-ukraine.
9. "Ukraine's Dangerous Independence," conversation with Rund Abdelfatah and Ramtin Arablouei, hosts, "Throughline," National Public Radio (Washington, DC), 10 March 2022, https://www.npr.org/2022/03/08/1085233552/ukraines-dangerous-independence.
10. "Appeasement," essay written in March 2022 in preparation for a book on the war that appeared in 2023 under the title *The Russo-Ukrainian War*.
11. "The Causes of the Russo-Ukrainian War," essay excerpted from a longer article, written at the invitation of the Minister of Foreign Affairs of Ukraine, Dmytro Kuleba, for *Viina i novi horyzonty: Lidery dumok pro s'ohodennia i maibutnie Ukraïny i svitu* (Kyiv, 2024), a volume that he edited concerning the outbreak and beginning of the war.
12. "Putin's War Is Banishing an Outdated Myth" first published under the title "Vladimir Putin's War Is Banishing for Good the Outdated Myth That Ukrainians and Russians Are the Same," *The Telegraph* (London), 3 March 2022, https://www.telegraph.co.uk/news/2022/03/03/putins-war-banishing-good-outdated-myth-ukrainians-russians/.
13. "Annexation," interview conducted by Jerzy Sobotta, first appeared as "Wir dürfen nicht vergessen, dass das nur Putins Plan B ist," *Die Welt* (Berlin), 2 October 2022, https://www.welt.de/politik/ausland/plus241380683/Historiker-Serhii-Plokhy-Wir-duerfen-nicht-vergessen-dass-das-nur-Putins-Plan-B-ist.html.
14. "The Russian Coup," written in late June 2023, appears here for the first time.
15. "The Ghosts of Chornobyl," written in early March 2022. Later integrated into the epilogue to the paperback edition of *Atoms and Ashes: A Global History of Nuclear Disasters* (New York, 2023).
16. "Who Is in Charge?" Interview conducted by Meghan Kruger, "'15 New Chornobyls': A Survivor's Fears about Putin's War," *The Washington*

References

Post, 2 March 2022, https://www.washingtonpost.com/opinions/2022/03/02/ukraine-war-nuclear-Chornobyl-zaporizhia-reactor/.

17. "Nuclear Terrorism," interview conducted by Tobin Harshaw, appeared under the title "Another Chornobyl Disaster? Russian Invaders Are Taking the Risk. A Q&A with Atomic Energy Expert Serhii Plokhii on Putin's New Form of 'Nuclear Terrorism,'" *Bloomberg* (New York City), 11 March 2022, https://www.bloomberg.com/opinion/articles/2022-03-11/another-chernobyl-disaster-in-ukraine-russian-invaders-are-taking-the-risk?embedded-checkout=true.

18. "Between a Rock and a Hard Place" was written as part of the epilogue to the paperback edition of *Atoms and Ashes: A Global History of Nuclear Disasters* (New York, 2023).

19. "Atoms for Peace and Atoms for War," Answers to questions from *LatePost* (Beijing), October 2023.

20. "Nuclear Plants Could Become Dirty Bombs" first appeared under the title "Nuclear plants could become dirty bombs in Ukraine," *The Economist* (London), 16 June 2023, https://www.economist.com/by-invitation/2022/06/16/nuclear-plants-could-become-dirty-bombs-in-ukraine-warns-serhii-plokhy.

21. "Hiroshima Diary" first appeared under the title "There's one way to avoid repeating the horrors of Hiroshima," *The Spectator* (London), 20 May 2023, https://www.spectator.co.uk/article/theres-one-way-to-avoid-repeating-the-horrors-of-hiroshima/.

22. "Magical Thinking," interview conducted by Oliver Gehrs, first appeared under the title "Das magische Denken," *Fluter* (Bonn), 29 March 2023, https://www.fluter.de/serhii-plokhy-interview-ukraine.

23. "Germany and Ukraine," interview conducted by Katja Hoyer, *Zeitgeist* (London and San Francisco), 19 and 22 August 2023, https://www.katjahoyer.UK/P/Germany-and-Ukraine-a-history-part; https://www.katjahoyer.UK/P/Germany-and-Ukraine-a-history-part-B48.4.

24. "Why the Delays?" first appeared under the title "Serhii Plokhy's diary: The trains are still running in Ukraine—unlike the West's planes" in *Prospect Magazine* (London), December 2023, https://www.prospectmagazine.co.uk/views/63720/serhii-plokhys-diary-the-trains-are-still-running-in-ukraine.

25. "Worrying Signs," interview conducted by Manuel Cudel. First published as "Guerre en Ukraine: des 'signes inquiétants' désormais pour Volodymyr Zelensky et ses alliés occidentaux, analysent des experts," *Midi Libre* (Montpellier), 7 January 2024.

26. "The War That Neither Ukraine nor the West Can Afford to Lose," first published in the *Wall Street Journal* (New York City) on 12 December 2023, https://www.wsj.com/world/russia-ukraine-war-stakes-nato-2ac4150e.

27. "The Trump Card," interview conducted by Jens Uthoff. Originally published under the title "Harvard-Historiker über den Krieg," "Noch

gibt es Hoffnung für die Ukraine." "Harvard-Historiker Serhii Plokhy erklärt, was Donald Trumps Wahl für den Krieg in Osteuropa bedeutet —und welche Rolle Deutschland jetzt hat," *TAZ*, 5 December 2024, https://taz.de/Harvard-Historiker-ueber-den-Krieg/!6051172/.

28. "Writing History as It Happens," interview conducted by Maria Ramirez, first published under the title "Hay esperanza de que la guerra en Ucrania termine con una paz justa," *El Diario* (Madrid), 25 February 2023, https://www.eldiario.es/internacional/serhii-plokhy-historiador-hay-esperanza-guerra-ucrania-termine-paz-justa_128_9972201.html.

29. "Not Since World War II," interview conducted by Petro Dolhanov, first published in Ukrainian in *Ukraina Moderna*, 9 September 2023, https://uamoderna.com/backward/serhiy-plokhiy-shche-zhodna-viyna-z-chasiv-druhoi-svitovoi-ne-bula-nastilky-chitkoiu-ne-tilky-dlia-ukraintsiv-ale-y-svitu-v-tsilomu/. Translated into English by Marta D. Olynyk and published as part of a project supported by the Canadian non-profit charitable organization Ukrainian Jewish Encounter.

30. "Turning Back the Clock of History," first published under the title "Turning the clock on history. The Kremlin's attempt to recreate the Russian Empire," *Times Literary Supplement* (London), 17 February 2023, https://www.the-tls.co.uk/articles/putins-wars-mark-galeotti-overreach-owen-matthews-invasion-luke-harding-book-review-serhii-plokhy/.

31. "The Zelensky Effect," first published under the title "Zelensky's heroic wartime leadership has deep historical roots," *The Washington Post*, 9 March 2023, https://www.washingtonpost.com/books/2023/03/09/zelensky-effect-review-onuch-hale/.

32. "The Sources of Russian Conduct," first published as "Russia's Great-Power Complex," in *The New Statesman* (London), 24 June 2024, https://www.newstatesman.com/culture/books/book-of-the-day/2024/06/russias-great-power-complex.

33. Originally presented as a paper at the conference entitled "The Unpredictable Past: Revisiting European, Russian, and Ukrainian Historical Studies," Canadian Institute of Ukrainian Studies, University of Alberta, 11 May 2023. This text later appeared as a chapter in *The Unpredictable Past? Reshaping Russian, Ukrainian, and East European Studies*, eds. Volodymyr Kravchenko and Marko Robert Stech (Edmonton and Toronto, 2024), 208–13.

34. "We Have to Make the Russians Think Differently," first published in Ukrainian under the title "Pro rosiiu pislia putina, Ukraïnu bez Zelens'koho ta dialohy z rosiianamy. Interv'iu z istorykom Serhiiem Plokhiiem" (On Russia after Putin, Ukraine without Zelensky, and Dialogues with the Russians. An Interview with the Historian Serhii Plokhy), *Hromads'ke*, 4 June 2024, https://hromadske.ua/viyna/225257-pro-rosiiu-pislia-putina-ukrayinu-bez-zelenskoho-ta-dialohy-z-rosiianamy-interviu-z-istorykom-serhiyem-plokhiyem.

Index

Abdelfatah, Rund, 70
Abkhazia, 11, 91
Additional Protocols to the 1949 Geneva Conventions, 125–6, 127, 138
Afghanistan, 60, 203, 228
Africa: Soviet influence in, 213
Alekseev, Mikhail, 107
Aliev, Alim, 44
Al Tuwaitha nuclear complex in Iraq, 126
Andriewsky, Olga, 220
Andrukhovych, Yuri, 44
appeasement: policies of, 88, 89, 93, 147, 158, 187
Applebaum, Anne, 217
Arablouei, Ramtin, 70
Armenia: conflict between Azerbaijan and, 9, 12; democratic development of, 7, 8; GDP per capita, 9; Russian forces in, 9. See also Nagorno-Karabakh war
Association for Slavic, East European and Eurasian Studies (ASEEES), 218, 219
Atoms and Ashes: A Global History of Nuclear Disasters (Plokhy), 130, 131
Atoms for Peace program, 129
Atucha I Nuclear Power Plant in Argentina, 126
August 1991 coup, 6, 108–9, 110
Austria: *Anschluss*, 85, 89, 195; neutralization of, 59
Austro-Hungarian Empire: collapse of, 17, 38, 54
Azerbaijan: conflict between Armenia and, 9, 12; democratic development of, 8. See also Nagorno-Karabakh war

Babyn Yar massacre, 153
Bakhmut, Ukraine, 171
Baltic states: democratic development of, 7, 23; GDP per capita, 8; independence of, 39; "Popular Fronts," 5; Russian influence in, 146
Bandera, Stepan, 149, 153, 154
Ban the Bomb movement, 142
Belarus: democratic development of, 8, 194; falsified election, 22; mass protests, 22; nuclear disarmament, 9; opposition movement, 22–3, 56; political regime of, 7; Russian influence in, 39, 150; Soviet legacy in, 22
Berlin crisis of 1948-49, 60
Berlin Wall, 146, 147, 191
Bertelsmann Transformation Index, 8
Biden, Joe, 137, 175–6, 201
big Russian nation. *See* tripartite Russian nation
Bolsheviks: control of the former Russian Empire, 62, 96–7, 104, 135; rise to power, 53, 68
Brandt, Willy: *Ostpolitik* of, 147
Brezhnev, Leonid, 77, 78, 214
British Empire: collapse of, 17, 18
Bucha massacre, 206
Budapest Memorandum, 42, 43, 55, 148
Bush, George H. W., 54
Bush, George W., 90

Canadian Institute of Ukrainian Studies, 219
Carpatho-Ukraine, 28
Catherine II, Empress of Russia, 74
Caucasus: Bolshevik control of, 97; democratic development in, 23; frozen conflicts in, 16, 17; independence movement in, 6, 105; Russia's influence in, 11, 174
Central Asian states, 7, 23
Central Rada, 30, 68
Chamberlain, Neville, 88
Chaplyne, Ukraine, 162
Chebeliuk, Olena, 206
Chechen Wars, 16, 89–90, 93, 147, 202
Chechnya, 16, 105, 202, 224
Chernobyl. *See* Chornobyl
Chernobyl (HBO/Sky blockbuster), 113, 120
Chernobyl: The History of a Nuclear Catastrophe (Plokhy), 130
China: international influence of, 196; market economy in, 14; relations with Kazakhstan, 174; relations with Russia, 51, 215, 225; Taiwan dispute, 174, 176
Chornobyl (Chernobyl) nuclear disaster: books about, 130–1; consequences of, 79, 130, 133, 140–1; major contributing factor to, 116; Ukrainian perception of, 29, 78, 79, 128
Chornobyl (Chernobyl) nuclear power plant: confinement structure over the damaged reactor, 117, 120, 121; danger of releasing radiation from, 127; electricity supply, 127, 138; emergency generators, 120, 139; exclusion zone, 113, 114, 130; Russia's military takeover of, 95, 113–15, 117–19, 120–2, 124–5, 131, 141, 165, 189; shut down of last reactor at, 138; theft of radioactive elements from, 127; Ukrainian personnel at, 117, 120; withdrawal of Russian troops from, 127
Chornovil, Viacheslav, 31
Chotiner, Isaac, 61
Chubais, Anatoly, 10

Churchill, Winston, 188
Cold War: beginning of, 12, 60; bipolarity paradigm of, 197, 200, 212; danger of nuclear war, 136; end of, 17; resurgence of, 211–12; Soviet conduct during, 212–14; trans-Atlantic cooperation, 136, 188, 196, 200
collapse of the Soviet Union: absence of large-scale wars, 9, 54; in comparative perspective, 17, 135; consequences of, 15, 16–17, 52, 54, 159; as end of history, 4, 14–15; popular attitudes toward, 3; preconditions for, 192; Ukrainian independence movement and, 39–40, 59, 97, 109; United States and, 54–5, 80
Commonwealth of Independent States (CIS), 10, 53–4, 55
Communist Party of Lithuania, 5
Conflict in Ukraine, The, (Rajan Menon and Eugene Rumer), 41

Cossacks, 72, 73–4, 75
Crimea: de jure status of, 24; ethnic Russian population of, 65; integration into Russian Federation, 86; military logistical hubs in, 171; pseudo-referendum in, 85–6; Putin's approval ratings in, 65. *See also* Russia's annexation of Crimea
Crimean Tatars, 44, 187
Cuban missile crisis, 59, 60, 134, 213–14
Cudel, Manuel, 168
Curzon Line, 15
Czechoslovakia: Nazi annexation of, 195; post-war development of, 229; radical nationalism in, 153

D'Anieri, Paul, 40, 41
democracy: in post-Soviet states, 7–8, 9, 23, 40, 147, 194; in the Soviet Union, 14
Denysenko, Larysa: "Majority as a Minority," 44
Digital Atlas of Ukraine, 26

Index

Dnipro, Ukraine: Russia's bombing of, 161–3
Dnipro University, 167
Dolhanov, Petro, 190
Donbas (Donets Basin) region: de jure status of, 24, 204; destabilization of, 55; hybrid warfare in, 11, 19, 21, 56, 98, 102; industrial workers' strikes, 6, 29; propaganda in, 193; pro-Russian attitudes in, 146; puppet states in, 98, 201, 204; rejection of the oligarchic model in, 25; Russia's recognition of "independence," 201, 204; Soviet identification in, 21, 65
Donetsk, Ukraine, 104, 176
Donetsk-Kryvyi Rih Republic, 67
Drach, Ivan, 29, 31
Dunkirk evacuations, 89

Eastern Europe: decolonization of academic study of, 199–200; German influence in post-Cold War, 157; Hitler's war in, 153; NATO presence in, 96; Soviet influence in, 146, 158
East Germany, 155, 156, 158
Eisenhower, Dwight D., 129, 177, 228, 229
empires: definition of, 135; disintegration of, 13, 15, 135, 223
end of history: idea of, 4, 14–15
Enerhodar, Ukraine, 115, 118, 122
European Commission, 123, 128
European Union: anti-Americanism in, 187; attitudes toward Russia, 124, 147, 158, 187; Baltic states in, 11, 23, 90; former Eastern bloc and, 146; "green" economic agenda, 123–4; international influence of, 196, 197; Russo-Ukrainian war and, 172, 173; Ukraine's aspiration for membership in, 10, 11, 55, 81, 97, 150, 170, 184–5, 188; US policies toward, 196

famine of 1932-33. *See* Holodomor (famine of 1932-33)
Fergana massacre of 1989, 19

First World War, 15, 17
France: nuclear energy in, 123; policy of appeasement, 89
Freedland, Jonathan, 205
French Empire: collapse of, 17
Friedrich, Klaus, 86, 88
FSB (Federal Security Service, Russia), 109
Fukushima nuclear disaster, 118, 121, 128, 132, 134, 189
Fukuyama, Francis, 4, 14

Galeotti, Mark, 203, 204, 207; *Putin's Wars: From Chechnya to Ukraine,* 202
Gates of Europe, The (Plokhy), 184, 185
Gaulle, Charles de, 228–9
Gehrs, Oliver, 145
Georgia: applications for NATO membership, 90–1; democratic development of, 7, 8; GDP per capita, 9; Russia's invasion of, 11, 16, 81, 91–2, 147, 187, 190, 202; territorial issues, 92
German Democratic Republic. *See* East Germany
German Empire: in First World War, 68–9
Germany: at Bucharest summit of 2008, 90; crimes of the Red Army against, 197; energy sector, 123–4; financing of universities in, 199–200; as intermediary between the West and Russia, 158–9; international status of, 228; *Ostpolitik,* 147, 158, 159, 160; populist parties in, 179; radical nationalism in, 153; relationship with Ukraine, 37, 104, 148, 151–2, 153, 157, 158, 159–60, 172, 178–9; responsibility for Nazi crimes, 148, 153, 157; reunification of, 146, 157–8, 229; Russo-Ukrainian war and, 159, 179, 184–5; security policy, 158; Slavic studies in, 199–200; social system in, 195; in trans-Atlantic alliance, 196; Treaty of Rapallo, 62

Gorbachev, Mikhail: American support of, 10; control of nuclear weapons, 214; efforts to preserve the Soviet Union, 97; foreign policy of, 214; KGB revolt against, 108–9; lack of historical vision, 15; Primakov and, 196; resignation of, 6, 52
Grachev, Pavel, 108
Great Britain: policy of appeasement, 89
Green World (political party in Ukraine), 29
Grossi, Rafael Mariano, 114, 125, 141–2
Grozny: Russian siege of, 90
Guchkov, Aleksandr, 107

Habsburg, Wilhelm von, 154
Hale, Henry E., 209, 210; *The Zelensky Effect*, 208
Harding, Luke, 205, 206, 207
Harshaw, Tobin, 120
Harvard Ukrainian Research Institute, 219
Hegseth, Pete, 177
Herashchenko, Anton, 113
Hiroshima: atomic bombing of, 140; comparison to Chornobyl, 140–1; G-7 meeting in, 140
Hiroshima Peace Memorial (Atomic Dome), 140, 142
Hitler, Adolf: *Anschluss* of Austria, 85, 89, 93, 195; appeasement of, 88, 89, 93; attack on the Soviet Union, 148; denunciation of the Treaty of Versailles, 87; idea of "Greater German Reich," 102; occupation of Czechoslovakia, 89, 93, 195; occupation of Rhineland, 89
Hnatiuk, Ola, 44
Holodomor (famine of 1932-33), 63, 78, 152
Honcharuk, Oleksii, 201
Horyn, Mykhailo, 29, 31
Hoyer, Katja, 151
Hrushevsky, Mykhailo, 30, 68, 185, 209
Hrytsak, Yaroslav: "Ukraine: A Brief but Global History of Ukrainian Bread," 44

Hutchinson, Erin, 219
hydrogen bomb testing, 136

International Atomic Energy Agency (IAEA): creation of, 129; governance of, 125, 142; lack of legal instruments, 128; plan to reduce the EU's reliance on Russian hydrocarbons, 124; responsibilities of, 127, 139; statements on Russo-Ukraine War, 114, 119, 137, 141–2
"International Fronts," 5
International Humanitarian Law: Rule 42 of, 127
Iran: Bushehr nuclear plant, 126; Russo-Ukrainian war and, 172; Soviet influence in, 213; war with Iraq, 126
Iron Curtain, 12, 155
Israel, 126
Italy: radical nationalism in, 153

Jaczko, Gregory, 132
Japan: transformation of social system in, 195
Jaulmes, Adrien, 58
Jews, 72, 98, 152, 187, 209, 210
Johnson, Boris, 205
Johnson, Lyndon B., 177

Kadyrov, Ramzan, 224
Kakhovka Dam, 165, 172
Kaliningrad enclave, 3
Kazakhstan, 6, 7, 9, 56
Kebuladze, Vakhtang, 44
Kellogg, Keith, 176, 178
Kennan, George F., 4, 212, 213; "Long Telegram," 211; "The Sources of Soviet Conduct," 211
Kennedy, John F., 134, 136, 215
Kerensky, Aleksandr, 107, 108
Kharkiv, Ukraine, 118, 127, 161–2, 168
Kharkiv Institute of Physics and Technology, 127
Kherson, Ukraine, 168, 176
Khmelnytsky, Bohdan, 28
Khrushchev, Nikita, 60, 77, 134, 136, 213–14

Index

Kirienko, Sergei, 203
Kirill, Patriarch of Moscow, 99
Klitschko, Vitali, 159, 165
Koeberg Nuclear Power Station in South Africa, 126
Korean War, 177
Kornilov, Lavr: march on Petrograd, 107–8, 110
Kosovo, 215
Kostenko, Yuri: *Ukraine's Nuclear Disarmament*, 42–3
Kotkin, Stephen, 189
Kotsiura, Khrystyna, 223
Kravchenko, Volodymyr, 220
Kravchuk, Leonid, 31, 53
Kriuchkov, Vladimir, 108
Kruger, Meghan, 117
Kryvyi Rih, Ukraine, 163, 206
Kulakov, Andriy: "Tabula rasa, or How to Find a Ukrainian Terra Incognita," 44
Kurkov, Andrei, 44, 45
Kvit, Serhiy, 165
Kyiv, Ukraine: monuments to historical personalities, 20, 68; as Russian city, idea of, 35, 100; Russia's bombing of, 99, 101, 165
Kyivan Chronicle, 100
Kyivan Rus´, 73, 100, 101, 200
Kyiv Mohyla Academy, 72, 161, 164, 165–6, 167
Kyrgyzstan, 8

Landsbergis, Vytautas, 5
LatePost, 130
Lavrov, Sergei, 196
Lebed, Aleksandr, 108
Lemkin, Raphael, 63
Lenin, Vladimir: as "creator" of Ukraine, 67, 186, 202, 209–10; formation of modern Russia, 69; recognition of Ukrainians as separate peoples, 62, 69, 96; rise to power, 76; Ukrainian social media on, 67–8; vision of world revolution, 62
Letterman, David, 207
Leyen, Ursula von der, 123
Lithuania, 5–6
Little Russians, 103–4

Luhansk, Ukraine: Russian control of, 176
Lukashenko, Alexander, 7, 11, 22, 56
Lviv Book Forum, 200

Macron, Emmanuel, 178
Maidan protesters, 66
Manafort, Paul, 41
Mao, Zedong, 213
Maoist People's Revolutionary Army, 126
Mariupol, Ukraine: Russia's destruction of, 98
market economy in communist states, 14–15
Martin, Terry, 219
Matlary, Janne Haaland, 87, 88
Matthews, Owen, 204–5, 207; *Overreach: The Inside Story of Putin's War against Ukraine*, 203
McConnell, Nadia, 24
McMahon, Linda, 179
Merkel, Angela, 158, 178, 203
Meskhetian Turks, 16
Millennium of Christianity, 29
Minsk agreements, 169, 173, 177
Moldova: declaration of independence, 6; democratic development of, 7, 8, 23; GDP per capita, 9
Molotov-Ribbentrop Pact, 5, 6
Moscow Patriarchate: jurisdiction of, 99
Munich Agreement, 89
Munich-The Edge of War (Netflix film), 88
Mykolaiv, Ukraine: Russian bombing of, 161–2

Nagorno-Karabakh war, 16
nationalist movements, 146, 153
NATO: Bucharest summit of 2008, 90, 92, 158; expansion of, 51, 56, 59, 146, 158, 184; formation of, 56; Membership Action Plan (MAP), 91; Putin's relations with, 95–6; Russo-Ukrainian war and, 174; Ukraine and, 56, 150, 170, 176, 177, 188

Navalny, Aleksei, 189, 203
Nazi Germany: *Anschluss* of Austria, 85, 89, 195; comparison to Putin's Russia, 93–4, 102; crimes of, 153–4; foreign policy of, 5, 88–9, 148, 195; invasion of Ukraine, 101; policy of appeasement toward, 85, 88–9
Nicholas II, Emperor of Russia, 106, 107, 110
9/11 terrorist attack, 126
Nixon, Richard, 177
Nolan, Christopher, 133
Nord Stream 2 pipeline controversy, 18, 124, 159
North Korea: Russo-Ukrainian war and, 172, 174
nuclear disarmament, 9
nuclear energy: EU status of, 123; future of, 138; production of, 132, 138; public and government attitudes toward, 132; Russia's war on Ukraine and, 124
Nuclear Folly: A History of the Cuban Missile Crisis (Plokhy), 130
nuclear power plants: accidents at, 131, 133, 189; control systems of, 138; future of, 139; investment in safety of, 129; lack of legal protection of, 128; military attacks on, 138; technological systems, 131; vulnerability of, 128; wars and, 115, 139, 190; worldwide statistics of, 131, 137, 142
nuclear terrorism, 120, 122, 125, 126
nuclear weapons, 138, 142, 214

Obama, Barack, 92
Onuch, Olga, 209, 210; *The Zelensky Effect*, 208
Onuphry (Berezovsky), Metropolitan of Kyiv and All Ukraine, 99, 100
Oppenheimer (film), 133
Oppenheimer, J. Robert, 133
Orange Revolution, 147
Organization of Ukrainian Nationalists, 20, 28
Orlov, Dmytro, 115
Orphanage, The (Zhadan), 45–6

Orthodox Church in Ukraine: division in, 99–100
Orwell, George: *1984*, 70, 71
Osirak nuclear research facility, 126
Ottoman Empire: collapse of, 15, 17, 54
Overreach: The Inside Story of Putin's War against Ukraine (Matthews), 203

Patrushev, Nikolai, 204
Peskov, Dmitry, 203
"Phony War" of 1939-40, 89
Pilsudski, Józef, 228
Poland: civilian casualties during WWII, 149; membership in NATO, 56, 158; post-war development, 229; radical nationalism in, 153; Russian influence in, 146; Russo-Ukrainian war and, 184
Polish-Lithuanian Commonwealth, 72, 74
Pomerantsev, Peter, 43
Poroshenko, Petro, 20, 21
post-Soviet identity, 23, 45
post-Soviet space: democratic development in, 8; disintegration of, 4; economic transformation of, 3, 8, 13; future of, 10; GDP per capita, 8–9; new international actors, 12; nuclear weapons, 9; rule of law in, 8, 12–13; Russia's control of, 56, 59, 80–1
Prigozhin, Yevgeny: attempted coup of, 106, 107, 108, 109, 110, 171; background of, 107; Bakhmut operation of, 171
Primakov, Yevgeny, 196
private property: in communist and post-communist states, 14–15
Prypiat, Ukraine, 141
Przemyśl (Peremyshl'), Poland, 165
Putin, Vladimir: on annexation of Crimea, 11; anti-West rhetoric, 215; approval ratings, 226; Chechen War, 90; comparison to Hitler, 85, 87, 88, 93–4; Covid isolation of, 203, 204; denial of Ukraine's right to statehood, 52, 67, 77, 202, 209–10; foreign policy of, 10, 52, 214; "Greater

Index

Russia" project, 102; idea of big Russian nation, 20, 62, 96, 185, 202; interpretations of history, 192–3; meeting with Zelensky, 204; mindset of, 32–3; nuclear threats, 137; policy goal toward Ukraine, 46; political regime of, 109; recognition of puppet states in Ukraine, 67, 201–2; rejection of Soviet-era policies, 65; relations with NATO, 95–6; rise to power, 7–8, 90, 202; on Russo-Ukrainian unity, 19, 22, 33, 38, 52, 71, 217–18; war on Ukraine, 60, 71, 85, 95, 96, 103, 201, 202–4, 207, 210, 215

Putin's Wars: From Chechnya to Ukraine (Galeotti), 202

Radchenko, Sergey, 212, 213, 214; *To Run the World: The Kremlin's Cold War Bid for Global Power*, 211, 215
Rafeyenko, Volodymyr, 44
Ramirez, Maria, 183
Rapallo, Treaty of, 62
Reagan, Ronald, 215
Reichardt, Adam, 14
Revolution of Dignity, 20, 206
Reznikov, Oleksii, 113
Roell, Sophie, 38
Rosatom (Russian nuclear monopoly), 142
Rosgvardiia (Russian National Guard), 110, 138
Rukh (the Popular Movement of Ukraine), 29, 30, 31, 35, 79
Russian Empire: ban of Ukrainian language publications, 61, 96; collapse of, 38, 76, 96–7, 104; emergence of, 18; European and Asian parts of, 145; "friendly" states on the periphery of, 19–20; nationality policies in, 199; relationships with Ukrainian Cossacks, 76; serfdom in, 74–5, 76
Russian Federation: authoritarian regime of, 7, 40; coup of 1993, 6; democratic development of, 9, 193–4; Far Eastern region, 3; foreign policy of, 58; gas industry in, 124, 158–9; imperial ambitions of, 57, 184, 185, 192, 193, 194–5, 214–15; independence of, 77; insecurity of, 211; international influence of, 11, 196–7; nationalism, 34, 65, 224; NATO relations with, 39, 56, 90; nuclear threats, 9, 128; partnership with the West, 124, 214–15; post-war scenarios for, 224–6; relations with China, 197, 215, 225; relations with US, 9–10; sanctions on, 124, 168–9; Soviet legacies in, 225–6; support for Lukashenko, 56; threat of disintegration of, 104, 105; trade relations, 147, 158–9; ultimatum to the West, 51; Western appeasement of, 89, 147, 158, 187
Russian identity, 34, 38, 41, 58, 185, 227
Russian Provisional Government, 107
Russian Revolution of 1917, 96
Russians and Ukrainians as one people: idea of, 33, 52, 96, 192, 225
Russian World (*russkii mir*), 34, 103
Russia's annexation of Crimea: consequences of, 56, 57, 187, 190; Navalny's statement on, 189; popular uprising in Ukraine and, 11, 55, 81, 97–8, 102; root causes of, 16; Western response to, 93–4, 148, 175, 201
Russo-Georgian War of 2008, 91–2
Russo-Ukrainian relations: books on, 40; crisis of, 58–9; discourse of brotherhood in, 66; energy sector and, 6; in historical context, 40, 62, 147; NATO and, 59; post-Soviet space and, 59; prospects of, 34–5; Russia's approach to, 38–9, 55, 58; Stalin policies, 63
Russo-Ukrainian War (Plokhy), 161, 166, 191
Russo-Ukrainian war in 2014, 11, 21, 46–7, 56, 64, 67, 81, 85, 98
Russo-Ukrainian war in 2022–25: analysis of, 202–5, 207, 217–19,

221–2; as anti-colonial war, 221; anti-Semitism narrative in, 186, 193; atrocities of, 161–3, 164–5, 206; casualties, 47, 164, 167, 171, 225; causes of, 95–8; coping mechanism in Ukraine, 46; discussion of "land for peace" settlement, 171, 173–4; effect on Ukrainian society, 46, 81–2, 162–3, 164–5, 166–7, 205–6, 208–9; failure of the Russian offensive, 106, 172; North Korean soldiers in, 172; nuclear danger of, 135, 137, 141; origins of, 183–5, 192, 216–17; outbreak of, 95, 99, 134, 204, 205; outcomes of, 66, 104–5, 173–4, 188–9, 207; political and economic cost of, 136; predictions about, 122, 124, 191, 204; preparations for, 95, 169, 201, 203–4, 217–18; prospects of ending, 35, 136, 169, 176, 177, 188, 229; puppet states and, 67; Putin's justification of, 96, 99, 149, 192–3, 202–3; refugee crisis, 95, 164; Russian propaganda on, 86–7, 149, 186–7, 193, 206; Russian troops in, 171–2; Trump policy toward, 175, 176–8, 179; turning points of, 168; Ukrainian resistance in, 98, 103, 183, 190, 216–17, 223; as war against the West, 203; warnings about, 100; weapons, 165, 172; Western response to, 89, 93, 148, 163–4, 166, 168–9, 172–3, 178–9, 195–6

Ruzsky, Nikolai, 107

Saakashvili, Mikheil, 92
Sakharov, Andrei, 133
Sarkozy, Nicolas, 92
Scholz, Olaf, 159, 178
serfdom, 74–5
Sheiko, Volodymyr, 36
Shelest, Hanna: "Insecure Security of Ukraine," 44
Shevchenko, Taras, 33
Shoigu, Sergei, 204
Shulgin, Vasily, 107

Shushkevich, Stanislav, 53
Skoropadsky, Pavlo, 28, 68, 152
Slavic studies, 199–200, 219–21
Snyder, Timothy, 154, 191, 217
Sobotta, Jerzy, 102
South Ossetia, 11, 91, 92
South Ukraine Nuclear Power Plant, 115, 116
Soviet Russia: creation of, 77
Soviet Ukraine: Bolsheviks' policy in, 67, 186, 202, 209–10; Declaration of Independence, 6, 24, 28, 30; Declaration of Sovereignty, 30; democratic elections in, 30; East German relation with, 156–7; economic development of, 77; mass mobilization, 29–30, 31; nuclear weapons in, 80; peasant uprisings in, 76; referendum on independence on 1 December 1991, 31–2, 53, 59, 79, 97; russification of, 63, 210; status of Ukrainian language in, 63; during World War II, 153, 156
Soviet Union: atomic project, 213; Cold War and, 212–13; as continuation of the Russian Empire, 15; creation of, 53, 69, 76; imperialism of, 212; importance of Ukraine for, 97; influence in Eastern Europe, 146; nationality policies in, 199; opposition to the center in, 5, 63; travels abroad in, 156. *See also* collapse of the Soviet Union
Stalin, Joseph: concessions to Ukrainians, 186, 210; death of, 177, 226; revival of Russian language and culture, 63; state building, 62; at Yalta Conference, 213
Steinmeier, Frank-Walter, 158
Sudetenland, 89, 93
Surkov, Vladislav, 204

Tairova-Yakovleva, Tatiana, 226
Taiwan: China claims on, 174, 177
Tajikistan, 7, 8
Teller, Edward, 133
Thomas-Greenfield, Linda, 125

Index

Tokayev, Kassym-Jomart, 56
To Run the World: The Kremlin's Cold War Bid for Global Power (Radchenko), 211, 215
Transnistria, 9, 11, 39
tripartite Russian nation: idea of, 20, 52–3, 62, 96, 103–4, 185, 202
Truman, Harry S., 215
Trump, Donald, 175, 176–8, 179, 196
Turkey, 12, 213
Turkmenistan, 7, 8, 9

Ukraine: armed forces, 216–17; aspirations for freedom, 206, 209; ban of the CPSU, 31; as borderland, 27, 145–6; Commonwealth of Independent States and, 10; comparison to South Korea, 189; corruption in, 18, 150; critical infrastructure of, 19; cultural unification of, 19; democratic development of, 8, 23, 40, 147, 194; deoligarchization of, 25; dependence on Russian gas, 55; division between eastern and western, 21, 61; economic crisis, 26; European aspirations in, 145, 170, 184–5, 188, 202, 203; foreign policy of, 204; GDP per capita, 8; Germany and, 151–60; history of, 219, 220–1; language divisions, 64; loyalty to institutions in, 34; mobilization against Russian aggression, 6, 21, 22, 26–7, 65, 205–9; modernization and urbanization of, 64; national anthem, 73; nationalism, 53, 149, 152–3, 154–5, 186; nation building, 27, 33–4, 38–9, 186, 187, 195, 209, 229; NATO and, 56, 90–1, 150, 170, 176, 177, 188; nuclear disarmament of, 9, 42–3, 148; Orange Revolution, 10; post-war scenarios for, 229–30; presidential elections in, 21; Putin's denial of statehood of, 19, 38–9, 96; Russian-speaking population of, 34, 74, 103, 146, 210; Russia's annexation of territories of, 102, 201–2; social issues, 19; Soviet legacy in, 18–19; support from Ukrainian diaspora, 35–6; territory of, 24, 72, 169, 229; understanding of nationality in, 103; Western powers and, 37, 80, 147, 158. *See also* Soviet Ukraine
Ukraine in Histories and Stories: Essays by Ukrainian Intellectuals, 43–4
Ukraine's Nuclear Disarmament (Kostenko), 42–3
Ukraine's State Nuclear Regulatory Inspectorate, 114
Ukraine: What Everyone Needs to Know (Yekelchyk), 41–2
Ukrainian Academy of Sciences, 152
Ukrainian diaspora, 35–6
Ukrainian Greek Catholic Church, 29
Ukrainian independence: Bolshevik Revolution and, 63–4, 151; celebration of anniversary of, 161; collapse of the Soviet Union and, 39–40, 59, 79, 97, 109, 209; Putin's views of, 32–3; US recognition of, 80
Ukrainian Institute, 36
Ukrainian Insurgent Army, 154
Ukrainian national identity: elements of, 61, 62, 70, 71; formation of, 24, 26–7, 146, 208–9; Putin's denial of, 38, 185, 192; Russo-Ukraine war and, 66
Ukrainian Nuclear Regulatory Inspectorate, 125
Ukrainian Orthodox Church, 99, 100
Ukrainian People's Republic, 28, 68–9, 209
Ukrainian Security Service, 163
Ukrainian volunteer military formations, 87
United Kingdom: Ukrainian refugees in, 164
United States: atomic project, 213; as dominant power, 18; relations with Ukraine, 37, 80; sanctions on Russia, 124
University of Dnipro (Dnipropetrovsk), 155, 156
Unmaking Imperial Russia (Plokhy), 185

Uthoff, Jens, 175
Uzbekistan, 7, 8

Vance, J. D., 177
Vernadsky National Library of Ukraine, 152
Vienna, Austria: anti-war protests in, 85
Viking princes, 101
Vilkul, Oleksandr, 206, 207
Vilnius massacre of 1991, 16
Vladimir (Bogoiavlensky), Metropolitan of Kyiv, 68
Volodymyr, Prince of Kyiv, 20, 100
Vyhovsky, Ivan, 28

Wagner group, 106, 107, 171
Waltz, Mike, 177
War and Punishment (Zygar), 226
What Everyone Needs to Know (book series), 41
World War I, 151
World War II, 17, 18, 89, 101, 153, 193, 197–8, 224, 229

Yalta Conference, 5, 136, 213
Yanukovych, Viktor, 11, 55, 97, 228
Yazov, Dmitry, 108
Yekelchyk, Serhy, 43; *Ukraine: What Everyone Needs to Know*, 41–2
Yeltsin, Boris: Belavezha Accords, 53; coup of 1991 and, 108–9, 110; democratic image of, 194; First Chechen War of, 16, 202; foreign policy of, 214; on formation of the CIS, 54; George H. W. Bush and, 54; political career of, 5, 69, 109; suspension of Communist Party, 6; Ukrainian question and, 97, 158; vision of the post-Soviet space, 10; Western support of, 89, 147
Yermolenko, Volodymyr, 206; "Steppe, Empire, and Cruelty," 44

Zaluzhny, Valerii, 168, 228
Zaporizhzhia, Ukraine, 161–2, 163, 176
Zaporizhzhia nuclear power plant: damages to, 135, 138; location of, 115, 122; missiles attacks on, 141; Russian occupation of, 95, 121, 122, 127, 135, 141; shut down reactors, 121; size of, 118, 189
Zelensky, Volodymyr: approval ratings, 228; criticism of, 169; election of, 21, 150; first government of, 201; hometown of, 163, 206; meeting with Putin, 204; nationality of, 146; on nuclear terrorism, 125; personal courage of, 208; on policy of appeasement, 88; rise to power, 20; on Russian takeover of Chornobyl nuclear plant, 114; as wartime leader, 66, 205–6, 208–9, 210, 227–8
Zelensky Effect, The (Onuch and Hale), 208
Zhadan, Serhiy: *The Orphanage*, 45–6
Zolotov, Viktor, 110
Zubov, Andrei, 85, 86, 88, 93
Zygar, Mikhail: *War and Punishment*, 226

Harvard Series in Ukrainian Studies
Recently Published

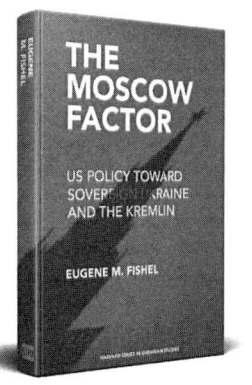

The Moscow Factor: US Policy toward Sovereign Ukraine and the Kremlin

Eugene M. Fishel

This unique study that examines four key Ukraine-related policy decisions across two Republican and two Democratic US administrations. Fishel asks whether, how, and under what circumstances Washington has considered Ukraine's status as a sovereign nation in its decision-making regarding relations with Moscow.

2022 | 324 pp., 2 figs.
ISBN 9780674279179 (hardcover) | $59.95
9780674279186 (paperback) | $29.95
9780674279421 (epub)
9780674279193 (PDF)

Harvard Series in Ukrainian Studies, vol. 82

Read the book online

The Frontline: Essays on Ukraine's Past and Present

Serhii Plokhy

The Frontline presents a selection of essays drawn together for the first time to form a companion volume to Serhii Plokhy's *The Gates of Europe* and *Chernobyl*. Here he expands upon his analysis in earlier works of key events in Ukrainian history.

2021 (HC) / 2023 (PB) | 416 pp. / 420 pp.
10 color photos, 9 color maps
ISBN 9780674268821 (hardcover) | $64.00
9780674268838 (paperback) | $19.95
9780674268845 (epub)
9780674268852 (PDF)

Harvard Series in Ukrainian Studies, vol. 81

Read the book online

Ukrainian Nationalism in the Age of Extremes: An Intellectual Biography of Dmytro Dontsov

Trevor Erlacher

Ukrainian nationalism made worldwide news after the Euromaidan revolution and the outbreak of the Russo-Ukrainian war in 2014. Invoked by regional actors and international commentators, the "integral" Ukrainian nationalism of the 1930s has moved to the center of debates about Eastern Europe, but the history of this divisive ideology remains poorly understood.

2021 | 658 pp., 34 photos, 5 illustr.

ISBN 9780674250932 (hardcover) | $84.00
9780674250949 (epub)
9780674250956 (Kindle)
9780674250963 (PDF)

Read all chapters online

Harvard Series in Ukrainian Studies, vol. 80

Survival as Victory: Ukrainian Women in the Gulag

Oksana Kis

Translated by Lidia Wolanskyj

Hundreds of thousands of Ukrainian women were sentenced to the GULAG in the 1940s and 1950s. Only about half of them survived. With this book, Oksana Kis has produced the first anthropological study of daily life in the Soviet forced labor camps as experienced by Ukrainian women prisoners.

Based on the written memoirs, autobiographies, and oral histories of over 150 survivors, this book fills a lacuna in the scholarship regarding Ukrainian experience.

2020 | 652 pp., 78 color photos, 10 b/w photos

ISBN 9780674258280 (hardcover) | $94.00
9780674258327 (epub)
9780674258334 (Kindle)
9780674258341 (PDF)

Read all chapters online

Harvard Series in Ukrainian Studies, vol. 79

Forthcoming Titles
Harvard Papers in Ukrainian Studies

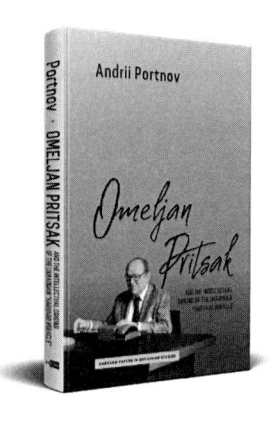

Omeljan Pritsak and the Intellectual Origins of the Ukrainian "Harvard Miracle"

Andrii Portnov

This is the first English-language intellectual biography of Omeljan Pritsak, the co-founder of the Harvard Ukrainian Research Institute (HURI) and the first professor of Ukrainian history at Harvard. Andrii Portnov places Pritsak's life and legacy in the context of Ukrainian and world historiography and illuminates the development of his scholarly interests.

Harvard Series in Ukrainian Studies

Breaking the Bonds of Corruption: From Academic Dishonesty to Corrupt Business Practices in post-Soviet Ukraine

Elena Denisova-Schmidt

This study makes an important contribution to the maturing study of informal practices in Ukraine and the region. Elena Denisova-Schmidt takes a broad view of corruption and its prevalence in societies globally and uses the case of Ukraine for examining the practices that are considered corrupt in their historical, social, and economic perspective. The author considers corrupt behavior in higher education internationally and in Ukraine, and examines the reliance on acts of corruption while doing business in Ukraine.

Find out more about these titles at https://books.huri.harvard.edu

Self-Organization: The Power and Limits of Ukraine's Informal Civil Society

Svitlana Krasynska

Civil society in Eastern Europe has long been labeled weak based on a general lack of citizen participation in formal civil society organizations—a key criterion for assessing civic engagement in comparative studies. However, such assessment of civil society fails to recognize the role and impact of informal civic engagement in contexts where informality permeates economic, political, and social spheres. Ukraine offers a valuable counterargument of the importance of informal civil society in Eastern Europe, especially in the post-Soviet countries. Using Ukraine as a case-in-point, Svitlana Krasynska engages diverse bodies of literature and rich empirical data to reveal the vital role and unique potential of below-the-radar civic engagement.

Jews in Old Rus´: A Documentary History

Alexander Kulik

This collection makes available for the first time a selection of documents on the history of Jews in Old Rus´ that provide a unique insight into Slavic-Jewish relations, offering both the original texts of the documents in Latin, Hebrew, Church Slavonic, and Arabic, and their English translations. Adding nuance to our understanding of the difficult relations Rus´ had with Khazaria, the volume also realigns the position of East European Jews within the larger diaspora of European Jews. This collection meticulously portrays legal rulings, religious and liturgical customs, practices regarding food and garments, linguistic acculturation, and the political loyalties of Jews in Old Rus´.

Find out more about these titles at https://books.huri.harvard.edu

The Eye of the Mind: Vision, Memory, and Meditation in Seventeenth-Century Ukrainian Preaching

Maria Grazia Bartolini

This study explores the role of vision, memory, and meditation in the sermons produced in Ukraine during the second half of the seventeenth century. It argues that the cognitive importance that vision and memory enjoyed in medieval and early modern culture informed their centrality in these sermons. *The Eye of the Mind* demonstrates how preachers used verbal and visual images to encourage the meditative re-creation of biblical events in the minds of their audiences. An investigation of the mental furniture of early modern Ukrainian preachers and their audiences, this book recovers a fascinating tradition that merged word and image to build "multimedia machines" for the spiritual elevation of the faithful.

Documentary Sources on the History of Rus´ Metropolitanate: The Fourteenth to the Early Sixteenth Centuries

Andrei I. Pliguzov

This work is an extensive collection of letters and documents relating to the late medieval Orthodox Church, edited and curated by the renowned medievalist Andrei Pliguzov. *Documentary Sources on the History of Rus´ Metropolitanate* is a rich resource for any reader interested in the controversies and preoccupations of the Orthodox hierarchy and the clergy throughout the Rus´ metropolitanate up to the early modern period. For the first time, the volume includes acts, edicts and decrees regarding the lands in the metropolitanate's jurisdiction, reports prepared for the metropolitans by their secretariat, and the letters of the hierarchs themselves

Find out more about these titles at https://books.huri.harvard.edu

Harvard Library of Ukrainian Literature
Recently Published

Signals of Being, or Verbum Caro Factum Est
Volodymyr Rafeyenko

Translated by Mark Andryczyk

It's the early days of Russia's 2022 invasion of Ukraine. The lives of the inhabitants of the cottage community Blyzhni Sady (Nearby Orchards) have suddenly been shattered and they have now been thrust into attempts at individual and collective survival.

2025	156 pp.	
ISBN 9780674302631 (hardcover)		$29.95
9780674302662 (paperback)		$14.95
9780674302655 (epub)		
9780674302648 (PDF)		

Harvard Library of Ukrainian Literature, vol. 14

Read the book online

The City: A Novel
Valerian Pidmohylnyi

Translated with an introduction by Maxim Tarnawsky

This novel was a landmark event in the history of Ukrainian literature. Written by a master craftsman in full control of the texture, rhythm, and tone of the text, the novel tells the story of Stepan, a young man from the provinces who moves to the capital of Ukraine, Kyiv, and achieves success as a writer through a succession of romantic encounters with women.

2025	491 pp.	
ISBN 9780674291119 (cloth)		$39.95
9780674291126 (paperback)		$19.95
9780674291133 (epub)		
9780674291140 (PDF)		

Harvard Library of Ukrainian Literature, vol. 13

Read the book online

Love Life: A Novel

Oksana Lutsyshyna

Translated by Nina Murray
Introduced by Marko Pavlyshyn

The second novel of the award-winning Ukrainian writer and poet Oksana Lutsyshyna writes the story of Yora, an immigrant to the United States from Ukraine. A delicate soul that's finely attuned to the nuances of human relations, Yora becomes enmeshed in a relationship with Sebastian, a seductive acquaintance who seems to be suggesting that they share a deep bond. After a period of despair and complex grief that follows the end of the relationship, Yora is able to emerge stronger, in part thanks to the support from a friendly neighbor who has adapted well to life on the margins of society.

2024	276 pp.	
ISBN 9780674297159 (cloth)		$39.95
9780674297166 (paperback)		$19.95
9780674297173 (epub)		
9780674297180 (PDF)		

Harvard Library of Ukrainian Literature, vol. 12

Read the book online

Cecil the Lion Had to Die: A Novel

Olena Stiazhkina

Translated by Dominique Hoffman

This novel follows the fate of four families as the world around them undergoes radical transformations when the Soviet Union unexpectedly implodes, independent Ukraine emerges, and neoimperial Russia begins its war by occupying Ukraine's Crimea and parts of the Donbas. A tour de force of stylistic registers and intertwining stories, ironic voices and sincere discoveries, this novel is a must-read for those who seek to deeper understand Ukrainians from the Donbas, and how history and local identity have shaped the current war with Russia.

2024	248 pp.	
ISBN 9780674291645 (cloth)		$39.95
9780674291669 (paperback)		$19.95
9780674291676 (epub)		
9780674291683 (PDF)		

Harvard Library of Ukrainian Literature, vol. 11

Read the book online

Earth Gods: Writings from before the War

Taras Prokhasko

Translated by Ali Kinsella, Mark Andryczyk and Uilleam Blacker
Introduced by Mark Andryczyk

This book presents Taras Prokhasko's early writings: genre-bending *Anna's Other Days*, the collection of reflections *FM Galicia*, and *The UnSimple*, an iconoclastic novel that offers an alternative history of the Ukrainian Carpathian mountains of the first half of the twentieth century. Collected here for the first time in one volume, these stylistically and conceptually virtuosic texts testify to the richness of contemporary Ukrainian literature.

2025 | appr. 400 pp.

ISBN 9780674291164 (hardcover)	$39.95
9780674291171 (paperback)	$19.95
9780674291188 (epub)	
9780674291195 (PDF)	

Harvard Library of Ukrainian Literature, vol. 10

Read the book online

A Harvest Truce: A Play

Serhiy Zhadan

Translated by Nina Murray

Brothers Anton and Tolik reunite at their family home to bury their recently deceased mother. An otherwise natural ritual unfolds under extraordinary circumstances: their house is on the front line of a war ignited by Russian-backed separatists in eastern Ukraine.

Spring 2023

ISBN 9780674291997 (hardcover)	$29.95
9780674292017 (paperback)	$19.95
9780674292024 (epub)	
9780674292031 (PDF)	

Harvard Library of Ukrainian Literature, vol. 9

Read the book online

Cassandra: A Dramatic Poem,

Lesia Ukrainka (Larysa Kosach)

Translated by Nina Murray, introduction by Marko Pavlyshyn

The classic myth of Cassandra turns into much more in Lesia Ukrainka's rendering: Cassandra's prophecies are uttered in highly poetic language—fitting to the genre of the dramatic poem that Ukrainka crafts for this work—and are not believed for that very reason, rather than because of Apollo's curse. Cassandra's being a poet and a woman are therefore the two focal points of the drama.

2024 | 263 pp, bilingual ed. (Ukrainian, English)

ISBN 9780674291775 (hardcover)	$29.95
9780674291782 (paperback)	$19.95
9780674291799 (epub)	
9780674291805 (PDF)	

Harvard Library of Ukrainian Literature, vol. 8

Read the book online

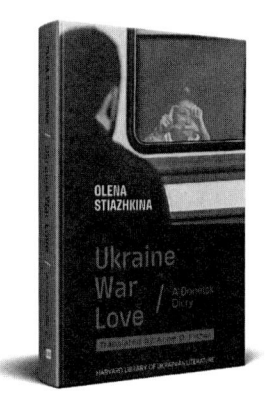

Ukraine, War, Love: A Donetsk Diary

Olena Stiazhkina

Translated by Anne O. Fisher

In this war-time diary, Olena Stiazhkina depicts day-to-day developments in and around her beloved hometown during Russia's 2014 invasion and occupation of the Ukrainian city of Donetsk.

Summer 2023

ISBN 9780674291690 (hardcover)	$39.95
9780674291706 (paperback)	$19.95
9780674291713 (epub)	
9780674291768 (PDF)	

Harvard Library of Ukrainian Literature, vol. 7

Read the book online

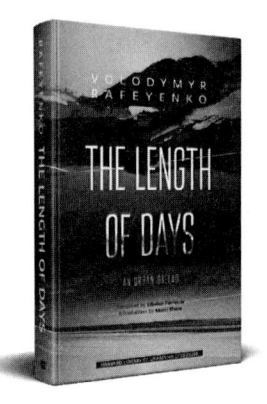

The Length of Days: An Urban Ballad

Volodymyr Rafeyenko

Translated by Sibelan Forrester
Afterword and interview with the author by Marci Shore

This novel is set mostly in the composite Donbas city of Z—an uncanny foretelling of what this letter has come to symbolize since February 24, 2022, when Russia launched a full-scale invasion of Ukraine. Several embedded narratives attributed to an alcoholic chemist-turned-massage therapist give insight into the funny, ironic, or tragic lives of people who remained in the occupied Donbas after Russia's initial aggression in 2014.

2023 | 349 pp.

ISBN 780674291201 (cloth)	$39.95
9780674291218 (paper)	$19.95
9780674291225 (epub)	
9780674291232 (PDF)	

Harvard Library of Ukrainian Literature, vol. 6

Read the book online

The Torture Camp on Paradise Street

Stanislav Aseyev

Translated by Zenia Tompkins and Nina Murray

Ukrainian journalist and writer Stanislav Aseyev details his experience as a prisoner from 2015 to 2017 in a modern-day concentration camp overseen by the Federal Security Bureau of the Russian Federation (FSB) in the Russian-controlled city of Donetsk. This memoir recounts an endless ordeal of psychological and physical abuse, including torture and rape, inflicted upon the author and his fellow inmates over the course of nearly three years of illegal incarceration spent largely in the prison called Izoliatsiia (Isolation).

2023 | 300 pp., 1 map, 18 ill.

ISBN 9780674291072 (cloth)	$39.95
9780674291089 (paper)	$19.95
9780674291102 (epub)	
9780674291096 (PDF)	

Harvard Library of Ukrainian Literature, vol. 5

Read the book online

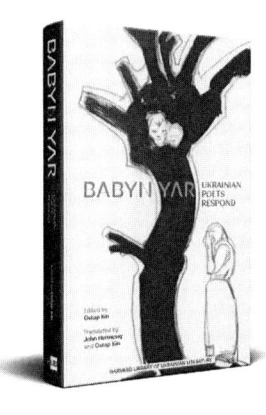

Babyn Yar: Ukrainian Poets Respond

Edited with introduction by Ostap Kin

Translated by John Hennessy and Ostap Kin

In 2021, the world commemorated the 80th anniversary of the massacres of Jews at Babyn Yar. The present collection brings together for the first time the responses to the tragic events of September 1941 by Ukrainian Jewish and non-Jewish poets of the Soviet and post-Soviet periods, presented here in the original and in English translation by Ostap Kin and John Hennessy.

2022 | 282 pp.

ISBN 9780674275591 (hardcover)	$39.95
9780674271692 (paperback)	$16.00
9780674271722 (epub)	
9780674271739 (PDF)	

Harvard Library of Ukrainian Literature, vol. 4

Read the book online

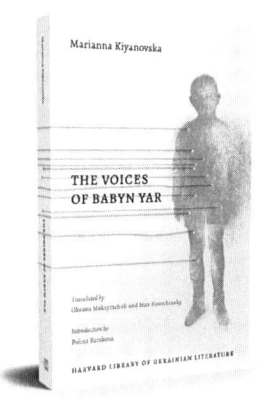

The Voices of Babyn Yar

Marianna Kiyanovska

Translated by Oksana Maksymchuk and Max Rosochinsky
Introduced by Polina Barskova

With this collection of stirring poems, the award-winning Ukrainian poet honors the victims of the Holocaust by writing their stories of horror, death, and survival in their own imagined voices.

2022 | 192 pp.

ISBN 9780674268760 (hardcover)	$39.95
9780674268869 (paperback)	$16.00
9780674268876 (epub)	
9780674268883 (PDF)	

Harvard Library of Ukrainian Literature, vol. 3

Read the book online

Mondegreen: Songs about Death and Love

Volodymyr Rafeyenko

Translated and introduced by Mark Andryczyk

Volodymyr Rafeyenko's novel Mondegreen: Songs about Death and Love explores the ways that memory and language construct our identity, and how we hold on to it no matter what. The novel tells the story of Haba Habinsky, a refugee from Ukraine's Donbas region, who has escaped to the capital city of Kyiv at the onset of the Ukrainian-Russian war.

2022	204 pp.	
ISBN 9780674275577 (hardcover)		$39.95
9780674271708 (paperback)		$19.95
9780674271746 (epub)		
9780674271760 (PDF)		

Harvard Library of Ukrainian Literature, vol. 2

Read the book online

In Isolation: Dispatches from Occupied Donbas

Stanislav Aseyev

Translated by Lidia Wolanskyj

In this exceptional collection of dispatches from occupied Donbas, writer and journalist Stanislav Aseyev details the internal and external changes observed in the cities of Makiïvka and Donetsk in eastern Ukraine.

2022	320 pp., 42 photos, 2 maps	
ISBN 9780674268784 (hardcover)		$39.95
9780674268791 (paperback)		$19.95
9780674268814 (epub)		
9780674268807 (PDF)		

Harvard Library of Ukrainian Literature, vol. 1

Read the book online